T0284941

WHAT WENT WRONG
WITH CAPITALISM

RUCHIR SHARMA

SIMON & SCHUSTER

New York   Toronto   London   Sydney   New Delhi

1230 Avenue of the Americas
New York, NY 10020

First Simon & Schuster hardcover edition June 2024

SIMON & SCHUSTER and colophon are registered trademarks of Simon & Schuster, LLC

Simon & Schuster: Celebrating 100 Years of Publishing in 2024

For information about special discounts for bulk purchases, please contact Simon & Schuster Special Sales at 1-866-506-1949 or business@simonandschuster.com.

The Simon & Schuster Speakers Bureau can bring authors to your live event. For more information or to book an event, contact the Simon & Schuster Speakers Bureau at 1-866-248-3049 or visit our website at www.simonspeakers.com.

Interior design by Carly Loman

Manufactured in the United States of America

1   3   5   7   9   10   8   6   4   2

Library of Congress Cataloging-in-Publication Data has been applied for.

ISBN 978-1-6680-0826-3
ISBN 978-1-6680-0828-7 (ebook)

CONTENTS

WHY I FELL FOR CAPITALISM

The young often rebel against the systemic injustices of their time and place. Today, in America and many wealthy countries, they are agitating against the excesses of modern capitalism: widening inequality, dominant monopolies, big corporate bailouts. They are drawn in their frustration to more government intervention or socialism as the answer, but they need to beware what they wish for.

I was born in the mid-1970s, when India was staggering under the burden of a homespun socialism heavily influenced by the Soviet Union. The government had nationalized any business that was big, thrown out many that were foreign, and started building a welfare state—before generating the revenue to pay for it. Shortages were routine; the economy grew at a painfully slow rate. Per capita income was falling behind the global average. I was drawn, during my early travels outside India, to capitalism as the answer.

My father had followed the path of opportunity in India at the time, which steered him into the government and a naval career. His postings kept us on the move, and I became the perennial new kid in town. In 1985 he was transferred to Singapore, which was developing a small and efficient state, with light taxes, simple regulations, and open doors, under the unchallenged rule of Prime Minister Lee Kuan Yew. Most Singaporeans did not seem to mind that elections were carefully managed, because with economic freedoms so well established, average incomes were rising by more than 10 percent a year—better than double the global average.

After the stagnation of India, Singapore was a liberating breath of fresh air. Lee's successes had earned him close ties to America and its president, Ronald Reagan, who seemed to go one better: loosening economic controls in a wide-open democracy. In my youthful exuberance, it seemed to me you could have it all—economic and political freedom. While in the West capitalism had already come to be synonymous in the eyes of many with greed and inequality, to me capitalism evoked endless possibility, not only for individuals but for my beloved home country. I became a passionate reader of classic economic texts.

When we returned to India, I was in my final years of high school. In May 1990, my teacher at Delhi Public School R.K. Puram assigned a debating topic for which I was, as luck would have it, well prepared: the relative merits of socialism and capitalism. The Soviet Empire was in its death throes, and many Indians were questioning the old socialist faith of the Congress Party, which had ruled the country almost without break since independence in 1947. I took the side of the questioners.

Why, I asked, was a democracy like India, so fiercely proud of its political freedoms, so unwilling to grant its people economic freedom as well? Surely citizens who could be trusted to vote and speak their minds could also be trusted to open businesses, set prices, and exercise the economic rights granted in other democracies as a matter of course. Wealth was rising and social welfare was improving faster in capitalist societies than in their socialist rivals.

The following year, 1991, would turn out to be one of the darkest in India's post-independence history. Decades of overspending had driven the country to the verge of default on its foreign debts. Prime Minister Rajiv Gandhi, a scion of the Congress Party's leading family, had taken tentative steps to open up India's economy. I admired Gandhi as a modernizer and was rooting for him in the upcoming national elections. But his life and his plans for India were cut short by a suicide bomber in May of that grim year.

Just out of high school, I went to work for a leading financial paper, writing a column on global markets—a beat no one else in India seemed to want at the time. Two months after Gandhi's assassination, my press credential got me in to see the maiden parliamentary address of the finance minister, Manmohan Singh, who captured all the pathos and promise of that moment. "As I rise, I am overpowered by a strange feeling of loneliness," said Singh, honoring the tragedy of Gandhi's assassination, before promising to push forward his economic agenda in a series of big-bang reforms.

I listened with so much excitement that it is surprising to look back at the speech now and find that the first flash of poetry was followed by thirty pages of jargon, dwelling on "credible fiscal adjustment and macroeconomic stabilization," which is to say budget restraint. Such was the tenor of the early nineties. The allure of socialism was fading, and pragmatic technocrats were in the ascendant. "Liberalization" was cool. Singh along with his Oxbridge and Ivy League team became the toast of the Davos crowd, praised for imposing budget discipline, thinning the regulatory thicket known as the "license raj," and opening India to the world.

Within a few years, India's economy pulled out of crisis. Under pressure from the old political establishment, still overwhelmingly socialist in its instincts, Singh slowed the pace of economic reform. I took a job at a global investment bank in 1996, and travel again gave me new points of comparison. East Asian nations like South Korea and Taiwan were, like Singapore, giving people far greater economic freedom and were seeing fast gains in income, alongside rapid declines in poverty and infant mortality. China was leaving India behind. In 1990, the two had similar average incomes: since then, China's has risen fortyfold to $12,500, while India's rose just sevenfold to $2,400.

To this day the standard Indian excuse is that the world's largest democracy can't force march development the way Communist China once did. But democracy is not the problem; many democracies have grown much richer than India. It is India's lingering attachment to a state that overpromises and under-delivers.

Even Congress's successors in the right-wing Bharatiya Janata Party (BJP) are steeped in the same ideals. BJP prime minister Narendra Modi campaigned for the job in 2014 promising "minimum government, maximum governance" and sounding like the Reagan of India. He criticized Congress for "welfarism" and said the poor want "work not handouts." Then Modi took power and, rather than restrain Congress's welfare programs, he topped them, offering every Indian family a "pucca" (concrete) home with gas and electricity.

India's critical mistakes included doing too little to expand economic freedom, and too much to build a welfare state, too soon. The government didn't spend more heavily than its Asian rivals, but it did spend less wisely, having introduced free social programs at a much earlier stage of development, before building the roads and schools that could generate incomes high enough to pay for those programs.

The imperious Indian state was quick to regulate, officiate, and pick winners, overconfident that its priorities were correct. Though Modi has in recent years tried to restrain welfare overspending, the central government remains notorious for its questionable choices, leaving critical services underfunded and understaffed. My grandfather died, after suffering a heart attack, when an unqualified aide in a public hospital tried to install a pacemaker.

Too often, Indian politicians sell aid to select businesses or industries as economic reform, when the measures in fact retard competition and growth. Pro-business is not the same as pro-capitalism, and the distinction continues to elude us.

The result: despite all of India's inherent strengths, from a strong entrepreneurial culture to world-class human capital, it will take longer to become a developed nation than it could have. In pursuit of the unreachable socialist ideal—equality of outcomes—India long denied itself the very real promise of capitalism: equality of opportunity.

Today the developed capitalist societies are turning onto the path that slowed progress in India, speeding the expansion of welfare and regulatory states. In its size and its reach into our economic lives, the U.S. government has, like its peers in Europe and Japan, grown steadily since the 1930s, when Franklin Delano Roosevelt launched New Deal spending programs to stop the Great Depression.

In 1980 Reagan had set out to reverse the New Deal and the growth of the state but ended up slowing its growth only in some respects, and temporarily. Now in the name of reversing the Reagan revolution, which never really happened, President Joe Biden is promising to fix the crises of capitalism by enlarging a government that never shrank. Biden aides call this recommitment to big government "the new Washington consensus," and they're not wrong.

Political and popular support for a larger state is higher now than it has been in at least half a century. Republicans are campaigning against Biden more on social issues than on his willingness to wield state power, since they are in many cases equally willing to impose government control on flows of people, money, or goods. Like populists on the left, many of those on the right share a sense that decades of free market ideology are behind today's economic ills.

This increasingly bipartisan and conventional wisdom is, I think, based on a fundamental misreading of economic history. Flaws that economists blame on "market failures," including inequality and inordinate corporate power, often flow more from government excesses. In particular, constant government support and intervention in financial markets has crippled the competition that would break up concentrations of personal and corporate power, were capitalism allowed to function properly. If frustrated young generations want to correct the growing ills of capitalism, the first step is to get the diagnosis right. This book reexamines the causes of those ills, and the possible way out.

WHAT WENT WRONG

> I've spoken of the shining city all my political life, but I don't know if I ever quite communicated what I saw when I said it. . . . In my mind it was a tall, proud city built on rocks stronger than oceans, wind-swept, God-blessed, and teeming with people of all kinds living in harmony and peace; a city with free ports that hummed with commerce and creativity. And if there had to be city walls, the walls had doors and the doors were open to anyone with the will and the heart to get here. That's how I saw it, and see it still.
>
> —*Ronald Reagan, Farewell Address, January 11, 1989*

L ove or hate him, few observers today would say Ronald Reagan was wrong when he declared victory for his revolution. Recalling why he had entered politics in the 1960s, Reagan said he was moved by concern for the direction of the country in a decade when regulators and tax collectors were taking a growing share of citizens' money, options, and freedom. His aim was to reenact, in a way, the American Revolution of 1776, which he described as "the first revolution in the history of mankind that truly reversed the course of government."

Reagan said his presidency had "stopped a lot of what needed stopping." His efforts to roll back government had unleashed the longest economic recovery since World War II—seven years and counting as he spoke, accompanied by a flowering of entrepreneurship and innovation. Aiming to change a nation, "we changed a world," inspiring other countries to abandon socialism and communism—"the ideologies of the past." Eleven months later, in November 1989, the Berlin Wall fell.

Looking back at the Reagan revolution, we can see where it worked and how it went wrong. The United States has had an astonishing run in the last four decades, losing nothing of its 25 percent share of the global economy over that time, while China was expanding its share rapidly—and entirely at the expense of Europe and Japan. As a financial superpower, the United States remains as strong as ever, the dollar by far the dominant currency in global trade, the U.S. stock and bond markets bigger than ever, relative to the rest of the world. And that also is where the flaws start to appear.

Reagan's farewell speech is remembered for the image of the "shining city." But there was a throwaway line, a caveat to his normally unshakable optimism that rings loudly now: "I've been asked if I have any regrets. Well, I do. The deficit is one."

Contrary to the narrative that prevails today, Reagan did not "reverse the course of government." The welfare state, the regulatory state, the national security state, all held steady or continued to grow, and government deepened its influence on our economic lives. What changed, starting in the late seventies and accelerating under Reagan, was the way government pays for itself—by borrowing to cover the perennial deficit. Four decades later capitalism is addicted to debt. While Donald Trump got mocked for calling himself the "king of debt," he captured in a phrase the rulers of a system who came to run on rolling over credit.

Capitalism is, to adapt a line from Winston Churchill, the worst system for allocating a nation's economic resources, "except for all the others that have been tried." When capitalism is working, it gives people freedom to vote in the marketplace, by investing in new ideas and growing companies. Their choices determine prices, and those prices reflect the public's best bet on which ideas and companies are poised to thrive in the future. The collective wisdom of millions of individuals, scrutinizing every deal closely, cannot be matched by the lone mind of the state, trying to steer capital from on high.

Capitalism is the economic soulmate of democracy, equally fair and flawed. With the partial exception of tiny Singapore, no wealthy, developed economy is not a fully formed democracy. And no centralized autocracy has ever grown rich in the modern era. China may never make it into the developed class, in part because it is in the process of bringing back big government.

Governments of the leading developed nations have played a more active role in allocating capital since the Depression of the 1930s, whether by rescuing and regulating, or spending and borrowing. Fear that the resulting debt bubbles will blow up and take down the economy has come to haunt policymakers, and has grown more acute since the crisis of 2008, when we witnessed the most damaging collapse of a debt bubble since the Depression. Today governments watch for jitters in the markets and rush in to support them with easy money and bailouts at the first sign of trouble.

When government becomes the dominant buyer and seller in the market—as it has in recent decades—it distorts the price signals that normally guide capital. Money starts to flow down the paths of least regulatory resistance, or most government support. Each crisis brings bigger bailouts, leaving capitalism more mired in debt, more dysfunctional and fragile. In the 2000s, and even more in the 2010s, the governments of advanced countries began injecting money into economies that were not in crisis. They were in recovery. Disappointingly slow recovery, but still. Intended to boost the pace of growth in these economies, these experiments had the opposite effect. By flooding the engines of capitalism with easy credit, they created more kings of debt, more excesses in the financial markets.

These distortions reached fun house mirror proportions amid the pandemic, with its record bailouts. Governments offered trillions of dollars in support to companies large and small, solvent or not, so investors no longer looked for companies with bright prospects. They looked to buy whatever assets the central bank was buying, or whatever companies the Treasury supported. That is what Ray Dalio, founder of the world's largest hedge fund, had in mind when he said in July 2020: "The capital markets are not free." Wealthy capitalists are now often as critical of "financialized" capitalism as socialists are.

The periodic financial crises—erupting in 2001, 2008, and 2020—now unfold against the background of a permanent, daily crisis of colossal capital misallocation. Its most visible symptoms are the big economic players who have the resources to thrive in a system awash in complex debt products. That is a major and overlooked reason why most American and European industries are concentrating in the hands of fewer companies, and the individuals who founded and lead those companies now measure their wealth in hundreds of billions, not mere billions.

Every big player on Wall Street knows in his or her heart that Bernie Sanders has a point when he calls modern capitalism "socialism for the very rich." Concentrating wealth in the hands of oligopolies and the billionaire class is a critical symptom of capitalism gone wrong, both inefficient and grossly unfair. I agree with Sanders, but my diagnosis of how it went wrong could not be more different.

4

In the Sanders view, the story begins with leaders like Reagan shrinking government. Over the next four decades they gutted regulations, which left rich capitalists free to run wild, and downsized the welfare state, which left the poor to get poorer. Sanders always pairs his critique of "socialism for the very rich" with "rugged individualism for the poor." The problem is a shrinking government, he says, so the answer must be more regulation and welfare spending—a view that captivates many Americans, especially the young.

In 2016, the youth vote helped turn Sanders from a Vermont sideshow in American political life to the first socialist ever to make a serious run for the presidency from one of the major parties. By 2020, only half of American adults under forty approved of capitalism, a third were willing to try communism as an alternative, and 70 percent said they were likely or extremely likely to vote for a socialist. For the first time since the Pew polling agency started posing the question in the early 1990s, a majority of under-forties said yes when asked if the government should "do more to solve problems."

They did not get an avowed socialist in 2021, but they did get Joe Biden, who saw himself as a throwback to Franklin Delano Roosevelt. The original big-government president, FDR launched the New Deal spending programs to counter the Great Depression. The prospect that Biden would launch a second New Deal inspired headlines from the *New York Times* to the *Washington Post* and the *Guardian* heralding the end of "the era of small government" or the "age of neoliberalism," which is to say the free market reforms that began with Reagan and Margaret Thatcher in the United Kingdom. Even conservative publications like the *Wall Street Journal* accepted the basic premise—that big government had disappeared—by warning that it was "back."

That narrative was misleading. Government had been growing steadily since the 1930s, and during the pandemic matched peaks of spending and debt reached in World War II. Capitalism has been twisted into an unfair and inefficient form, but not mainly by rules stacked in favor of big companies and tycoons. It has been distorted above all by governments and central banks pumping more money into the economy than the markets can possibly invest effectively. More than just socialism for the very rich, the underlying issue is socialized risk for everyone—the government extending the safety net beyond the poor to the middle class and the rich, at a pace and scale that have corrupted capitalism with debt. Bigger government will only magnify the distortions.

A TURN OF THE MIND

In 2022 and 2023, a series of landmark histories of capitalism hit the bookstores and bestseller lists, and all tell the story of the Reagan revolution in the same basic way. In Gary Gerstle's taxonomy of capitalist orders, the "New Deal order" begins to erode under President Jimmy Carter in the 1970s, and the ascent of the "neoliberal order" begins in earnest with the 1980 election. In Jonathan Levy's account of capitalist ages, the postwar "Age of Control," in which big government and big corporations control flows of capital, gives way in 1980 to the "Age of Chaos," in which the unleashed markets steer capital to chaotic ends. In *Slouching Towards Utopia,* Berkeley economist Brad DeLong describes how "thirty glorious years of social democracy" fell apart in "the neoliberal turn," starting in the 1970s and accelerating under Reagan.

In these "grand narratives," as DeLong calls them, the implication is that big government rose to new heights in the 1950s, '60s, and '70s, then fell back sharply under one aggressively capitalist leader after another, starting with Reagan and Thatcher.

There is wonderful depth in these books, which take readers inside the culture wars and the change in corporate mindsets that defined this shift from the early to late postwar eras. All of this happened. The public conversation did often attribute to free markets a kind of magic and focused on ways to push government out of the way by cutting regulations and deficits. The "neoliberal turn" was very real, but it was, for the most part, a turn of the mind.

The neoliberals resurrected the ideas of classic liberal thinkers like Adam Smith and John Stuart Mill, who were the original apostles of small government and free market capitalism. The neos rejected the way the word "liberal" had been repurposed, starting in the New Deal and continuing through Lyndon Johnson's Great Society in the 1960s, to describe people in favor of a larger welfare state. Starting in the fifties, the neoliberals had been plotting to overthrow the New Deal and much that followed. Clustered around economists and political scientists at the University of Chicago, they developed the agenda of cutting—taxes, spending, and regulation—that Reagan brought to the White House in 1980.

In practice, however, neoliberalism did not slow the momentum of big government. There was some slowdown at least in spending under Reagan, even a brief and isolated retreat under Bill Clinton in the 1990s, but not to the degree talk of new ages and orders implies. After 2000, government was booming again. By selectively stitching together the many episodes in which neoliberal thinking did shape policy over the last four decades, under both parties, commentators create what appears to be a persuasive picture of government retreating, leaving big companies and tycoons free to take over the economy.

Any leader who at any time followed any piece or pieces of the neoliberal agenda—from tax cuts to deregulation, privatization of state companies, free trade deals, or a rhetorical concern with containing public deficits and debt—is cast as one of them. From Bill Clinton to Barack

Obama in the United States, Tony Blair in Britain to Gerhard Schroeder in Germany, and Emmanuel Macron in France—all populate these narratives as neoliberal descendants of Reagan and Thatcher.

Follow the data, not the debate, and the story reads differently: government grew steadily bigger everywhere in the capitalist world, with a few surprising exceptions, including the Nordic welfare states so beloved of the American left. On many measures, they are less socialist than most people think.

THE "ERA OF SMALL GOVERNMENT" ENDED LONG AGO

There was an era of small government, but it ended in the United States with the Depression. Washington circa 1930, before FDR was first elected to the White House, would be entirely unrecognizable today. Half the government departments had yet to be created, and those that did exist were a sliver of what they would become. Half of all federal government employees worked for the post office. The Capitol, the citadel of democracy, would soon be dwarfed in scale by the temples of New Deal bureaucracy, first the headquarters of the Commerce Department and then in 1936 of the Agriculture Department—the world's largest office building at the time. Income taxes, introduced in 1913, were still relatively light, so Washington raised revenue largely through tariffs and tolls. Federal government spending was so low, less than 4 percent of GDP, even a large deficit would not have had much impact on the economy. Deficits were not only rare, they were a breach of the prevailing post-Victorian ethos, which saw debt as a moral failing and bankruptcy as a criminal offense. Compared to the capitals of Europe, Washington was like a small company town.

Since the 1930s, public spending has grown steadily as a share of every large capitalist economy, punctuated by two upward spikes during World War II and the pandemic of 2020. There was never a sustained retreat anywhere in the leading capitalist economies, which I'll call the LCEs. Owing to limited historical data for others, I include in this group the United States, Japan, the United Kingdom, and the four major members of the European Union: Germany, France, Italy, and Spain. Since 1930, spending by government—including state and local—has quadrupled on average to 48 percent of GDP in the LCEs, but within a broad range, rising from 4 percent to 36 percent in the United States and from 19 percent to 58 percent in France.

While free market ideology spread worldwide after 1980, and shaped policy episodically, governments in the western world were extending their reach into economic lives. In the United States and Europe alike, parties of the center right and left launched bouts of deregulation, which generally entailed rewriting and replacing regulations with longer ones. Overall, the regulatory state grew dramatically—more rules, more restrictive rules, more rule-makers, and more rule-making agencies with bigger budgets.

The legislators cut some taxes, raised others, and overall the government's tax take didn't change much. "Hauser's law," really just a factual observation, states that while the sources of tax revenue shift constantly, the total tax burden hasn't changed for decades. Including state and local government, it has hovered slightly above 20 percent of GDP on average in the LCEs, and slightly under 20 percent in the United States. If revenues are so steady over time, how can it be that government is growing more expansive?

The big change was that the large capitalist countries began running significant deficits (larger than 1 percent of GDP) virtually every year starting in the late 1970s. Under Reagan, the spending choices shifted from welfare to defense, butter to guns, and the deficits grew. Rather than pay for the growing edifice of state agencies by raising taxes, or making cuts elsewhere in the budget, governments borrowed more. Central government debt in the LCEs crept up from 21 percent of GDP in 1970 to 30 percent in 1980, surging to almost 120 percent on the eve of the pandemic and 140 percent during the pandemic.

The Reagan revolution spawned a conviction, which soon spanned the capitalist world, that deficits and debt don't matter. From 1980 on, Republicans would propose tax cuts as the solution to every problem, claiming they would pay for themselves by generating more economic growth. Even if public debt rose, the economy would grow faster, easing the burden. Democrats would make the same case for spending on schools, health, or subsidies for manufacturing, arguing that social spending is "an investment" in the future. Either way, growth in the economy never kept up. The burden of public debt— measured as a share of GDP—mostly kept climbing. The two main exceptions—public debt receded a bit in the United Kingdom under Thatcher in the 1980s, and in the United States under Clinton in the 1990s—prove the general rule.

Slowly the developed world became addicted to debt, and to constant support from governments that had come to define their jobs as ensuring stable expansion of the economy. The Keynesian idea, born in the Depression, that governments should run deficits to create jobs in hard times, and surpluses in good times, had given way to running deficits all the time. Democracies were losing the capacity to make hard choices.

Elected legislatures were fracturing along partisan lines, often over issues of race, immigration, and other social conflicts not directly related to the economy. Divided lawmakers found it difficult to come to spending decisions, even during crises. Voters had come to expect the government to keep the economy growing, but responsibility for that task was passing by default to unelected central bankers, who came to see themselves as the last institutions standing between the world and the next Great Depression.

This fearful, backward-looking mindset is destructive for all countries, and a particularly odd fit for the United States, which sees itself as younger, bolder, tougher, and more "future-oriented" than soft Europe or aging Japan. Yet for much of this century, the mantra of officials facing a crisis has been variations on "better to be early and overreact," or "err on the side of being generous," or the "risks of doing too little are far greater than the risks of doing too much."

This shift mirrors exactly the "revolution in pain management" that, also over the last two decades, helped hook America on opioids. Accepting any pain is seen as a legacy of crude, nineteenth-century medicine, so modern doctors should dose their patients with OxyContin even for moderate injuries. The public—particularly homeowners, stockholders, and bondholders—came to expect more help in every crisis; they put more pressure on politicians and central bankers to deliver more relief, culminating in the shockingly large doses of government aid in 2020. Though inspired by a kind of paternalistic fear, these rescues are delivered with growing certainty that the cure is not worse than the disease.

Gradually, a safety net once meant to catch the poor at the precipice of hunger was extended under the financial markets, where the big beneficiaries are far from hungry. In the seven largest capitalist economies, cited above, the combined stimulus from governments and central banks rose from about 1 percent of GDP in the recessions of the early 1980s and 1990, to nearly 3 percent in 2001, to more than 12 percent in 2008 and 35 percent in 2020.

As governments and central banks flushed more money into the economy with each crisis, they inflated the size of the financial markets. Liberal critics cast the post-Reagan boom in financial markets as a result mainly of deregulation, which did play a big role—but only in widening the options for investors. Their capital came mainly from governments and central banks, and their overconfidence was built on the promise of public bailouts.

Since easy money inflates the prices of all financial assets—equity and debt, stocks and bonds—the financial markets grew even more bloated than the debts alone. From slightly larger on average than the large capitalist economies in the 1970s, the financial markets had grown to nearly four times larger by the eve of the pandemic, when they rose even higher. In the United States, where the "everything bubble" was the most extreme, the financial markets are now worth $120 trillion, four and a half times U.S. GDP.

Though stocks comprise roughly 30 percent of global financial markets, the rest is in debts of all kinds, from simple government and corporate bonds to increasingly exotic packages of loans—for cars, college, consumer credit, mortgages, anything. The markets are the big city street corners where debt addiction plays out.

Central banks used to be conservative institutions that bought only short-term government bonds to push money into a troubled economy, but in the crises of 2008 and 2020 they turned radical and experimental, expanding what kinds of bonds they would buy and from whom, to the point that in 2020 they were buying the junk debt of failing companies known as "sinking demons" and purchasing those debts from "shadow banks" like hedge funds and other private investors.

They pushed easy money straight into the hands of the biggest players on Wall Street, which, despite their scale, can't steer that many trillions efficiently. By the time the pandemic hit, capitalist economies were already being overtaken by monopolies and oligopolies, by the billionaires who own them, by firms that make no profit, and by a growing class of "zombie companies" that make too little profit to cover even the interest on their debt and survive by taking out new debt. All these creatures of credit thrived in the bailouts of 2020, which were seen by many as a creative emergency response to a hundred-year storm. Yet each new rescue built on those that came before, pushing the century-long expansion of the bailout culture to a risky new height, and setting a higher bar for the future.

HOW BIG GOVERNMENT SLOWS GROWTH

Economies began to slow in the 2010s, not only in the LCEs but worldwide, in part for a reason beyond government control. The social revolutions of the 1960s and '70s gave women the freedom to have fewer children. Birth rates started to fall, which meant fewer young adults entering the workforce in subsequent decades. Many governments would try to counter the population slowdown—for example, by giving families bonuses for having more children—but to little or no avail.

Economic growth is a simple function of how many people are working, and how much each worker is producing. To boost economic growth in an era when fewer adults are entering the workforce, governments need to raise productivity—output per worker. Productivity growth allows companies to raise worker pay without increasing prices— generating higher economic growth without inflation. It has been called the magic key to prosperity, which it is. But like population growth, productivity growth has slowed sharply since 1980. Despite a recent uptick, productivity growth is down by more than half in the United States to an average barely over 1 percent a year since 2010, and down even more sharply in the United Kingdom, Japan and the four largest European economies, where it averaged just one quarter of a percent.

The productivity slump is the most important mystery of modern capitalism, and mounting evidence suggests that a widely overlooked piece of the puzzle is bigger government and its by-products: ballooning debt and metastasizing capital misallocation. To revive capitalist economies, the most essential thing governments need to do is boost productivity. Instead, their efforts are backfiring. It is likely no accident that productivity has fallen more sharply to even lower levels in Europe than in the United States, at a time when the European Union is building what scholar Anu Bradford calls a global "empire of laws and regulations."

When capitalism works, it does so through what the Austrian-born economist Joseph Schumpeter called "creative destruction." Competition in the markets allows new firms to rise up and destroy the complacent ones, making the economy ever more productive over time. This process generates vast pools of wealth, personal and corporate, but *only temporarily*, as cut-rate competitors raze monopoly profits and concentrations of power. The downsides of this rough cyclical justice are more downturns in the economy and churn in the markets. The upside is human progress.

This is what capitalism is losing, daily. Government rescues made recessions few and far between, and less deep than they otherwise would have been. As more old and weak firms survived each downturn, America ceased to be the land of second chances, because so few established businesses were allowed to fail in the first place. As what researchers have called "the cleansing effect" of recessions disappeared, recoveries started to last longer but at a slower pace of growth, particularly after the dot-com crash of 2000.

The rhythm of the markets started to change, too, calmer and steadier but less discriminating. Investors came to assume that good economic news was good for the markets yet so was bad news—because it would trigger more government support. As a growing government stifled competition and crippled the process of creative destruction, the largest firms kept getting bigger. And markets with no downside were a boon to the super-rich. Billionaires barely existed worldwide before 2000, but have since surged in number to more than 2,600, rising with the financial markets.

All of this—the bloated markets, weaker recoveries, and shorter recessions with fewer bankruptcies, the general stupefaction of a business culture pickled in debt—might be of less social consequence were it not conspiring to slow economic growth. Who, after all, wants harsher or more frequent recessions, more bankruptcies, or a scarier ride in the stock markets? By smothering capitalism's competitive fire, big government is slowing productivity growth, which is lowering economic growth in the long run, thus shrinking the pie and concentrating what's left in fewer hands.

Millennials, the next ruling generation, have embraced a narrative that is clear on the problems of capitalism and way too certain of the causes. Like the media establishment, many Americans seem to assume that the story of shrinking government is true. They juxtapose it against the stark facts of giant corporations dominating the economy: the stock market value of the largest company skyrocketing above $3 trillion, the fortunes of the richest tycoons breaking $200 billion, CEO pay topping four hundred times the average staffer's pay. If these distortions arose in a period of shrinking government, they figure, then bigger government must be the answer. But if the era of shrinking government never happened, that is exactly the wrong answer.

AMERICA IS NOW "EXCEPTIONAL" IN THE WRONG WAYS

Since its earliest stirring in the seventeenth century, the term "American exceptionalism" has described the unique culture of a country in which individual freedoms flourished because government was too young and small to be entrenched or overbearing. Reagan's "shining city on a hill" was a metaphor for this origin story. And though the American style of democratic capitalism continued to outperform its rivals into the late 2010s, at least in economic competition, the U.S. intelligentsia did not recognize, much less boast of, its achievements. Perhaps the establishment was reluctant to highlight American successes when Donald Trump, a man it despised as a rogue populist, occupied the White House.

Then Trump lost, and "American exceptionalism" made a comeback. Even writers who normally avoid a patriotic tone began to laud "the power of American capitalism," or the "marvel" of how it had held its ground against China, and the lessons this "astonishing economic record" have for Old Europe and Japan. What impressed establishment publications from the *Economist* to the *New York Times* and the *Washington Post* was U.S. dominance in financial markets, the might of the dollar, and the fact that the biggest American companies were growing even bigger. While U.S. tech giants accounted for most of the world's ten largest companies, and had for more than a decade, many investors thought they would remain on top for another decade.

Most Americans, however, were not joining in this round of applause and awe. Riding the back of what was still the fastest-growing economy in the developed world, Biden was said to be perplexed by why he was so unpopular, and why voters were still so frustrated. Late in his first term, Biden's approval ratings were the lowest since Jimmy Carter in the 1970s; only two in ten Americans thought life in this country was "better" than fifty years ago, and one in ten expressed confidence in their economic future.

Make no mistake, America has had an exceptional run, relative to other developed countries, for the past decade in particular. But it has been outrunning a field of competitors who have all slowed dramatically. The weaknesses of modern capitalism are increasingly clear to the majority, and not only in the United States. They see that the system is unfair, out of balance, less and less capable of lifting all boats. In many ways, the economic crisis is not merely brewing, it is here. The debate over how to fix capitalism needs to start with a clear understanding of what went wrong in the first place.

BIDENOMICS

By 2023 the White House was pitching "Bidenomics" as a geopolitical masterstroke and a historic turning point. Its premise, as outlined by national security adviser Jake Sullivan, was that after World War II, the United States had built a global economic order that lifted millions out of poverty and "sustained thrilling technological revolutions." In recent decades, however, this order had faltered on an "oversimplified" faith that "markets always allocate productively and efficiently." Left to their own devices, it was the markets that had allocated capital to the rich over the middle class, to finance not manufacturing, and to China not the United States, leaving the construction of a green economy to Beijing. Thus the first pillar of Bidenomics was an "economic mentality that champions building."

It put government in charge of allocating capital—through spending and subsidies, regulations and trade barriers—to where the executive branch thinks it is needed most. Denying any intent to "pick winners," the administration would aim instead to "unlock the power and ingenuity of private markets" through financial incentives, said Sullivan. And yet it had already picked three very specific winners indeed: advanced semiconductors, green technology, and precious minerals required in many green technologies, such as lithium, cobalt, nickel, and graphite.

This "modern American industrial strategy" was part of "the new Washington consensus," in which "like-minded" Western countries would rally to fight climate change and compete with China. Sullivan's speech was titled "Renewing American Economic Leadership."

The muscular nationalism inherent in Bidenomics might rally support at home, but it was inherently divisive abroad, pitting capitalist countries against China—and against one another. After complaining that a modern American industrial policy would hurt them as much as China, American allies began racing to match it, barrier for barrier, subsidy for subsidy. The European Union rolled out a "Green Deal Industrial Plan," including schemes to match U.S. clean energy subsidies. The head of the European Central Bank touted the plan, and so did French president Macron, who was once a champion of free markets. Japan launched $150 billion in green tech subsidies of its own. German officials warned German companies in unusually blunt terms to reduce ties to China.

The leader of the capitalist world was leading its peers toward a bigger, more active government. Biden had campaigned for the presidency on promises of a "cradle-to-grave" expansion of the welfare state, from childcare to community college to health and pension benefits for retirees. By 2022, after some defeats for his social spending agenda in Congress, the Biden team had shifted focus, emphasizing the "modern American industrial strategy" more than the social spending. None of its speeches failed to mention China, the rival supposedly provoking this strategic response.

The timing was odd. Biden was said by aides to harbor a "burning sense of competition to prove that democratic capitalism can work," yet he was, in rough outline, following the lead of China, where the state still plays the guiding role in investing capital—with increasingly disastrous results. As paramount leader Xi Jinping reimposed state control in the 2010s, China's GDP growth rate slowed from well over 10 percent a year in nominal dollar terms to less than 5 percent by 2023. At that pace, China was no longer growing fast enough to surpass the United States as the world's largest economy in the coming decades, if ever. Why follow the lead of a faltering rival? Former U.S. trade representative Robert Zoellick called Biden's vision a "Washington Ordered Economy," and warned that its barriers, rules, and subsidies, once embedded, would be "hard to reverse."

By mid-2023, Biden had launched nearly $8 trillion in new spending, the largest surge ever, outside a world war or depression. Of that sum, roughly $2.3 trillion did go to the kind of investment in research and infrastructure that could be called "industrial policy." But some $1.7 trillion went to Covid relief, $2 trillion to the military, and more than $2 trillion to new welfare benefits, including Medicare subsidies, disability benefits, and student loan forgiveness.

As Biden rolled out new spending, the governments of Europe and Japan were exercising more restraint, particularly after the return of higher interest rates started pushing borrowing costs upward in 2022. Though U.S. spending habits were once pretty typical for an advanced economy, the United States was turning into an outlier, exceptional in self-defeating ways, the biggest deficit spender in the capitalist world. It was putting its competitive advantages at risk.

In early 2024, the Congressional Budget Office estimated that federal government spending would remain near 25 percent of GDP through the 2020s, higher than at any point in the prior century. The deficit thereafter would remain at record levels—close to 6 percent of GDP, roughly double the average of recent decades. The scale of this shift is hard to overstate. Before the pandemic, the U.S. deficit was only slightly larger than average for a developed economy. In the coming years, it is on track to be six times larger, because rivals are cutting back while the United States ramps up.

And deficits mean more debt. Already third highest in the developed world after Italy and Japan, the U.S. government debt (including state and local) is expected to rise between 2023 and 2028 by 14 points, to 137 percent of GDP. It was growing nearly twice as fast as the public debt of the United Kingdom, more than five times faster than that of Japan and ten times faster than the average for the four largest European states. Meanwhile, public debt was poised to decline through 2028 as a share of smaller European economies, including the Nordic states, such as Denmark and Sweden.

To date, capitalism has arguably gone more wrong in Europe, where the state has been even more inclined to rescue, bail out, and regulate, and growth in productivity and average incomes has slowed more than in the United States over the last two decades. Now, however, the two sides of the Atlantic may be swapping places, as big government grows faster in the United States.

Part I of this book will retell the story of the last century, showing how government has evolved from limited before the Depression to omnipresent in this century. Part II will explain the cumulative effect of expanding government, and how it has distorted the capitalist system, as the symptoms of dysfunction became clear after the year 2000. Fueled by easy money and rising debt, those distortions include, most prominently, the increase in income and wealth inequality, the spread of zombie firms that live on fresh infusions of debt, and the rise of "bad" monopolies and oligopolies—the kind that thrive less on innovation than on strangling competition. Part II will end with a new explanation for the mystery of the global productivity slowdown, which can be traced, in good part, to these symptoms of debt addiction, enabled by government.

There is no returning to the nineteenth century, when the government barely existed as a provider of welfare services or a regulator of economic behavior, much less the major player in the financial markets, the way it does now. No rational person would imagine it possible to return to an era when the federal government didn't do much more than deliver mail and wage war. The intellectual consensus today, however, assumes that there is plenty of room for government to grow bigger, and more active, because it has been shrinking since the Reagan presidency. Flawed history will lead to misguided solutions. Expanding government from this new base—many times larger than it was in 1980—is likely to make the ongoing crisis of capitalism that much worse.

PART I

THE RISE AND RISE AGAIN OF BIG GOVERNMENT

———————————

ONE

THERE WAS NO GOLDEN AGE

Government as Americans know it is traceable to one of the founding fathers, Alexander Hamilton. He wanted to establish a strong government to develop the young country, anchored by a central bank that would serve as the foundation for a private credit system, which in turn would fund the spread of commerce and industry, and the rise of cities.

A financial visionary, Hamilton was ahead of his time. He tried to persuade his skeptical peers, steeped in Puritan values of self-reliance, that issuing public debt would be good for the economy. Only the interest would have to be repaid, while the principal would serve in essence as collateral for private lending, over time greatly expanding the credit supply—and the economy. "A national debt if it is not excessive will be to us a national blessing; it will be a powerful cement of our union," he said. Hamilton would prevail, but only long after he was dead.

America's emergence as a credit-driven, urban-industrial society was resisted for much of the nineteenth century by the descendants of Hamilton's archrival, Thomas Jefferson. The Jeffersonians envisioned America as a land of farmers, blessed by what they saw as the rugged virtues that come with landownership. And they saw Hamilton as the enemy, intent on turning America into old Britain: aristocratic, mired in corrupt commerce, built on a financial system that favored the rich city elite over the rural majority. In fact Hamilton did model his plans for a central bank on the Bank of England, which was one of the governing institutions through which sinecures and self-dealing enriched the Victorian elite.

Throughout the nineteenth century, Jeffersonian democrats managed to thwart the creation of a central bank as too powerful by definition, concentrating too much control over money and credit in one set of hands. Bank wars were a center-ring feature of American politics. Nonetheless, a loosely Hamiltonian system started to work, albeit through a chaotic network of private banks, many issuing their own currencies—which numbered around eight thousand up to the Civil War.

Credit began to flow in the familiar cycle of boom and bust, fueled on the way up by growing optimism and popped at the peak by obvious signs of excessive lending. Early on these cycles tended to spring out of the fields, usually of wheat or cotton, and on the frontiers—the South or West. They ended in the major panics of 1819 and 1837. Painful as they were, these crises punctuated but did not slow the economic expansion. In this period, the American South was growing richer than any nation other than England, yet it was falling behind the American North.

The Industrial Revolution had started in England and by the 1820s it was crossing the Atlantic, seeding the first small textile mills in the northeastern states. Powered first by water and the labor of women and children, later by steam engines and immigrants from Europe, "the

Northeast was likely the fastest-growing and richest economic region on earth," writes historian Jonathan Levy. Between 1840 and 1860, its industrial output quintupled.

The origins of the modern U.S. financial system date to the Civil War. The North was, in essence, a one-party state under Republican rule. President Abraham Lincoln needed funds to support the vast Northern armies and delegated the task of raising those funds to his secretary of the Treasury, Salmon P. Chase, an imperious figure said by contemporaries to regard himself as the fourth member of the Holy Trinity. Chase greatly expanded the government's authority to levy business taxes and tariffs and introduced its authority to sell Treasury bonds. The public debt tripled on his watch, and the government began steering capital as it never had before, investing heavily in munitions plants, bakeries, and all the other enterprises needed to keep the Union army in the field.

Chase created a network of national banks that were required to hold reserves in their largest member, located in New York. He also consolidated the swarm of state and local currencies into two, which were further consolidated after the Civil War into the new dollar, backed by gold. The inherent scarcity of gold naturally limited the supply of dollars, which would further concentrate capital—and the power to decide where it would be lent and invested—on Wall Street.

The war and the boom that followed made many men rich. American newspapers revived a medieval phrase, "robber baron," to describe a new breed of Wall Street tycoons, such as John D. Rockefeller, Jay Gould, Andrew Carnegie, Cornelius Vanderbilt, and J. P. Morgan. As banker-industrialists, they were able to guide capital into their own ventures. The action was in railroads, the hot network of the age, built with steel, powered by oil and electricity. Unrestrained by any national plan, rival tycoons were racing to finish competing rail lines between every pairing of major cities, including, most importantly, New York and Chicago.

Most of those rail lines collapsed in the next big credit busts—the financial panics of 1873 and 1893. The United States still had no central bank to save anyone, had it been so inclined. The intellectual founder of central banking, English journalist Walter Bagehot, had defined their role quite narrowly. In a crisis, they would offer emergency financial support only to solvent private banks, against stiff collateral, and nothing to other kinds of businesses. In practice central banks were even more strict than Bagehot suggested; in response to crises—one economist would later write—they tended to "protect their own gold reserves first, turning away their correspondents in need."

As the tycoons poured money into expanded production, the U.S. rail network began linking factories across the Northeast and Midwest; this region was emerging as the center of the Industrial Revolution. Workers enjoyed rapidly rising wages but declining living standards, typically in urban factory neighborhoods lacking sewers and health services. Blue-collar workers were dying younger than fellow Americans in the countryside. Chicago, the western terminus of this industrializing corridor, was an explosively growing marvel of new industry and a nightmare of soot-stained tenements. As the robber barons built the faux European castles that still dot the East Coast, America had the worst labor violence in the world.

The result was a populist revolt. Where Jefferson and his early successors feared centralized government power, by the late nineteenth century, their successors feared the private rail, steel, and oil monopolies and thundered against the plight of the factory worker. The Progressive movement, led by presidents Theodore Roosevelt and Woodrow Wilson, would in the 1910s pass the Sixteenth Amendment to legalize income taxes, create new agencies to regulate commerce and fight the exploitation of labor, and to break up monopolies.

Wilson also abandoned the traditional populist resistance to a central bank. The financial crises of the age, including the global panic in 1907, tended to start when England's central bank raised its interest rates, which attracted money from all over the world. As U.S. dollars flowed to London, credit would dry up on Wall Street, triggering panics. To defend the dollar at moments like these, the United States would need its own central bank after all. Still, lingering resistance would delay the establishment of the Federal Reserve until 1913.

The financial center of the world was shifting. World War I broke out in 1914, turning continental Europe into a battlefield, and the United States into a safe and flourishing haven. Gold pooled up in the United States. New York replaced London as the global financial capital—and the epicenter of future financial crises. They would not be long in coming—but by now the upsides of creative destruction were becoming clear.

Before the early nineteenth century, asking humans whether they expected to be better-off than their ancestors, or five years in the future, would have been absurd. The answer was obviously no. After 1820, the Industrial Revolution had started to generate sustained gains in average incomes for the first time in human history, first in England, then in a few other nations of northern Europe, then most rapidly in America. Worldwide, per capita income growth jumped roughly tenfold, from less than two-tenths of a percent in the prior century to around 1.5 percent a year by the late nineteenth century, with virtually all the gains concentrated in the crucibles of Western capitalism.

Those inclined to romanticize early capitalism overlook the fact that even after 1820, as people in Europe and the United States moved to rapidly industrializing cities, where life could be deadly, they were growing shorter in stature and sometimes lifespan as well. Germans, for example, lost nearly two inches in height in the early nineteenth century, and similar if smaller losses were found in the United Kingdom and much of Europe. Broad pockets of humanity were still trapped in the Malthusian dilemma: economic growth was never fast enough, so bursts of population growth were checked by failing food supplies and famine.

There was a sudden turn for the better after roughly the 1870s, when the Industrial Revolution accelerated, powered now by electricity and softened by a growing state. Though the forces that began to ease the struggle for subsistence were complex, one clear step forward was a more active government in some of the largest economies: big enough to start providing basic services, and to start regulating away some of the worst excesses of unfettered capitalism—ghettoes choking in coal dust, slaughterhouses deadly to human labor, children working in factories. But not so big as to get in the way. Finally, economic progress was allowing for longer, healthier lives. Since 1880, the typical American has gained forty years of life and four inches in height; the typical German grew even more during this period and is now half a foot taller than in 1880.

From 1875 to 1915, the United States under a small government saw per capita GDP growth near 2 percent a year; that was significantly faster than the average for other developed countries including Germany, which was seeding the welfare state, and France, where the industrial boom spilled over the northern border but didn't penetrate the heartland. One reason was a statist French legal tradition that would become associated—in every country where it took hold—with weaker enforcement of property rights, heavier regulation, more corruption, easier evasion of bankruptcy, and slower growth.

No rulers stood more firmly in the way of progress than the Austro-Hungarian emperors, whose lands extended from modern-day Belgium across Eastern Europe and into Italy. They resisted the construction of factories, the import of machines, and the development of railways, in particular steam railways, "lest the revolution might come into the country." More than half a century after the United States launched steam engines, the Austrians were still pulling rail cars with horses. While more open societies were booming in the late nineteenth and early twentieth centuries, per capita GDP shrank in the Austro-Hungarian empire. The emperors had prevailed, and their people remained peasants, watching the global rise in prosperity from the sidelines, on state orders.

THE PINNACLE OF CREATIVE DESTRUCTION

In the 1910s Henry Ford raised wages to $5 a day, an unheard-of sum, in part, he said, so that his workers could afford the Model Ts rolling off his assembly lines. At River Rouge, outside Detroit, Ford built the largest factory complex the world had ever seen. Its 1,200-acre network of ninety buildings had a production plant for almost every part of an automobile, from leather for the seats and glass for the windshield to steel for the frame. Over the course of the decade, cars replaced horses on the streets of New York, and the electrified assembly lines pioneered by Ford began turning out new generations of consumer gadgets, from radios to spin dryers. The artists of this period were often less terrified than "thrilled" by industrial marvels like River Rouge and the promise they held for the future.

The rush to prosperity peaked in the Roaring Twenties, which began with a downturn so harsh it has been called the "Forgotten Depression." During World War I, government borrowing had tripled to 40 percent of GDP, and as American soldiers flooded home from European battlefields after 1918, inflation took off. The Fed responded over the next two years with sharp rate hikes, and real interest rates hit 20 percent, wiping out many weak borrowers. Five hundred banks failed. Industrial production fell by 25 percent in 1920–21, and unemployment tripled to 12 percent. Prices fell at an annual rate of 15 percent, foreshadowing the deflation of the 1930s. Only in this case, the Treasury and the Fed—still less than a decade old—let the crisis unfold.

The result was a quick cleansing of weak links in the economy. The depression was over by 1922, which is why it was so easily "forgotten." Later, President Herbert Hoover's light-touch response to the early stages of the Great Depression would be informed by his experience of this flash downturn; according to his biographer Charles Rappleye, Hoover never tired of detailing the progress made, the millions of new homes, cars, and other new consumer luxuries built in the 1920s by a capitalist system "without interference or regulation by the government."

The boom of the twenties was phenomenal, with GDP growth averaging 8 percent a year by mid-decade, driven by rapid gains in output per worker. Blue-collar lives started to lengthen and living conditions to improve. U.S. life expectancy was extended by six years, a record for any decade, as if humans had evolved in short order to a more durable form. Soon after it was introduced to grocery store shelves in 1928, Americans began praising the most practical innovations as "the greatest thing since sliced bread."

Strong productivity growth helped to restrain consumer prices, and with inflation low, the Fed argued that it could keep interest rates low indefinitely. Starting in 1924, enabled by the newly loosened gold standard, the New York Fed pioneered what would become "open market operations," buying some $500 million in government securities to push rates down further. Even as obvious signs of excess started to appear, the Fed ramped up asset purchases and cut rates in mid-1927. The American economy was booming, racing ahead of its European allies but also toward the credit meltdown that still haunts U.S. policymakers today.

To this point the Hamiltonian finance system had funded commercial endeavors much more than consumption. Early American Protestantism had cast all indebtedness as sinful, though less damnably so if loans were taken out to finance industry rather than to indulge consumer desire. Amid the new abundance, old mores began to break down. Consumer borrowing was emerging from the dim realm of loan sharks into the fluorescent light of the department store installment plan. By 1926 most cars and many other big-ticket consumer goods were sold on credit.

All this was achieved in a period when the government was pumping far less money into the economy than it does now, and borrowing had a cost: even the 4 percent rates in the 1920s were nowhere near as low as rates near or below zero in the 2010s. The merger waves of this early period often generated what economists call good monopolies—the kind that by revolutionizing industries from autos to steel produced spectacular gains in productivity and national prosperity.

The go-go '20s got truly crazy only in the final two years. New lending for cars and other big purchases drove consumer credit up to 140 percent of GDP—a level not matched again until the 2000s. More and more lending started to flow not into factories but into stocks and real estate. Property bubbles inflated in local markets from Florida to Chicago and New York, as developers planned to push new skyscrapers to record heights. Manufacturers diverted profits into real estate ventures and the financial markets, sending stock valuations skyward as well. The number of Americans who owned stock had mushroomed sixteenfold, and by the end of the decade they accounted for 25 percent of the population.

If this sounds familiar, it should. All of these excesses—manic trading, manic borrowing to trade, newbie investors joining the party and driving stock prices to irrational heights as the super-rich get richer—are classic signs of a bubble.

"IF IT IS NOT EXCESSIVE"

Admirers of capitalism before the New Deal marvel at its achievements, detractors recoil at its failings, and both can make a solid case. There was no golden age of capitalism, when government got its role just right. The state has always been and will always be searching for the proper balance, but the credit-fueled booms before and immediately after World War I were for the most part what Hamilton had hoped for: dynamic and productive, even if often accompanied in late stages by speculative excess and ending in crashes.

This is the potential capitalism lost, in the new age of Treasury and Fed expansion and free money. It has lost its dynamism, suffering fewer recessions, thanks to constant stimulus, each with less cleansing effect, thanks to bailouts, leaving behind more bad monopolies, more corporate deadwood. The result is that productivity growth is more and more disappointing, slowing overall growth, and leaving the capitalist system with less and less potential to advance the greater good.

Hamilton would win in the end but perhaps too convincingly. His vision of a powerful central government, anchored by a powerful central bank, keeper of a significant store of national debt, would expand in future crises to a degree that might have alarmed even him. Recall his caution: "A national debt *if it is not excessive* . . ." The credit system he had envisioned would grow bloated, increasingly dysfunctional, no longer serving its public purpose: to build nationwide prosperity.

======

TWO

NONE OF US ARE
KEYNESIANS NOW

The worst global pandemic in memory was a vivid reminder of how deeply major crises have shaped the evolution of capitalism. Periods of maximum anxiety—war, joblessness, poverty, and viruses—have gradually eroded the original American fear of concentrated power and authority. Over time, this process has greatly strengthened Washington's role in the economy. The Jeffersonian conviction, that to be democratic a government had to be small and constrained, died out slowly.

Through the New Deal and World War II, the United States was again a virtual one-party state, as the North was during the Civil War, only this time led by Democrats under President Franklin Delano Roosevelt. During his first year in office, FDR was warning privately that to avoid popular calls from the "Nazi-minded" for an autocratic government to ease the Depression, his administration would have to address the economic pain.

It was during the New Deal that government started to grow big as both a rule maker, in the Progressive-era sense of busting trusts or regulating conditions in slaughterhouses and factories, and as a major player—a buyer and seller—in the financial markets and the overall economy. Roosevelt would turn government into an agent of relief, pushing federal spending from under 4 percent to more than 10 percent during the 1930s.

The 1930s signaled an end to the cautious approach to bailouts recommended by Bagehot. New legislation allowed the Fed "in unusual and exigent circumstances" to extend emergency loans to a wide array of companies, not just commercial banks, against looser collateral, not just gold and other hard assets. The Fed used these powers only sparingly in the 1930s, extending around 125 loans—one to a vineyard, secured by barrels of wine—and rarely at all for the rest of the twentieth century.

The impulse to rescue was not yet programmed into the thinking of politicians or central bankers, and it would be many decades before any bank was considered too big to fail. Then in 2008, and even more aggressively in 2020, the Fed reached back to those powers created in the 1930s and deployed them to save many hundreds of banks and other companies from "unusual and exigent circumstances."

In the absence of bailouts as we know them today, with the Fed and the Treasury mobilizing the full power of the U.S. government to rescue the financial markets as a whole, the Depression created chaos—surprisingly creative chaos. As sales collapsed, many businesses went under. General Motors, Ford, and Chrysler survived alongside a few independent auto companies like Packard, in the rubble of an industry that had around 40 carmakers by 1930, down from around 250 in 1910. The industrial shakeouts of the Depression era are very well known; less well known is that the survivors continued to invest, not at first in new factories but in upgrading old ones. The car companies added faster conveyor belts, quick-drying lacquers. Packard cut the factory space it needed to produce a car by half. Greater efficiency allowed carmakers to raise real wages as the Depression began to lift.

The United States saw a productivity boom that has not been matched since. The core measure, technically known as total factor productivity, reveals in effect not just how much more skilled labor and machinery businesses are putting to work but how much more efficiently labor is using machines. More output per worker allows businesses to raise wages without raising prices and inflation, and is the key to economic progress. According to Congressional Budget Office records going back to 1870, the U.S. economy has never been more dynamic than it was in the 1930s, when core productivity grew at an average annual pace of 3 percent. Historian Alexander J. Field would describe the Depression as the most intense period of creative destruction in American history. He titled his book on the 1930s *A Great Leap Forward*.

WRONG LESSONS OF THE DEPRESSION

Many of the basic assumptions of economic authorities today have roots in the harsh experience of the 1920s and '30s. One is that consumer prices could reveal all they needed to know about the economy. If prices were low and relatively stable, the economy was thought to be in balance, interest rates were thought to be about right, and supply was thought to be meeting demand. Central banks could therefore ignore all other warning signs—particularly signs of bubbles in the financial markets—as secondary symptoms. Consumer price stability became both the goal of economic policy and its guide.

Thus it was that in 1928, as stock prices were spiraling toward a crash, the economic elite saw no reason to worry. They understood "inflation" as a risk only for consumer prices, not stock and bond prices. British economist John Maynard Keynes said "there was 'nothing which can be called inflation yet in sight.'" Not realizing the stock market crash was near, Treasury secretary Andrew Mellon hailed persistently low inflation, despite persistently low interest rates, as proof government had tamed "the vagaries of the business cycle." New York Fed chairman Benjamin Strong argued that with consumer prices stable, there was no need to fret about stock prices. On balance, taking action to calm the stock market would do more harm than good for the economy as a whole.

They were warned of the risks. Austrian school economists led by Friedrich Hayek predicted in 1928 that the downsides of easy money were already showing up in runaway lending, speculation, and "malinvestment" in the financial markets. The warnings went unheeded. Indeed, by brushing away Hayek and his school as cull-the-weak Darwinists, mainstream economists managed in the same gesture to brush off warnings about how loose credit and malinvestment enrich mainly the financial tycoons. Nearly a century later, economists still dismiss these same warnings, even though the role of finance and financiers in the economy has grown spectacularly in the intervening decades.

The lessons of the Depression are still open to interpretation because the Fed waffled so much in response, veering between loosening and tightening the money supply. The main point here is that officials came to see the fall in consumer prices—deflation—as the defining problem of the 1930s, the symptom to be avoided at all costs. But was deflation triggered by hawkish central bankers raising rates too aggressively in 1929 and then sticking to a tight monetary policy even after the market crash? Or was it caused by the dovish cuts of 1927, which sent the boom to its manic peak, and sowed the seeds of a deflationary bust? The view of many observers at the time was, with Hayek, that the dovish cuts kept too much deadwood alive, leading to a depression more "devastating" and long-lasting than any that had come before. The standard narrative now is that a hawkish central bank "tried overzealously to stop the rise in stock prices," but in raising rates too high, ended up deepening the downturn.

Fed leaders are still haunted by criticism of their confused response to the Depression, which goes a long way to explaining their conviction that it is now "better to err on the side of excess." At the time, however, there was no political support for the Fed to save the financial markets, even as the suicide rate climbed after the crash of 1929. The role of the Fed as lender and "buyer of last resort" had yet to be invented. When the pandemic hit, the problem was that central bankers were still focused on the threat of deflation, which largely disappeared after the Depression.

Ever since the 1930s, the link between consumer prices and economic growth has been "episodic and weak," according to a 2015 study by the Bank for International Settlements, which is the global bank for central banks. Stop and think for a second, and this point is obvious: consumer prices had been low and stable for decades, but those decades were hardly free of financial crises, often leading to serious and prolonged downturns. The growing instability of increasingly bloated markets revealed itself with a bang in 2008, when three out of every four developed countries suffered a severe crisis, starting with the United States.

The resulting Great Recession was global. And yet central banks continued to insist that their main job was stabilizing consumer prices, not asset prices—even if asset prices had become a more powerful warning signal for both financial crises and recessions.

Government and central bank officials patted themselves on the back in 2008 and even more loudly during the pandemic for preventing a return to the bankruptcies and breadlines of the 1930s. Recalling the panic of early 2020, Trump Treasury secretary Steven Mnuchin said that "never in the history of the Fed" had it coordinated action so closely with the Treasury, with such glowing results. "I think that if we had collectively not done what we did . . . we would have had a Great Depression."

The rescues were largely unquestioned at the time and remain popular now. Expectations have changed over the past century. Accepting a tough recession is no longer politically viable. But in embracing the faith that they had fended off another Depression, policymakers were fueling a different crisis, built on rapid asset price inflation and mounting debts.

GOVERNMENT THRIVES ON WAR

The New Deal reached its peak in World War II. The existential threat posed by powerful fascist states eroded much of the remaining opposition to big government, and the Fed fell in line behind the Treasury, agreeing to fix interest rates at 2 percent to ensure cheap financing for the war effort. Federal government spending spiked during the 1940s from just over 10 percent to 44 percent of GDP, and its debt nearly tripled to more than 100 percent of GDP. The share of American households whose members paid income tax rose from 5 percent to 60 percent. As in the Civil War, Washington started to steer capital to an unprecedented degree.

The Pentagon supplanted the Agriculture Department headquarters as the world's largest office building. The Defense Plant Corporation—using new powers that a *New York Times* columnist cast as "totalitarian"—funded a third of the new armament factories. The navy and army funded much of the rest. By the end of the war, the government was the majority owner of the rubber, aircraft, magnesium, and machine tools industries, and owned a significant share of many others. To prevent the new government spending from driving up consumer prices, the war planning offices imposed wage and price controls similar to those the Supreme Court had ruled unconstitutional just a decade before.

The government also halted or restricted the manufacture of many goods that were not weapons: cars, furniture, refrigerators, and other consumer appliances. Officials banned sliced bread, on the theory that it was too convenient and encouraged overconsumption, but were soon forced by a popular outcry to rescind the order. Sweeping state shutdowns of private business would not be imposed again for another eight decades, until the Covid-19 outbreak of 2020.

Though the Depression left a deep fear of joblessness, World War II created a new expectation that government could put just about everyone to work if it chose. Going into the war, joblessness was no longer a problem in countries that started preparing early for battle, like Germany and Japan. In the United States, which had no intention to fight, unemployment was in double digits but would drop quickly when FDR started to mobilize the "great arsenal of democracy."

When the war was won, the promise of full employment was codified in law and political culture. FDR declared that the war had been waged in the name of four freedoms, of which "freedom from want" would become the highest priority. GIs returning from Europe would not be left wanting for a well-paid job, to provide food for their families. American artist Norman Rockwell rendered *Freedom from Want* as a Thanksgiving holiday, three generations gathered around the grandmother, who is easing what looks to be a thirty-pound turkey onto the dining table. For many Americans, this was the future. Though unemployment had remained stuck above 10 percent for a decade during the Depression, it would rise that high in only fifteen months after 1945.

In the GI Bill, Congress assured returning veterans that they would have access to jobs and to government health, education, and other social benefits. But welfare programs would not grow as fast in the United States as in Europe, where socialism had deeper roots, in nations where social stratification went back centuries. Europe after the war was a land of bombed-out cities and scarred battlefields, where demands for government relief were for many a matter of survival. Desperation and political tradition made Europe more willing to embrace a larger state while America, largely untouched, looked forward in relief and optimism to life under a relatively limited government.

From the wartime highs, government spending fell much faster to lower levels in the United States than in Europe—by two-thirds in the United States, to 15 percent of GDP, and by just half, to 35 percent of GDP, for example, in the United Kingdom. In subsequent years, government expanded everywhere, but from a much higher starting point in Europe. By 1950, the "essential components of the welfare state were in place in Europe," writes economist Thomas Piketty. Welfare spending alone amounted to nearly a third of national income in the United Kingdom, France, Germany, and Sweden, making the large European welfare states roughly half again larger than the U.S. federal government as a whole.

This history throws in stark relief the ironies of the current moment, as the United States continues to roll out new spending plans in the wake of the pandemic—the worst crisis since World War II. Instead of demobilizing more rapidly than Europe, the United States was still mobilizing. Government spending (including state and local) is on track to rise in the United States by around 3 points, to 39 percent of GDP, by 2025, while it falls in the developed economies on average by an equal margin, to around 46 percent of GDP. It's as if the two had traded psychic places, America feeling battered and afraid of the future, Europe ready to return to something closer to normality and balance.

To a large degree, the Biden administration was justifying its call for a "New World Economic Order" on national security grounds, including trillions in spending and a firewall of new rules, regulations, and tariffs to defend America from the competitive threats posed by China and Russia. Though the president was often compared to FDR, Roosevelt had told Americans that "the only thing we have to fear is fear itself," while Bidenomics plays on fear—fear of China especially. The 2023 speech introducing the White House's vision for the world economy was not delivered by the secretary of the Treasury, Commerce, or State: it was delivered by the president's national security adviser, Jake Sullivan.

RESCUE SPENDING, REGARDLESS

In Biden's new order, the administration will behave like a wartime regime, stepping in to mobilize capital, but in the absence of war or depression. This approach, though entirely novel, follows unsurprisingly from nearly a century of growing government momentum.

John Maynard Keynes, the intellectual godfather of government intervention, died in 1946, so we can't be sure how he might have judged what followed. Suffice it to say that constant government intervention departs sharply from the original Keynes prescription. He argued that governments should borrow and spend to make up for weak demand in hard times, then save in good times, to build a surplus to spend in the next crisis. He saw government stimulus as a crisis measure, not the permanent feature of capitalism it was to become.

For a while, the traditional Keynes ruled. The first postwar president, Harry Truman, a Democrat, deliberately followed the Keynes playbook, raising government spending in response to the recession of 1948. His Republican successor, General Dwight Eisenhower, had learned while leading an army of millions in Europe "a deep respect for what government—and a well-organized bureaucracy—could do." Eisenhower defended the wartime tax regime, with personal rates topping 90 percent, as necessary to cover the rising cost of pensions, unemployment, farm subsidies, and other social programs. To his brother he remarked that "should any political party" threaten to cut back the emerging welfare state, "you would not hear of that party again in our political history."

When Eisenhower took power, the U.S. economy was still suffering a full-on recession every three to five years. He had to deal with downturns in 1953, 1957, and 1960. Memories of the Depression were still fresh, and Eisenhower assured voters before the '57 recession that "everything the government can do, every single force and influence it has to bring to bear, will be brought in timely fashion and not after any such catastrophe occurs." His Treasury department would respond in the new Keynesian style, increasing spending to ease the downturn, aided by Fed rate cuts. "We are all Keynesians now," a comment later attributed to Richard Nixon, among others, was first uttered as a lament by a Republican critic of Eisenhower, *Newsweek* columnist Henry Hazlitt. Still, Eisenhower remained true to the original Keynes, building up surpluses during the recovery of the mid-1950s, and warning as he left office of excessive spending by the "military-industrial complex."

Eisenhower was followed by a Democrat, John F. Kennedy, who took office the month that the recession of 1960 ended and set in motion a landmark break with the original Keynes. Tax cuts have a stimulative effect on the economy similar to government spending increases, by leaving more money in the hands of consumers. Kennedy proposed a tax that would be approved in 1964—after his assassination—establishing a first for U.S. economic policy: stimulus to fuel an expansion. The action was seen as "revolutionary, even heretical," at a time when balancing the budget was still sacrosanct, writes former Fed vice chairman Alan Blinder in his history of U.S. economic policy since 1961. Kennedy's team went through "mental gymnastics" to argue that his deficits would not top the peaks hit under Eisenhower.

For a while the Kennedy stimulus worked. Inflation remained quiet as GDP growth nearly tripled, to more than 8 percent between 1963 and 1965, creating a feeling that at least in economic terms the visions of Camelot inspired by Kennedy had been realized under his successor, Lyndon Johnson. This inflation-free boom made economic technocrats the toast of Washington. In 1966 former Kennedy aide Walter Heller went so far as to say that "we now take for granted that the government" should stay on "constant, rather than intermittent, alert" to step in and "provide the essential stability at high levels of employment and growth that market mechanisms, left alone, cannot deliver."

This new claim of control over the business cycle was unfortunately timed. Nineteen sixty-six was also the year the consequences of over-stimulating the economy became apparent, as growth petered out and inflation rose sharply. Johnson's aides urged him to restrain spending on the Vietnam War or on his Great Society welfare programs—or both. Johnson, determined to be "a leader of war and a leader of peace," re-fused for more than two years. He had expanded Social Security and created Medicare, legacies he did not want to let go. When he relented, agreeing to a tax hike in 1968, it was the first and possibly the last time in U.S. history that the government even attempted to use its budget authority—tax hikes or spending cuts—in an effort to contain inflation.

With that the original Keynesians gave way to a new generation, who tended to argue for stimulus all the time. The idea that taxes and spend-ing should ever be used by government to reduce demand in an overheat-ing economy was superseded by political reality: these tools "in the future would be used (with rare exceptions) only to expand demand," writes Blinder. Tax hikes and spending cuts were just too politically difficult to push through Congress. Keynes had argued for "symmetric" policies, with surpluses in good times funding deficit spending in bad times, but his ideas would become "asymmetric" in practice. When cutbacks were the order of the day, the government would either leave the job of imposing restraint to central banks or ignore it altogether.

Government hubris was growing. In his inaugural speech in 1969, Nixon said that "we have learned at last to manage a modern economy to assure its continued growth." He would, however, prove neither economic thinker nor manager, since he pulled the levers of power mainly to advance his own political prospects. Before the 1972 election, Nixon took steps to ensure victory by ramping up government spending. Having appointed a friend named Arthur Burns as Fed chair, Nixon pressured Burns to ease credit conditions before the vote—and let it be known that Burns would "get it right in the chops" if he did not deliver.

The scheme was almost too successful. In the summer of 1971, when growth accelerated to nearly 7 percent, threatening to send inflation skyward, Nixon shocked the country by imposing controls on wages and prices, a tool he had denounced as "a scheme to socialize America" just a month earlier. This was the only time wage and price controls have been used in the United States outside of war, and it worked as a political strategy. A roaring economy with falling inflation helped to reelect Nixon in 1972.

As soon as Nixon was back in the White House, he lifted price controls, and inflation broke out again. He and Burns switched from juicing growth to "double-barreled restraint" in fiscal and monetary policy. The resulting recession, like the boom before it, was so clearly a result of Nixon's machinations that future presidents have not dared manipulate the economy in ways so nakedly timed to benefit them at the next election.

Brought down by his attempt to cover up the Watergate scandal, Nixon paved the way for Jimmy Carter, who presented himself as an honest, responsible alternative. Steeped in homespun Georgia thrift, Carter took office when the economy was growing again but unemployment and inflation were still high. Many Americans were deeply dissatisfied. Reluctantly, Carter agreed to take the JFK path—stimulus in a recovery—with a big spending bill in his first year and a tax cut in his second. Even some advisers to Carter later said that this was an excessive "jolt" to a growing economy.

Carter also presided over a critical transition, as deficit spending became a permanent habit of big government, and not only in America. The backdrop was the gradual shift away from the gold standard, which had placed a natural limit on the supply of money and credit, including borrowing by governments.

DAWN OF THE DEFICITS

During the Depression, FDR had suspended the basic promise behind the gold standard—that the United States would use its gold to buy dollars on demand—as a way to keep cash in the economy and fight deflation. Then after World War II the United States and its victorious allies, eager to revive growth, created at Bretton Woods a new currency system, which fixed the price of the dollar to gold, and fixed the price of all other currencies in dollars, with some wiggle room.

The United States had emerged from the war as the most dominant economy in history, and its wealth included 70 percent of the global gold supply. It was hard to imagine a day when gold reserves would dwindle to the point of limiting the supply of dollars, which had displaced British sterling as the currency of global commerce. Most imports and exports were priced in dollars, even if no American was involved on either side of the sale.

But the gold did run out. By the 1960s, spending by the U.S. government on wars and welfare, and by American consumers on Japanese and German imports, was driving up U.S. debt to the rest of the world—and eroding its gold surpluses. In the twenty years before 1970, the U.S. gold stock fell by more than half. In 1971 the United States ran its first trade deficit of the twentieth century. Over the next two years, the Nixon administration pulled the dollar off the gold standard for good.

The demise of Bretton Woods freed governments and central banks to focus less on maintaining the value of their currencies and more on spending to achieve their new postwar mission—full employment. This freedom was empowering for all governments but especially for the United States. Since the dollar was the currency of international trade, it was also the currency foreign central banks overwhelmingly preferred to hold in their reserves. Usually, central banks held dollars in the form of U.S. Treasury bonds—so widely traded they are almost like cash. Virtually limitless global demand for Treasuries, greased by the postwar rise in international capital flows, meant virtually limitless support for U.S. government borrowing.

The only remaining barrier to more spending was political will, which proved a thin barrier indeed. Given more leeway to borrow and spend, politicians did just that. Before the 1970s, the governments of developed countries rarely ran a deficit outside of wartime, but since then they have run deficits virtually all the time. On average, the leading capitalist economies have run a significant deficit (larger than 1 percent of GDP) every year since the early 1970s with one exception, in 2000.

The records for the United Kingdom go back a century further than most, all the way to 1689, and show the strongest pattern. For nearly three hundred years the government never ran deficits outside of a major war—not even during the Depression. The deficits of the early 1970s were the first ever in the United Kingdom during peacetime, and a turning point: the United Kingdom would run surpluses in only five of the next fifty years. Japan has not run a single surplus in the same period. France has not run a surplus since 1974, and Italy has run one surplus since 1925.

There is no major developed economy that consistently defied this trend. Between the 1790s, when records begin, and 1970, the United States ran consistent surpluses, with significant deficits only during five crises: the War of 1812, the Civil War, the Great Depression, and the two world wars. Since 1970, the United States has run a significant deficit every year but four, between 1998 and 2001 under Clinton, who did restrain spending. He also got help, however, from a windfall surge in capital gains tax revenue during the dot-com bubble.

Nonetheless, an illusion persists that government was a larger force in the economy from World War II through the Carter presidency than it is today. Often this period is seen as a "glorious" one for social democracy, when big government working with big unions and big corporations steered the flow of capital to generate growth and jobs. The war was still fresh in memory, and CEOs dared not buck the government's new commitment to full employment. The welfare state expanded under presidents of both parties. Top tax rates were much higher. Strict Depression-era financial regulations were still in place. Capital moved less freely, and built up in giant corporations like Exxon, AT&T, and IBM, which were comparable to the giants of today, measured by their share of profits or stock market value. Journalist William Whyte's book on "The Organization Man" became a touchstone for critics of an increasingly bureaucratized society. Yet economic growth was higher than it is today— proof to some that government control works.

The economy is a complex organism, and its growth is generated by many factors. But the role played by government was far smaller— as a spender, debtor, regulator, micromanager of business cycles, and financial market buyer and seller—in the 1950s, '60s, and '70s than it is now. Growth got a huge lift from the postwar baby and productivity booms, and in retrospect its healthy phase was quite brief. The relatively calm prosperity of the 1950s quickly gave way to the tensions of the 1960s, as cracks started to show, particularly in inflation boosted by deficit spending.

It was no coincidence that the first president to campaign against big government was Jimmy Carter, as inflation took off in the following decade. He waxed eloquent about the folly of asking the state to define our goals and dreams, or "mandate goodness," and urged Americans to understand that "even our Great Nation . . . cannot afford to do everything." Carter was also, however, the first president to talk up the virtues of balancing the budget while running constant deficits. No leader was willing to lower government spending when private demand was strong, as Keynes would have argued. None of us are traditional Keynesians now.

THREE

═══════════════

THE REAGAN EVOLUTION

I t's hard for someone who was a supporter of Ronald Reagan to admit, but the data shows quite plainly that his legacy was less a counterrevolution than an evolution in big government.

The stage was set by Paul Volcker. He became Fed chair in 1979, and created the financial stability that made possible the boom in government deficits and debt under Reagan. The spending unleashed by Johnson and Nixon had begun to drive up consumer prices even before the oil price shocks of the 1970s ushered in the era of "stagflation," which is stagnant growth with high inflation. Replacing his ineffectual predecessors, Volcker stepped in to stop inflation by hiking rates, and he stuck to his guns. That show of force was a first for the Fed since the Forgotten Depression of the early 1920s. And it would not be repeated for another four decades, when in 2022 the return of inflation compelled the Fed, under Chairman Jerome Powell, to get tough—albeit belatedly.

Volcker was nothing if not calm in a storm. Inflation was so deeply baked into the economy it refused to subside, peaking near 15 percent in 1980. To beat it back Volcker pushed up the Fed's base rate not once but twice to record levels, in the high teens. Both of those hiking cycles sparked recessions, in 1981 and 1982. Asked later how monetary policy crushed inflation, Volcker responded, "by causing bankruptcies."

Though Volcker is probably the most respected Fed chair ever, it is hard to imagine his successors describing harsh realities so plainly now. He was also acutely aware of the risks that arise when the central bank starts to fund the government. In *Keeping At It* (2018), he writes that the essential question facing central banks is: "How far should a central bank—shielded from political pressures—go in indirectly financing budget deficits and influencing the distribution of credit broadly in the economy?"

Volcker was more attuned than other Fed chairs to the flow of credit into the markets. He saw inflation in consumer prices and asset prices as "cousins" and understood that both needed to be contained to produce stable growth. The stock market dropped by 30 percent as Volcker pushed interest rates to new highs, and for imposing discipline the Fed chair received death threats. Critics sent Volcker little coffins in the mail, accusing him of "cold-blooded murder," on the grounds that tight money was killing small businesses and the American dream of homeownership. The second recession on his watch extended into 1982 and was quite severe, but the war on inflation was won.

The victory soon went global, as other central banks followed Volcker's lead. In advanced economies, the average inflation rate fell from 12 percent in the early 1980s to just 2 percent by 1991—and hovered near that mark into 2022. Defeating inflation cemented for the Fed a "preeminence in global economic policymaking that lasts to this day," despite what happened next.

Reagan arrived in office just in time to suffer through the second Volcker recession, though not quietly. When Reagan advisers later called Volcker into the Oval Office for a lecture on the need for easier money before the 1984 election, Volcker walked out of the meeting without a word. As Reagan ramped up military spending, aiming in essence to spend the bankrupt Soviet Empire into submission, Volcker grew openly critical. By pushing deficits to new highs, Reagan was undermining the central bank fight against inflation. In 1987, as these tensions festered, Reagan nudged Volcker to resign by commenting sparely on his prospects for reappointment. The growth of government as borrower and spender accelerated in the 1980s.

One source of confusion about the Reagan legacy is his tax cuts, particularly the ones that get the most attention, taxes on the rich. The top tax rate on individuals had peaked above 90 percent during the Depression and World War II, then dropped to 70 percent under Carter, before plummeting in steps to 28 percent under Reagan. Surely with revenue cuts that big, government had to be shrinking. But when top personal rates went down, some smorgasbord of other rates—on corporations, sales, investments—went up, typically with much less fanfare. The big Reagan cuts of 1981 were offset by hikes on everything from payroll to excise taxes in 1982, 1983, 1984, and 1987. The job of fully restoring the government's tax take would be completed in the 1990s by George H. W. Bush and Bill Clinton, who pushed the top rate on individuals back up to near 40 percent.

The same pattern held for other capitalist economies: top tax rates started to rise in the Depression and peaked above 90 percent in the United Kingdom, 80 percent in Germany, 70 percent in France and Japan. Then the top rates fell sharply after 1980, to a steady new band, ranging from 30 percent to 50 percent or more (in France and Japan). Yet government spending came down almost nowhere, with the interesting exception of Scandinavian socialist countries like Sweden, which realized in the 1990s it had built the welfare state too big.

Even with the U.S. recovery in full swing by the mid-1980s, the deficit was ascending to a new plateau. Having remained under 1 percent of GDP since World War II, the average deficit would triple to more than 3 percent during Reagan's two terms, and there it would remain, with spikes to 10 percent in 2008 and nearly 15 percent in 2020. That did not stop two of the next three Republican presidents, George W. Bush and Donald Trump, from repeating a basic assertion of Reaganomics: that tax cuts would generate enough growth to bring down the deficit and the debt. The Republicans became the party of tax cuts in all conditions, regardless of whether the deficit was large or small, or whether the economy was in recession or recovery.

Persistent deficits led to rising debts. Before the Reagan years, U.S. government debt had risen sharply only during major wars: the Civil War, World War I, and World War II. That changed dramatically after 1980, because Washington chose to wage a constant battle to keep growth alive and voters happy. U.S. government debt peaked at more than 100 percent of GDP at the end of World War II, fell steadily to around 30 percent of GDP in 1980, then rose again to top 100 percent of GDP in 2019 and 130 percent during the pandemic. And most of that increase was packed into the last two decades, even though this period saw no violent conflicts between great powers.

In a sense, the biggest achievement of the Reagan revolution was the Clinton administration, which did restrain government a bit. Federal government spending amounted to around 21 percent of GDP at the start and the end of the Reagan administration, remained at that level by the end of the George H. W. Bush presidency in 1992, then drifted down under Clinton to just over 18 percent in 2000. Spending around 18 percent of GDP turned the clock back to the mid-70s, not to the original era of small government before 1930. Still it was a step in the direction of downsizing. Public debt also declined a bit in the late Clinton years.

George H. W. Bush, arguably a throwback to the Eisenhower Republicans, laid some of the groundwork. He did not lower the spending or deficits he had inherited from Reagan, but he did make a landmark deal with Congress in 1990, aimed at controlling future deficits. In the past, presidents had cut similar deals, or empaneled blue ribbon commissions to outline deficit-reduction plans, to no effect. Future deals would be ignored, too. The 1990 deal was different: it required that new spending on entitlements like Social Security, which entitle every citizen to benefits based on age, income, or other conditions, had to be "paid for" with new revenue, from either tax hikes or cuts elsewhere in the federal budget. Amazingly, from today's perspective, the deal was honored. The now-familiar budget wars pitting the White House against congressional opposition, periodically shutting or threatening to shut the U.S. government, were already underway. Yet the 1990 agreement held. Washington politicians lived within the rules on spending restraint—for part of one decade.

The rewards were huge. The bond market had grown rapidly, worldwide, and so-called bond market vigilantes had started punishing spendthrift governments the decade before by selling off their bonds, which drove up their borrowing costs and threatened to stall the economy. The vigilantes loved the budget deal of 1990, and the steps Clinton took to make good on it. Clinton eschewed the accounting gimmicks his predecessors had used to make the deficit appear smaller than it was. He based deficit forecasts on realistic not maximally rosy estimates of economic growth. He raised taxes on the rich and cut some spending on at least one of the major entitlements, Medicare, demonstrating a credibility the markets had not seen before.

The resulting bond market rally drove down long-term borrowing costs, and helped fuel the boom in Silicon Valley. Rising tax revenues, particularly on capital gains, in turn helped balance the budget much faster than anyone expected, including the White House. The Clinton administration had foreseen significant deficits continuing into 1998; instead it got the first surplus since the 1960s. "For three decades, six presidents have come before you to warn of the damage deficits pose to our nation," Clinton said in his state of the union address that January. "Tonight, I come before you to announce that the federal deficit, once so incomprehensibly large that it had 11 zeroes, will be simply zero."

This appeared to be a turning point, but it was a false dawn. In the election of 2000, debate turned for the first time in U.S. history to how the candidates would spend this novel windfall. The Democrat, Al Gore, said he would use the surplus to pay down the national debt. George H. W. Bush had been replaced as the Republican standard bearer by his son George W., who said he would return the surplus to voters through tax cuts. As one might expect, Bush the younger won.

He promptly became, like LBJ in the 1960s, a president of war and peace. He ramped up spending on wars in Afghanistan and Iraq, and on new Medicare benefits. Instead of paying for new spending with revenue increases, as required by the 1990 budget deal, Bush and Congress scrapped the deal and cut taxes. With that, the second President Bush had abandoned the course set by the first. The surplus was gone as fast as it had appeared. By 2002, the deficit was back in the hundreds of billions—eleven zeroes—and growing toward new record highs. Yet somehow, the myth persists that the last four decades have been an age of relentless government "austerity."

It's worth looking at this claim more closely. In the forty years between 1980 and 2020, the U.S. economy was in recession for less than five years (fifty-six months, to be exact). The budget was in a significant deficit for thirty-six of those forty years. The overwhelming majority of the time, then, the government was borrowing to finance spending, yet the economy was not in recession. The habit of heavy spending had become so widely accepted, critics could describe deficit spending in good times as "austerity"—if they wanted even bigger deficits.

Austerity no longer meant spending cuts or tax increases. It meant running up debt and deficits just a bit more slowly than the previous year, which is criticized as austerity even if the economy is in recovery. Between 1980 and the start of the pandemic in 2020, the deficit has averaged 4 percent of GDP during recessions, and 3 percent during recoveries, with little variation from one president to the next. More than three-quarters of the government debt built up by the United States since 1980 has been amassed outside of recessions. In 2008, at the height of the financial crisis, U.S. public debt topped $10 trillion, and the "clock" in Times Square that tracked the debt in real time had to be replaced, because it had run short of digits.

In the jargon of today, it is said that the "fiscal impulse" is "fading" even when the deficit is still near record levels, so long as it is edging down, as it was in 2022. The question is no longer deficits, to be or not to be, it is deficits, how big will they be?

The same pattern repeated itself under President Barack Obama. Along with many leaders in Europe, Obama was attacked from the left for "austerity" when he failed to run even bigger deficits during the disappointing recovery from the Great Recession, which ended in mid-2009. No matter that in that downturn Obama passed two major tax relief and spending bills that made fiscal policy "more expansionary . . . than in any other recession since 1960." The deficit rose from 1.2 percent of GDP in 2007 to a "mind-boggling 10 percent of GDP in 2009," writes Alan Blinder in *After the Music Stopped*, his account of the crisis. The scale was "shocking" at the time, because the United States had not run deficits that large since World War II, and Obama would have kept the stimulus coming if cuts had not been forced on him by the newly ascendant Tea Party Republicans.

Nonetheless, fellow Democrats like former Clinton economic adviser Brad DeLong ripped into Obama and other leaders of the capitalist world. Writing in 2018, DeLong said they had failed to learn the lessons of the Depression, about the uplifting impact of stimulus. Instead, world leaders had "retreated to the balanced budget nostrums of the past," executing a "perverse turn to austerity" that arguably made the Great Recession worse than the Great Depression in terms of long-term impact on incomes and growth. History, which had made a hero of Roosevelt, would remember Obama and his peers as failures. But this picture of brutal "austerity" does not square with the reality of increasingly generous rescues, jointly staged by the government and the central bank.

HOW DEFICITS SLOW GROWTH

Liberal economists like to spoof the idea that cuts to government spending and deficits can promote growth as Hayekian "nonsense" with no real-life cases to back it up. To a Keynesian, says Blinder, "this sounded Orwellian: right is wrong, war is peace, up is down." If the government pumps less money into the economy, then the economy grows less rapidly, like a plant starved of water.

This is the view of a profession rooted in the 1940s, when the Roosevelt administration asked the economist Simon Kuznets to invent the broad measure of output that became gross domestic product. Economics became the study of aggregates like GDP, and broad flows of fiscal and monetary stimulus, from sixty thousand feet. Economists came to operate at a level far removed from the way money flows out of the government and central banks through markets, filters its way through millions of investors, large and small, and lands in the hands of companies, for better or worse.

A vantage point closer to the ground, closer to the quarterly reports of junk and profitless firms, reveals exactly how injecting too many dollars into the economy can slow growth: the impact does not show up immediately, it accumulates over time, as more of those dollars go to waste and malinvestment, drowning companies in debt. Plants are in reality no different: too much water can be as lethal to them as too little.

On the margins of the national conversation, an increasingly isolated band of conservative economists issued warnings that the rising deficit would trigger some ill-defined calamity in the future, involving inflation or a debt crisis. As years passed and the calamity never came, those warnings wound up distracting attention from the crisis unfolding in real time, in the form of trillions of dollars misallocated through distorted financial markets. The Orwellian thing to do is to pretend this is not happening.

One big reason governments could go on this spending spree was serendipitous. No one foresaw in the early 1980s that a falling inflation rate would allow central bankers to consistently lower interest rates for the next forty years, but that is what happened.

First came the Volcker shock; then larger forces came into play. Working-age populations were still growing, and many countries were poised to open doors to foreign trade for the first time in decades, if not centuries. The workers of Eastern Europe entered global labor markets after the fall of Communism in 1989; the workers of China followed, after Beijing joined the World Trade Organization in 2001. All those millions of workers put downward pressure on wages, which joined with other forces—including automation and intensifying global competition—to check consumer prices. And restrained consumer price inflation gave central bankers all the justification they required to drive borrowing costs—including government borrowing costs—down to lows never seen before.

Today Reagan's detractors blame him for creating a more brutal form of capitalism, and admirers credit him with unleashing a more dynamic capitalism. Who's right? What all camps now agree on is that even before Reagan left office, the United States was entering the Great Moderation, a long period of slower and less violent business cycles, which is very hard to square with the image of Reagan as a brutal capitalist reactionary. His administration had in fact slowed the expansion of government in some respects, for example, by flattening out the growth in regulation and welfare spending. Overall, however, Reagan did less to "reverse the course of government" than he had intended or than his haters—and his admirers—think he did.

Central Bakers Move to Center Stage

By 1988, when George H. W. Bush rode Reagan's coattails to victory, the business cycle was flattening out. Recessions would strike once every decade or so rather than every three to five years. The next arrived in Bush's second year, 1990, and his administration did not so much as broach the idea of government stimulus spending. Instead, they left the job to the Fed, which would consistently take the lead in future downturns. Chairman Alan Greenspan would become a global celebrity, nicknamed the "Maestro" for an almost mystic capacity to "fine-tune" stable growth.

Though mild and brief, the recession of 1990 marked a critical turn in the way capitalism had started breaking down. Earlier downturns tended to follow Fed rate hikes, but this one—and those that followed—

sprang from stresses in the booming financial markets. In 1990, the trouble was cascading failures of American savings and loans (S&Ls), lending institutions that dated to the nineteenth century. Founded to encourage homeownership and financial discipline, the S&Ls were also known as "thrifts," but they had gotten in trouble on reckless lending outside their traditional specialty, home mortgages.

The aftermath of the 1990 recession was also marked by a mysterious shift toward weaker recoveries. As usual, growth picked up, but less robustly than in previous recoveries, and instead of falling, unemployment continued to rise. Greenspan called these conditions "very unusual. . . . It's very much as though an economy which is picking up steam is running against a fifty-mile-an-hour headwind."

Later research would reveal that the force holding back the economy in the early 1990s was debt. A "debt overhang" from the 1980s, compounded by the serial failure of S&Ls, was depressing spending and new borrowing by consumers and businesses, leading to a recovery with weak growth and disconcertingly few new jobs. The long recoveries of the '90s, 2000s, and 2010s would be "jobless," weighed down in large part by rising debts.

By the time the pandemic surprised America amid its longest recovery ever, the old obsession with deficit reduction had faded so completely that Trump and Biden could combine to propose trillions in new spending, none of it "paid for" by revenue increases, driving up the deficit to a peacetime record 15 percent of GDP in 2020, and yet "nobody in Washington seemed to care," writes Blinder. He cites this as one of the clearest turns in U.S. economic policy since his book's history begins in 1961: the complete evaporation of concern about deficits. The standard government response to every recession and every disappointing recovery would be to spend more and run up more debt, which was likely to have an increasingly corrosive effect on growth in the future.

================

FOUR

THE ORIGINS OF EASY MONEY

lan Greenspan took over as Fed chairman in 1987 and just
two months later found himself in charge on Black Monday,
the worst stock market crash since 1929. The morning after,
Greenspan took steps to lower interest rates and spoke publicly and directly to investors, declaring the central bank's "readiness to serve as a
source of liquidity to support the economic and financial system." Wall
Street traders later came to describe this innocuous-sounding declara-
tion as the "Greenspan put"—a central bank guarantee to minimize market pain in future crashes. It is now remembered as the original promise,
to some the original sin, of the easy money era.

To be clear, "easy money" refers to a range of tools that governments
and central banks use to encourage borrowing. First and foremost, it
means lowering interest rates, or more recently, spending billions to buy

bonds, which is another way to push down interest rates. More broadly, the tools of easy money include emergency loans or other aid to stabilize jittery markets, or bailouts for individual banks or companies. Often, the mere promise of state-funded relief is enough to reinstill confidence in borrowers, and mollify the markets. Greenspan's "put" thus set the tone of the easy money era, which on many of these levels continues even today.

Encouraged by cheap borrowing costs and insured by the government against failure, the confidence of investors began to solidify into a near-permanent sangfroid in the 1980s. Though interest rates were still relatively high, they were trending down sharply and appeared likely to continue falling, since inflation was coming down as well. The new mood of fear-free borrowing was symbolized by the rise to prominence of the Predators' Ball, more formally known as the annual Drexel High Yield Bond Conference. It is where financiers made plans for the hostile corporate takeovers, funded with Drexel junk bonds, that defined this decade on Wall Street.

The 1980s thus saw the start of the process by which finance began to grow faster than other industries, and to extend its influence over capitalist economies. No doubt the "financialization" of capitalism was speeded up by deregulation, which began with the "big bang" reform of the London markets under Thatcher, continued under Carter and Reagan in the United States, and had parallels from Japan to Norway. While new financial regulations were never shorter or simpler, they did allow investors to move capital across borders with fewer prohibitions than before. But the capital itself originated primarily from governments and central banks, and so did the sangfroid, thanks to the emerging culture of bailouts and promises of official support anytime the markets stumbled.

How Interest Rates Fell Below Zero

The United States sets only loose term limits for the appointed Fed chair, and only four people have occupied that post since the late 1980s: Alan Greenspan, Ben Bernanke, Janet Yellen, and Jerome Powell. Together, these four responded to every new financial crisis by pumping more money into the economy than anyone would have thought possible as recently as the prior crisis. Their main tool is the "base rate" that the central banks charge on short-term loans to commercial and investment banks.

While the recession of 1990 was relatively mild, it was also pivotal. George H. W. Bush left the job of stimulating the economy to the Fed. Greenspan had started cutting the Fed's base rate before the brief recession began, and continued cutting sharply after it was over, motivated by the mysteriously "jobless" nature of the recovery. Between 1989 and 1992, the Fed would drop its base rate from around 10 percent to 3 percent, then a historic low, and hold it there for two years after the recovery began.

Greenspan thus became the first Fed chief to unleash central bank stimulus to juice up a recovery (just as Kennedy was the first president to roll out government stimulus in a recovery). He was also far from the last. Each new recovery would be met with easier money. The Fed would hold its base rate under 2 percent for three years in the early 2000s, and under 0.2 percent for seven years after the crisis of 2008.

When people talk about the era of "lower for longer" interest rates, they are referring to these elongating periods of historically low rates, but also to the diminishing peaks. When the Fed did start hiking, it stopped at less elevated highs, the lowest just 2.5 percent in 2020. Even central bank rate-hiking cycles were leaving borrowing costs historically cheap.

In their turn, the big commercial and investment banks took these cheap central bank loans and used them to extend long-term loans at lower rates to other businesses, and to consumers. This is the point where the rubber hits the road; easy money flowing out of central banks has such a profound impact on the economy because it lowers borrowing costs for people taking out longer-term loans to buy a home, or a car, or pay for college, open a business, or build a new factory.

Though interest rates are perhaps inherently boring, the drama that free money can stir up is epic. This was the aim of lower central bank base rates: to lower long-term rates for everyone and revive capitalism. Factor in inflation, which effectively lowers the cost of borrowing, and the "real" rate on longer-term loans fell in the United States to less than 1 percent from 2010 to 2022—more than a decade of virtually free money. For four of those years, the real cost of long-term borrowing fell below zero.

In other parts of the capitalist world, money would be even cheaper, and the historic precedents even more stark. Deutsche Bank Research has assembled records for central bank base rates in Europe going back as far as 1800. After hovering around 5 percent for nearly 120 years, base rates spiked to a record high around 20 percent in 1980. Then the great, gradual decline began. Following the consolidation of the continent's central banks into the European Central Bank in 1998, its base rate fell to record lows in the next decade, and below zero in 2014. There the basic price of borrowing in Europe remained, below zero, for the next eight years. And that was the base rate in "nominal" terms— before adjusting down for inflation.

As in the United States, the aim of central banks in Europe was to lower the rates that matter most to the economy, those paid by businesses and consumers. Those kinds of long-term loans for commercial or personal purposes have been around since long before the first central bank, which was founded in seventeenth-century Sweden. And in 2014, the real rate on long-term loans fell below zero in Europe for the first time since historical records begin in the early fourteenth century, for Italy.

The idea of an interest rate below zero is hard to get one's mind around, as customers of Jyske Bank of Denmark learned in 2019, when it became the first bank ever to advertise mortgages with a negative nominal interest rate. Skeptical customers asked the obvious question, "How is that possible?" The implication appeared to be that borrowers would get a monthly check from the bank, which was not quite right. Instead the principal they owed would fall by a sum larger than their monthly mortgage payment, but the bank would make up its losses on service fees. By the end of the mortgage, customers would have paid the bank a bit more than they had borrowed. Still, these were super-cheap loans.

Free or virtually free money, alas, did more to disorient and distort the capitalist system than to revive it. People made purchases and investments they would have dismissed as irrational or excessive in normal times, when borrowing has a price. Investors assumed that since consumer price inflation was so low, and had been for years, central banks would keep rates near zero indefinitely. The easy money era would endure for many years, and when it did finally end, no matter, the government would be there to help with bailouts.

PERMANENT CRISIS MODE

In 1992 the sluggish recovery helped Bill Clinton beat Bush and take the White House. Clinton, too, would leave "fine-tuning" largely to the Fed, and its stature grew. With growth reviving and inflation stable, a Wall Street analyst described these "not too hot, not too cold" conditions as a "Goldilocks economy," and the term stuck. It would be rolled out repeatedly over the next couple of decades by commentators who saw low consumer price inflation as proof of Goldilocks conditions—and ignored the big bear in the shadows, lurking in the form of rapidly inflating prices for stocks, bonds, and other assets.

Each time, easy money was feeding these asset bubbles. After 1992, the Fed kept interest rates below the growth rate in the economy for the rest of the decade, and while Greenspan expressed occasional concern about froth in the markets, he did not act on it. Quite the opposite. In another pioneering experiment, he began in 1995 to push "insurance" rate cuts, not to speed up the recovery but to extend its life and fend off the next recession. Fine-tuning was turning into steady support.

By the late nineties the "Greenspan put" had made the leap from Wall Street jargon to standard cable TV newspeak, where its effect was not so much calming as electrifying. Money was flooding into Silicon Valley, and the tech-focused Nasdaq index recorded the fastest rise in stock valuations ever seen in the United States, breaking the record set in the late 1920s. Having demonstrated that his words could move markets, Greenspan attempted to use them in 1996 to talk the markets down: in a televised speech, he warned that the markets were gripped by "irrational exuberance." But talk did not work: asset prices kept rising.

Two years later, some dissident Fed board members were making a push for higher rates to cool the tech bubble. Greenspan chose instead to cut rates, this time as "insurance" against the risk that Russia's recent default would ruffle nerves in the U.S. markets. His base case once again was that with consumer price inflation still low, easy money was safe. Doubters inside the Fed warned that cutting rates was like "pouring gasoline" on an overheating economy and a bubbly market, yet the cuts continued until consumer prices finally started to rise in early 2000.

The Fed responded by raising rates in steady increments. The dot-com boom went bust, triggering a mild "recessionette," to which Greenspan responded by once again cutting rates sharply. The Fed dropped its base rate from 6 percent to 2 percent between late 2000 and late 2001, when the 9/11 terror attacks reaffirmed its conviction that the economy, though recovering, would need more help. Thus in the aftermath of 9/11, the Fed's "state of emergency became almost permanent," writes author Christopher Leonard in *The Lords of Easy Money*.

The plunge in interest rates ushered in the next big bubble, this time in housing, which would melt down later that decade. Greenspan's defenders say the crisis of 2008 is no reason to question his legacy, because he saw property prices were rising fast and debts were mounting fast. To contain the risks of a credit bust, Greenspan and his successor, Bernanke, doubled the Fed's base rate to 5 percent between 2004 and 2006. Having hiked that sharply, how can these Fed chairs be criticized as enablers of the easy money era?

The mainstream view in the market was the opposite: Greenspan had been exposed as a serial bubble blower. His rate hikes were too little, too late to subdue the real estate mania. His attempts to contain the risks, through tightening or "jawboning"—as in the "irrational exuberance" comment—were erratic and inadequate. "When you keep rates very low—even if you're raising them but you keep them very low—you are inviting bubbles," Thomas Hoenig, the most persistent Fed dissenter throughout this period, would later say.

So why were the authorities shifting into permanent crisis mode? With economies growing but at a disappointingly slow rate after the turn of the millennium, and consumer price inflation below their target, they were concerned that weak growth could tip into outright stagnation and deflation. Their fear was the "Japan trap."

THE WRONG LESSONS OF JAPAN

Consumer price deflation was an unfortunate and untimely obsession, particularly for the United States by the early 2000s. After the long global bout of deflation that defined the Depression in the 1930s, the threat had all but disappeared. In subsequent decades, the only country large or small ever to suffer a bout of deflation lasting more than three years was Japan after 1990. Yet this one-off case had come to be seen as a universal warning for capitalist economies.

Japan was far from typical. For one, it had suffered from bad deflation, the kind that arises after a debt-fueled boom in housing or stocks turns into a bust—like the one that fueled the Depression. Japan's crash in 1990 had undermined consumer confidence and demand, which in turn started pushing down retail prices, as shoppers delayed purchases in the expectation that prices would fall further. The fact that sagging consumer prices dogged Japan for the next two decades stirred fear in other countries, despite vastly varied circumstances.

Deflation can also be the good kind, which is generated by innovations in technology or finance that raise productivity, lower costs, and boost economic growth. For leaders to focus on one highly unusual case of bad deflation was particularly ill-advised in the United States, which had seen plenty of the good kind before 1930. Between the 1870s and 1914, GDP growth averaged a steady 3 percent in the United States, but with 3 percent deflation during the first half of that period—as the Industrial Revolution accelerated—and 3 percent inflation during the second half. Good deflation also resurfaced during the 1920s, as a new generation of industrial innovations like the assembly line were pushing down prices while driving growth.

Similarly, inflation remained low in the late 1990s and early 2000s in part as a result of a productivity growth revival in the United States, driven by tech innovations. Yet after the dot-com boom went bust, fear that low inflation would tip into deflation began to grip policymakers. By mid-2003 a deflationary Japan trap had become Topic A in Fed board discussions.

In the 2010s, another weak global recovery inspired a new round of worry that low inflation would tip into deflation. The Japan trap was back. To assess the risks, researchers at the Bank for International Settlements took a look at the records for thirty-eight countries going back 140 years. They found that, after the 1930s, deflation had appeared mainly for short periods of a year or less—with no negative impact on the economy, on average. If anything, deflation had survived mainly in the good form, because growth was slightly faster during deflationary years.

Economic leaders were fighting the wrong war with good intentions. Convinced by a story of the Great Depression that links its worst effects to falling consumer prices, economic officials became obsessed with deflation—even as it disappeared after 1980. The worst crises since then—the dot-com bust of 2000, the housing bust of 2008, the pandemic of 2020—were not preceded by a serious outbreak of consumer price inflation. They were preceded by serious inflation in asset markets—stocks or real estate or both.

This is the tragedy: for more than two decades now, central banks have been flooding the world with easy money to stave off any hint of deflation even in good times, fueling asset bubbles that, when they pop, are the most likely source of bad deflation. By obsessing over the Japan trap, they were taking the steps most likely to make it a reality.

In 2004 Bernanke became the latest in the string of U.S. economic leaders to declare victory over the business cycle. For twenty years, he said, inflation and economic growth had become less volatile, and recessions had become shorter and less severe, across the developed world.

It was Bernanke who, as the housing bubble inflated, named this period the "Great Moderation," describing it as a felicitous turn in world history and crediting it, with due nods to other explanations, to central bankers.

After Bernanke was promoted to Fed chair in 2006, he made explicit the promises Greenspan had delivered implicitly—to always protect the markets. He would fight inflation in consumer goods and services but let the financial bubbles inflate, then step in after the crash to help mop up, using buckets of easy money. The message to investors was what one, Jeremy Grantham, called an "asymmetric promise to help if times get tough but to leave you alone when times are rolling." In short, the central bank was making the same "asymmetric" promise that presidents had started making in the 1970s—of government that never demands restraint.

THE JAPANESE-STYLE "EXPERIMENT" AFTER 2008

When the real estate markets started to collapse in 2008, central banks faced a quandary. They had dropped their base rates so low that they could not cut much further. So the Fed borrowed from Japan an experiment—once dismissed as unworkable—that it had launched to fight deflation following its own stock and real estate crash in 1991.

Central banks had long used the purchase of government bonds as one way to expand the supply of money and credit in hard times. The Bank of Japan's innovation was to expand the impact of its purchases by buying private debts as well. After 2008, the Fed and other central banks copied that practice, and began buying all manner of debt—government, corporate, and household. In the same way that government deficit spending became standard operating procedure in the 1970s, this new central bank role as buyer of last resort in the debt markets became a new feature of capitalist systems in the 2010s.

The Fed had launched its first round of bond buying during the recession of 2009 but continued with new rounds during the subsequent recovery, on the grounds that with unemployment still near 10 percent, government had to do more. The Obama White House could not get new spending bills passed in Congress, because the Tea Party Republicans were committed to blocking its every move. Any effort to "do more" would have to be undertaken by the central bank. In Washington, the Fed came to be seen, and to see itself, as "the only game in town."

Fed defenders bridle at the suggestion that it started "printing money," casting this as a technically ignorant mischaracterization crafted to make the central bank sound irresponsible. True, the Fed does not expand the money supply by ordering the mint to print more dollar bills. Its purchasing agents, working at the New York branch of the Fed, call up their contacts at a network of twenty-four "primary dealers," mainly big banks like JPMorgan, Citi, and Goldman Sachs. The Fed agent offers to buy a batch of bonds, agrees to a price, and then with a keystroke digitally sends payment to the primary dealer's reserve account, which is also at the New York Fed. The money is not "printed" per se, but it is digitally created out of thin air.

There was nothing new about the way money was created during or after the crisis of 2008. Instead the Fed expanded the range of assets it would buy, and from whom. Even banks as big as the primary dealers had only so many bonds to sell, so the Fed began buying from a wider array of sellers, including hedge funds, private equity firms, and other kinds of shadow banks. This suddenly expanded pool of sellers made it possible for the Fed to create billions more dollars per keystroke.

Second, and even more important, the Fed began for the first time to buy not only short-term but also long-term government bonds, including 10-year Treasuries. Up until then, the 10-year Treasury had been the daily bread of financial markets, a place where investors large and small, worldwide, could park their money for a reliable return. By buying 10-year Treasuries in multibillion-dollar batches, the Fed was deliberately pushing down the yield on those bonds, from 5 percent to less than 1 percent by 2020. Each fall in returns on these ultrasafe bonds landed like a stick, pushing investors to move into higher-risk debt, but accompanied by a carrot, the promise of government rescue if their bets failed.

The scale of these new bond-buying campaigns is hard to overstate: in barely more than a year, between late 2008 and early 2010, the Fed created $1.2 trillion dollars, more money than it had created over the prior century. Most of this was created by the Fed before Congress had finished debating Obama's first stimulus bill—a dramatic illustration of how much more quickly unelected Fed governors can act, compared to a divided body of elected representatives. And that was just the beginning—much more money would be created over the coming decade and in 2020.

Slowly, unelected central bankers were taking over from elected representatives the job of resuscitating economies in recession. In the United States, new stimulus spending by the federal government nearly tripled from 3.5 percent of GDP in the recession of 2001 to 9 percent in 2020. Those are huge increases, yet they pale in comparison to central bank purchases in the financial markets, which rose from 0.2 percent of GDP in 2001 to 9 percent in 2008 and 16 percent in 2020.

The same basic pattern holds across all the major capitalist countries, including the United Kingdom, Japan, and the eurozone. In the eurozone, government stimulus spending rose from 1 percent in 2001 to near 7 percent of GDP in 2020, but central bank stimulus rose from zero to 22 percent of GDP.

Most Americans don't pay much attention to this slow transfer of power and economic responsibility from the president and Congress to the central bank. The fishbowl that is life in the West Wing is far removed from the obscurity that surrounds Fed headquarters in the Eccles Building, a few blocks away. In a study of three hundred thousand news stories on the financial crisis in 2008, Obama was the lead character 8 percent of the time, Bernanke barely 0.1 percent of the time. Investors are so obsessed with the Fed, they tend to imagine the whole world is watching the central bank, but that is hardly the case.

As Bernanke wrote in 2010, one explicit aim of the bond-buying campaign was to drive up asset prices, so Americans would feel richer and spend more to lift the economy. By then, however, the Great Recession was over, and doubts about injecting so much money into a healthy economy were growing. Critics pointed out that even by the Fed's own estimates, for every $600 billion it pumped into the banking system, unemployment was likely to fall by just 0.03 percent.

For so little prospect of gain, the central bank was embarking on an experiment that was almost sure to distort financial markets. Though the Fed is dominated by economists with academic backgrounds, the internal dissenters were a minority, and often came to the central bank from Wall Street or jobs in the banking system. That minority included board members like Kevin Warsh and regional presidents like Richard Fisher, Jeffrey Lacker, and Thomas Hoenig, who warned that much of this newly created money was likely to be wasted—"misallocated"—rather than invested in ways that boosted growth or created jobs. It also included future chairman Jerome Powell, a veteran of the private equity industry, who began flagging the economic risks of building up so much debt as soon as he joined the Fed board in 2012.

The skeptics worried that many Americans would expect the program to continue until unemployment came down. Markets would become even more deeply hooked on low borrowing costs, and would put more pressure on the Fed to buy bonds, and on and on—what Fed board member Jeremy Stein called the "*Groundhog Day* scenario." Lacker warned that the Fed risked committing itself to "near-permanent intervention," inflating bubbles and thus "transferring income" from struggling savers to the rich, who own an overwhelming share of risky financial assets. In other words, people holding their money in bank savings accounts would lose out on low rates, while rich investors holding riskier assets, including high-yielding debts, would win.

The dissenters were overridden, and not only in Washington. Between 2008 and 2019, the four major central banks—of the United States, Europe, England, and Japan—expanded their stock of assets from $4 trillion to more than $13 trillion. In just over one decade, they spent more than twice as much buying financial assets—expanding their balance sheets—as they had in total over the prior fifteen decades, going back to the 1850s. The holdings of the Bank of England grew tenfold that decade, from 4 percent to 40 percent of GDP, smashing the record of 20 percent set in the late 1730s.

Unfortunately, central banks can create all the money they want, but cannot control where it will go. Instead of fueling growth in the real economy, as central banks hoped, easy money went into financial assets. Debts grew much faster than the economy, in most countries. As the problems created by easy money grew more obvious, the chorus of critics widened, at least within the financial world. Central bankers responded that they had not created the era of easy money, they were just coping, heroically and creatively, with forces beyond their control.

Worldwide, they argued, the supply of capital was growing, in the retirement funds of aging populations and in the accumulating wealth of emerging countries, particularly China. At the same time, demand for capital was falling, because those aging populations produced fewer young entrepreneurs, and because the world economy was shifting from manufacturing to industries like services and tech, which require less capital investment than building factories. In the view of central bankers, it was these impersonal forces of supply and demand that had been pushing interest rates—the cost of capital—down for decades.

Those impersonal forces were real. And yet, by the Fed's own estimates, the "neutral rate" of interest—at which supply and demand should balance—was 1 percent in real, inflation-adjusted terms throughout the 2010s. On average, the Fed had kept its real base rate two points lower than that estimate, at negative 1 percent, over the course of the decade. The reason it pushed real rates to zero and below, using risky experiments in bond buying to do it, was the new commitment to constant stimulus, the sense of personal responsibility central bankers felt for boosting growth all the time. When bickering politicians could not agree on spending, central bankers would have to display "The Courage to Act." That is the title of Bernanke's memoir on the crisis of 2008—pitch perfect for an era when central bankers had grown perhaps a bit too sure that their easy money experiments amounted to doing the right thing.

=======

FIVE

BAILOUT CULTURE

T hough many companies and banks have grown "too big to fail," in the eyes of the nanny state, that image hardly captures the reach of the bailout culture today. Over the last half century, governments have extended guarantees of survival from companies and banks to entire industries, pension and health systems, tunnels and other building projects, financial markets for assets of all kinds including stocks, bonds and housing, and to foreign countries large and small.

Company Bailouts Become Industry Bailouts

In the United States, direct corporate bailouts started out as one-off and highly controversial rescues. A hint of what was to come surfaced during the 1930s and 1940s, when the new Reconstruction Finance Corporation became a kind of back channel for relief spending of all kinds, including cheap but often inadequate emergency loans for distressed banks and businesses. Banks still failed by the hundreds. Railroads that got RFC loans were still more likely to go bankrupt than rivals. As prosperity returned in the 1950s, the idea of "reconstruction" seemed out of date, and the RFC was shut down.

The first postwar bailouts emerged from the suffocating regulatory environment of the 1960s, which was strangling America's oldest and sixth-largest company, Penn Central railroad. Regulations demanded that the railroad keep running trains even if the cars were empty; union contracts demanded it pay workers who were not on the job. Desperate to make up for mounting losses, Penn Central managers began borrowing in European markets, which were less heavily regulated than U.S. markets. They used these loans to invest in property, buying swaths of the land under Lexington, Park, and Madison Avenues in New York. America's leading railroad had quietly become its largest real estate company.

When recession hit in early 1970, Penn Central could no longer service its loans. Its bosses had powerful friends, and they went to the White House to ask for loan guarantees. The Nixon administration found a way to say yes, using an obscure rule that would allow the Pentagon to bail out the railroad on "national security" grounds, in exchange for an ownership stake. The leading liberal economist of the era, John Kenneth Galbraith, praised the bailout of Penn Central and predicted it would lead to further nationalization of troubled giants. He delighted in chiding conservative Republicans for leading this campaign, in a piece titled "Richard Nixon and the Great Socialist Revival."

Galbraith spoke too soon. The country wasn't ready. Congressional leaders blocked the deal, asking why they should bail out corporate giants rather than small businesses or homeowners. Instead, Nixon's friend at the Fed, Arthur Burns, stepped in, opening a new "discount window" that eased fears of a broader seizure in the credit markets. Penn Central was forced into a reorganization that ultimately cost taxpayers some $4 billion, securing a place in the early history of corporate bailouts.

Soon America's twentieth-largest bank, Franklin National on Long Island, was going the way of Penn Central, getting into trouble on heavy borrowing in Europe. Again Congress would not help. Again the Fed would, reassuring Franklin's investors in 1974 that the bank would get financial support—even after the bank's chief shareholder tried to escape accountability by faking his own kidnapping. The stress in the markets melted away. "The entire financial world can breathe more easily, not only in this country but abroad," said Burns.

That was it, outside of a few midsize banks and a relatively small loan guarantee for Lockheed Martin, for bailouts in the early 1970s. The rescue response was not yet automatic. In 1975 New York City, then awash in street crime, found its coffers depleted by an exodus to the suburbs and pleaded for federal help to stave off default. President Gerald Ford's abrupt refusal inspired the legendary tabloid headline: "Ford to City: Drop Dead."

A turning point came in 1984, with the first financially costly bailout of a major bank, Continental Illinois. The nation's largest commercial and industrial lender, Continental had gotten involved with a small Oklahoma bank run by Bill "Beep" Jennings, who was, according to Christopher Leonard, "the sort of person who drank beer out of a cowboy boot to impress clients." Jennings was also an early pioneer in financial securitization, the same repackaging of risky loans into supposedly secure assets that would come back to haunt America in the 2000s.

Amid the oil boom of the 1970s, Jennings sold investors on packages of loans to oil companies that he called "participating loans," which were premised on the faith that oil prices could only go up, and aided by stratagems that allowed him to dodge limits on how much he could lend to any one customer. When oil prices started to drop in the early eighties, the government allowed Jennings's little bank to fail.

But soon it emerged that his biggest customer was Continental Illinois, which had a complex string of loans and connections to more than two thousand other banks. Spooked customers were withdrawing cash by the millions. Concerned that the run on Continental would lead to a broader stampede, and accepting collateral "no private actor would accept," the government extended emergency credit along with a promise of unlimited protection for depositors. Greeted at the time as an "extraordinary" departure from past practice, the bailout would establish "one of the most important legacies" of the 1980s, with Continental becoming the first bank that the United States declared "too big to fail." The total cost to taxpayers came to $11 billion.

The first sweeping industry bailout came in the late 1980s and early 1990s, in the savings and loan crisis. Like others before them, S&Ls got caught up in dubious foreign borrowing, and their troubles grew as the easy money era got rolling. Ultimately, the taxpayer bill for folding roughly 750 S&Ls and shoring up the many hundreds of faltering survivors would come to around $125 billion, many times the record set in the Continental Illinois bailout.

With global markets growing rapidly, and more interconnected, the Fed was ever more watchful of worldwide contagion effects, which rose high on the radar during the crises in Asia and Russia of the late 1990s. In September 1998, the hedge fund Long-Term Capital Management was getting into very short-term trouble, having borrowed heavily to make bets across many asset classes. Managing as much as $100 billion for fewer than a hundred clients, including foreign countries, LTCM had about $30 in debt for every $1 of capital. And its creditors included most major Wall Street firms.

Fed officials feared markets might panic and "cease to function" if even an investment house like LTCM, which was led by Nobel laureates in economics, could not find buyers for its more exotic assets. First Greenspan cut the Fed funds rate to ease fear in the markets, and a week later the chair of the New York Fed brought together nearly a dozen of Wall Street's largest banks to defend themselves from contagion by financing a private $5.6 billion infusion for LTCM. This was another first, establishing the habit of bailouts to preempt rather than respond to recessions. Saving LTCM ushered "in an era of extreme moral hazard that continues to this day," wrote economist Jim Reid of Deutsche Bank Research. "Pure capitalism that has been the catalyst for over two centuries of economic growth was being replaced by an increasingly state-managed capitalism that involved larger and larger bailouts."

The next industry bailout was for the airlines after the 9/11 terror attacks, at a relatively low cost of $25 billion, but all previous rescues would be outdone by the government response to the financial crisis of 2008.

MR. BAILOUT AND THE CRISIS OF 2008

In the 1990s and early 2000s, easy money had encouraged mergers across American industries, including finance, leaving the daisy chain of mortgage lending in the control of five investment banks, three commercial banks with investment arms, three ratings agencies, two thrifts, and one mega-insurer, AIG. On the eve of the crisis, it was no secret that for all the apparent scale and diversity of the global housing market, the debts on which it depended were channeled through this narrow circle of giant companies.

The lending chain started with big thrifts—survivors of the S&L crisis—selling mortgages to homeowners. Wall Street banks got in the game, extending lines of credit to the thrifts or buying the thrifts directly. The banks started bundling mortgage loans into multilayered securities, with bundles of riskier loans paying the highest interest. As the market for these "mortgage-backed securities," or MBSs, expanded worldwide, with $4 trillion in new issues in the four years before 2008, banks grew more confident that size and diversification equaled security.

The thrifts and other creditors started selling mortgages to ill-qualified borrowers including the NINJAs—customers with no income, no job, and no assets to offer as collateral. Investment firms began packaging these "subprime mortgages" into another multilayered security, collateralized debt obligations, or CDOs, with $700 billion sold in the four years before 2008. The ratings agencies came to judge at least the senior (most solid) layer of these packages as less risky than individual subprime mortgages, and thus found a way to rate bundles of junk loans AAA—no risk at all.

Encouraged, the banks began creating "CDOs squared"—bundles of CDOs. Insurers, led by the big one, AIG, began offering insurance on these bundles and other assets, which they called credit default swaps, or CDSs. As the guesstimated value of assets insured by these contracts, which came to cover much more than mortgages, departed from underlying reality, their "notional value" skyrocketed in the four years before the crisis, from around $6 trillion to $58 trillion—a sum roughly matching global GDP.

If confidence faltered at any step in the lending chain, the entire structure could come down. When home prices started to fall in 2006, and subprime lenders started to go bankrupt the next year, the end was inevitable. When it came, the government took over and ran the market, rescuing most of the big financial firms or rolling the weaker ones into the stronger ones.

A narrower circle of finance industry giants emerged after 2008 with each member stronger. By early 2009 the government, through a blizzard of new emergency lending and rescue vehicles, had extended some $2.3 trillion in bailout funds. Nearly a thousand U.S. financial institutions got help, but so did two large automakers, GM and Chrysler, foreign central banks, and commercial banks in Japan, Switzerland, Scotland, and France. The government also rescued its own mortgage lenders, including Fannie Mae, created during the Depression to make homeownership more accessible, and its younger brother, Freddie Mac. The mortgage agencies had been encouraged by President George W. Bush to "use the mighty muscle of the federal government" to make homes even easier to buy in the 2000s, but they, too, had gotten carried away in the subprime lending frenzy.

Working in tandem, the Treasury and Fed had become the lender of last resort for global markets, and the dealmaker—bringing together buyers and sellers—should lending fail anyway. Bankers started calling NY Fed chair Tim Geithner "eHarmony," for his smooth matchmaking. As if to set his own efforts within the bounds of long-established tradition, Geithner in his inside account of the crisis praises Alexander Hamilton as "America's original Mr. Bailout."

To stem the financial panic of 1792, Hamilton had made novel use of Treasury funds to buy assets and calm the markets—in ways that did indeed foreshadow Treasury's role in 2008. However, in the intervening centuries, this kind of rescue was rare, limited, and piecemeal, and the government often left banks to fail before the bailout culture began laying down roots in the 1980s. What Geithner did, then, was to radically expand the budding bailout culture, not build on tradition.

When many of the government loans were paid back after 2008, defenders could argue that the borrowers had never been insolvent deadbeats after all, and that the rescues had profited the taxpayer in the end. But the distorting impact on capitalism remained. The message to markets, that government would treat an ever-wider range of companies and financial institutions as too big to fail, was life-changing.

During the crisis, Sheila Bair was chair of the Federal Deposit Insurance Corporation, an agency created in the 1930s to restore public faith in the banking system by insuring depositors. She thought the government went too far in 2008. By bailing out mismanaged institutions "instead of using the crisis as an opportunity to clean out the system . . . we repeated the mistakes of Japan's 'lost decade' and of our own savings-and-loan debacle," Bair wrote. Propping up failures would only hurt well-run institutions. "We cannot rely on our capitalist system to allocate resources for their most productive use unless we let the inefficient or mismanaged fail."

INDUSTRY BAILOUTS BECOME GLOBAL MARKET BAILOUTS

Fear of cross-border financial contagion gave U.S. officials a growing sense of responsibility for generating constant growth not only at home but worldwide. In the mid-1990s, the Fed under Greenspan had first established itself in a formal way as a global lender by extending swap lines—effectively, emergency credit lines, swapping dollars for foreign currencies—to the central banks of Mexico and Canada. These became critical tools in subsequent years.

Starting in 1997, as dollar-denominated debts in Asia began to implode, the same bailout machinery mobilized to save LTCM extended its reach worldwide. The Fed cut rates to calm the markets, and worked with the Treasury and the International Monetary Fund to organize rescue loans including $55 billion for South Korea and $23 billion for Russia. Greenspan would remark much later that the threat of contagion from Asia had inspired a "major rethinking at the Fed," by bursting for good the assumption that the United States "can remain an oasis of prosperity" in moments of global stress.

It was during the crisis of 2008 that the Fed became the "lender of last resort to the world," Ben Bernanke writes. Though central banks from Europe to Japan were also doing everything they could to ease panic in the markets by supplying euros, yen, or other currencies in abundance, they could not supply dollars—the currency most often used in international lending. To prevent a shortage of dollars from magnifying the crisis, the Fed extended swap lines to fourteen central banks from Brazil and Mexico to Sweden and Denmark.

By the next decade, because global markets were so sensitive to any sign of Fed tightening, it was difficult for Fed leaders to slow the flow of easy money. In 2013, Bernanke hinted that it was time for the central bank to slow or "taper" its bond buying, and the global markets threw a "taper tantrum," dropping rapidly until Bernanke backed off. In late 2018, the Fed again tried to start the return to normality, by purchasing fewer bonds each month. Again the markets dropped suddenly, and again the Fed felt it had no choice other than to continue buying in bulk.

Less than a year later, the economy was growing, unemployment was at a half-century low, and again the Fed cut rates in a recovery, as insurance against a slowdown. What could possibly go wrong? A lot, it turned out. Even as it cut rates, the Fed was trying to restore normal lending conditions by selling off the assets on its books—at a safe pace, or so it thought. In September 2019, an obscure yet vital arm of the global money markets suddenly seized up. The "repo" crisis was on.

Repo loans have been called the "beating heart" of the financial system. Traditionally, they were extended by the big Wall Street banks, using their Fed reserves, to other banks, which used them to fund daily operations. After 2008, the repo market had been opened to shadow banks, including hedge funds, which had started using super-cheap repo loans as collateral to borrow up to fifty times more, making huge leveraged bets on Treasury bonds. When the Fed began selling assets in 2019, big banks started to worry about the adequacy of their own reserves, and suddenly jacked up rates for repo borrowers.

The Fed was not sure what was happening—yet—but stepped in to offer its own repo loans at rock-bottom rates. Though its aim was to save the banking system, it ended up saving the hedge funds as well, closing the circle. Private investors had borrowed billions of dollars created by the government to bet big on government bonds, only to be bailed out by the Fed when those bets failed. Chris Leonard, citing the estimated cost of $400 billion, calls this episode the "invisible bail-out," because it took place in a vast corner of the global market that is little known to the public. To keep markets settled, the Fed returned to buying assets in subsequent months, and it worked: every 1 percent increase in the Fed balance sheet was matched by a 1 percent gain in the S&P 500.

The lesson is that every new bailout begets much more of the same: at the start of the pandemic, one of the Fed's first moves was to offer cheap repo loans at a scale far higher than those of 2019. Another was to revive all fourteen swap lines it had extended to central banks in 2008—five of which had become permanent in the interim. And the powers used by the Fed and Treasury to extend bailouts to corporate borrowers in 2020 and 2008, and to Mexico in 1994, had all been created for emergency use back in the 1930s and had been sitting dormant on the books for decades. Once created, rescue powers do not just disappear.

EUROPEAN RESCUE CULTURE

In the 1990s, four nations on the "periphery" of Europe had through profligate spending habits earned the distrust of global financial markets. Portugal, Italy, Greece, and Spain came to be known as countries that could not be relied on to cover their debts. Investors shunned their currencies, which would crash if their debts did. But all that changed when they adopted the new continental currency, the euro, at its launch in 1999. Investors knew that Europe would not let member nations default, for fear their failure would undermine the euro, and with it the political project of unification.

Investors began lending to these troubled countries on easier and easier terms, betting that Europe would rescue these debtors in a pinch. By 2007, Greece, for example, was paying a quarter point more interest than Germany. That implied investors saw only a 1-in-400 chance Greece would default on its government bonds, which had in fact been in default half the time since records began in 1829—shortly after the country declared independence. And so Greece and its fellow debtors went on a borrowing spree that imploded in the crisis of 2008. Portugal and Greece were dubbed "the subprime" and Spain "the Lehman Brothers" of Europe.

As expected, the European Union stepped in to bail out Greece and company, with financial support for their $2 trillion in debt to foreign lenders. In creditor nations like Germany and France, many voters were angry at their leaders for spending taxpayer money to bail out profligate neighbors. Their leaders, however, were less worried about saving the Greeks than saving the system. With global debt levels at record highs, one sovereign default could trigger others. Contagion threatened the creditors, including many of the largest German and French banks, that had loaned heavily to nations on the periphery. The easy money culture was making the entire global system more fragile, begetting more bailouts.

Greece ended up suffering a lost decade in the 2010s. Though it initially resisted demands for belt tightening in return for official bailouts, the markets left the country no choice. Investors sent rates on Greek debt skyward in 2010 and again in 2015, forcing even a socialist prime minister, Alexis Tsipras, to embrace financial discipline—ultimately to Greece's benefit. In recent years Greece has been one of Europe's fastest-growing economies, and unemployment has fallen from a crisis peak near 30 percent to less than 10 percent. Greece was forced in the end to change its ways, but discipline was imposed primarily by the markets, tired of financing such gargantuan debts, not by fellow governments.

Indeed the government bailout culture was alive and well. By 2020, the amount of government debt that had fallen into default was still near record lows worldwide. Even nations that had defaulted in the recent past could sell bonds offering improbably low returns. Cyprus issued new twenty-year debt yielding just 1 percent, a rate so low it showed investors were supremely confident the little country—which had defaulted on its debts as recently as 2013—would get saved by fellow governments if it faltered again.

When inflation returned worldwide in 2022 and central banks started raising rates, it looked like tight money might force government leaders to reconsider these increasingly costly bailouts, but they did not.

Rising rates were bound to tip reckless borrowers over the edge— the question was where trouble would appear first. The answer came from California, where Silicon Valley Bank, better known as SVB, catered to the community of tech entrepreneurs and venture capitalists. SVB had extensive holdings of Treasury bonds which plummeted in value as rates rose. Depositors started to flee. The authorities stepped in, stretching the rules to insure the deposits of SVB's wealthy clientele in full, and to preempt any contagion effects by promising other smallish banks that the government would buy their Treasuries at the original price, not the plummeting price.

SVB was folded into a larger bank. Unlike SVB's depositors, its investors were not protected, leading many to argue this was not a bank bailout. But it was effectively a bailout of the banking system, including as it did new Fed lending and other measures to prevent the run on SVB deposits from spreading. The conversation behind official doors was once again, according to a staffer at the New York Fed, about whether this was 2008 all over.

SVB was also a bailout of Silicon Valley itself. In Texas, the mayor of Fort Worth said that business leaders there were asking whether, if SVB had served the oil industry, the government "would have stepped up the same way." Indeed, the bailout was more about defending U.S. technology companies, the main beneficiaries of the administration's new industrial policy, than "prudent finance," wrote *Bloomberg* columnists John Micklethwait and Adrian Wooldridge. Combined with the rescue of other banks in California and Switzerland, these government interventions "may not have pleased Adam Smith, but they would have brought a smile to Jean-Baptiste Colbert, Louis XIV's finance minister and the father of dirigisme. The idea that finance is an arm of the state is back—and global banking is likely to be reshaped by it." Not for the better. Micklethwait and Wooldridge warned that the downsides of Colbertism were vividly foreshadowed by China, where state banks have been conduits for misdirecting capital into ghost cities and the like for years.

The system had internalized new reflexes, with markets automatically looking to the Fed for help, and the central bank automatically assuming that the wisest course of action was instant, overwhelming rescues, before crises took root.

SOCIALIZED RISK

"Socialized risk" refers to the government safety net, which was originally designed to protect the weakest members of capitalist societies from hard times but now extends under the feet of everyone, poor and rich, all the time.

Again, no matter how solidly policymakers can justify any particular bailout in the short term, borrowing to pay for them all matters in the long term. The Biden administration had increased government spending and borrowing so fast that interest payments on the public debt are on track to exceed spending on the military or welfare programs. Amounting to 2 percent of GDP in 2022, interest payments on the federal debt alone are now expected to exceed 6 percent of GDP by 2050. Along the way, those payments were expected to surpass the Pentagon budget and the Medicaid budget around 2030, and to surpass the largest entitlement programs, Medicare and Social Security, in the late 2040s.

When the *Economist* tried in the fall of 2022 to put a number on the size of the "bailout state," it found the task greatly complicated by promises of bailouts in the future. These "contingent liabilities" will one day require enormous outlays. They include, for example, the UK government promise to support the Channel Tunnel if it falls into disuse, insurers in the event of terrorist attack, and pensioners if their retirement funds go under. The United States insures bank deposits, health care payouts and, in recent years, more than half of all home mortgages. Taken together, contingent liabilities have grown faster than the economy for at least two decades, and by 2022 were more than six times total U.S. output. In Europe, they were leading to about ten rescue programs a year, up from just two on average in the 1990s.

It was hard to tell where central banks left off and governments began, because both were offering generous corporate bailouts, often jointly. In late 2022, historian and market analyst Russell Napier argued that governments were taking over "the power to control the creation of money" by guaranteeing bank credit. To those who objected that these guarantees were a one-off response to the Covid crisis, Napier pointed out that the practice continued across capitalist countries, inspired by new emergencies, including the war in Ukraine and the resulting energy supply crunch. "This is the new normal," wrote Napier.

European governments continued in late 2022 to roll out new guarantees for new bank loans to corporations. Over the previous two years, the German government had guaranteed 40 percent of all new bank loans to corporations, and the French government had guaranteed 70 percent. Italy went one step further. By rolling old guarantees into new ones, it was guaranteeing more than 100 percent of the new loans. Much of this financial relief was a preventive response to the war in Ukraine and the jitters it might cause. The economic war-fighting mentality was tightening its grip on governments, not easing as the price of money rose.

The fighting in Ukraine was also driving up energy prices, and European governments mobilized to help. France and the United Kingdom rolled out emergency energy subsidies reaching 3 to 7 percent of GDP, nearly the opposite of what they had done to address energy shortages in the harsh winter of 1973–74. During the 1970 oil crisis, very few governments had offered help to consumers, and many European leaders had advised their people to drive less and dress more warmly. The energy subsidies of 2022 were thus a sign of how automatic the bailout reflex had become. In late 2022 Biden touted a $36 billion bailout for the Teamsters retirement plan as the largest ever for a union pension system—a historically large bailout, lost in the line items of his multitrillion-dollar spending plans. Yet the mainstream view was still that bailouts are almost endlessly affordable, because the rest of the world will never lose faith that America can cover its debts.

SIX

THE SURREAL LOGIC OF 2020

S trangely, writers who in 2020 welcomed the end of "the neoliberal era" were counting even outgoing president Trump as a neoliberal, on the grounds that at times he bashed big government and his main accomplishments were tax cuts and deregulation.

But Trump followed in the path of no one. He instituted tax cuts later in a recovery than any previous president, pushing the practice of constant stimulus to a new extreme. In doing so, he had driven the government deficit to a peacetime record, even before the pandemic hit, supported by the many conventional Republican economists who continued to argue that tax cuts would solve every problem, including deficits. Investors had learned to expect that the White House will roll out spending and tax cuts as campaigns heat up, which is why stocks typically do so well in the year before presidential elections; as usual, the preelection year of 2019 was a particularly strong one for the S&P 500.

Trump's exercise of presidential authority to personal ends through the medium of Twitter has no parallel in American history. He insisted that "my gut tells me more sometimes than anybody else's brain can ever tell me," which is to say he rejected membership in any school of thought.

Trump's attacks on the deep state often followed less from market logic than from conspiracy theories about how the CIA and the FBI were trying to run him out of office. Most days Trump was thumbing his nose at free markets: building a wall to block immigrants, threatening to impose punitive tariffs even on allies in Europe, Mexico, and Canada, calling out U.S. companies to stop them moving facilities abroad, cheering on the stock market, publicly ridiculing the Fed chair as "clueless" and its governors as "boneheads" for refusing to make easy money even easier. Trump not only intruded in the markets, he named the names of people and companies he didn't like in the markets, giving the term "bully pulpit" new meaning. Should the precedents set by Trump be followed by his successors, they are more likely to widen than restrict the scope of central government power.

HOW 2020 FOLLOWED THE LOGIC OF A GROWING BAILOUT CULTURE

This was the situation when the pandemic hit in early 2020. The world economy was highly vulnerable to another financial crisis because it was already so riddled with debt, and it was riddled with debt because governments had offered more easy credit and bailouts to soften the impact of every crisis since the 1980s.

During previous global pandemics, going back to the Spanish flu of 1918 and the Asian flu of 1957, no major government had ever seriously considered shutting down the economy to thwart the spread of a virus. By

2020, popular expectations of government protection required both lock-downs to slow the virus and public spending to ease the pain of lockdowns.

What happened next was the story of the last four decades—the rapid socialization of economic risk—only this time telescoped into a matter of days and weeks and magnified to previously unimaginable scale. The government had been gaining confidence in its capacity to manage the economy for decades, and in 2020 its interventions would not only ease the pain but overcompensate tens of millions of people for difficulties imposed by lockdowns.

It is probably fair to say that never before had modern capitalist economies run so directly on government command. At the signing of the $2.2 trillion relief package in March, Steven Mnuchin said his brief was to fight a "war on the virus," and so it was. Within months, total U.S. government spending shot up to 45 percent of GDP, edging past the World War II record. The deficit shot up to 15 percent of GDP, second only to World War II. The recession of early 2020 was the shortest since records begin, in 1850, snuffed out by government relief after just eight weeks. It ended in May, even though stay-at-home orders were still in effect in forty-two of the fifty American states.

Looking back, the pandemic was so out of step with the past experience of "recessions" that it probably needs a new word to capture it. In the United States, output fell by more than 9 percent and joblessness shot up from 4 percent to more than 14 percent. These were the worst declines since the Great Depression, and they unfolded faster. Tens of millions of Americans were suddenly out of a job, with all the misery and uncertainty that entails. Yet for many it did not feel like a recession, much less a depression.

Aiming to preempt critics who said that the 2008 bailouts had helped only big banks and Wall Street, the authorities resolved to leave no one out. Most Americans got unconditional relief checks. The unemployed got $600 supplemental benefit checks, which for many made it profitable not to work: in nearly four of five states, the combined benefits exceeded the average wages of the jobs that were lost.

Knowing how fragile capitalism had become, governments and central banks felt compelled to throw a safety net under businesses of all shapes, sizes, and financial conditions. Though the trigger was different—this crisis was triggered by natural disaster, not decades of mounting debt—the government response built once again on all those that had come before.

Small businesses got "forgivable loans," which is to say grants, if they agreed to keep workers on payroll. Midsize businesses got direct Fed loans, financed by the Treasury, through the Main Street Lending Program. For bigger corporations, the authorities would buy both existing bonds and newly issued bonds, even those rated as junk or near junk. These supports extended to fallen angels like Ford and Kraft Heinz, which had recently been demoted into junk status, and sinking demons, which were already junk but were descending into a lower circle of financial hell.

The Fed was opening new discount windows for short-term emergency loans—traditionally reserved only for banks with strong collateral—to all kinds of companies, large and small, financially strong or deeply troubled. For all the coverage devoted to the thousands of small businesses that had to shut down, the rate of personal bankruptcies and mortgage loan defaults actually fell during the pandemic. According to the research firm Oxford Economics, a recession as big as the one in 2020 would in the past have triggered a 20 percent increase in corporate bankruptcies; instead, bankruptcies fell across the big capitalist economies, from the United States to Germany, the United Kingdom, France, Italy, Canada, and Japan.

All these forms of support were either totally unprecedented or unrivaled since World War II. And the interventions came on top of amped-up versions of the 2008 rescues for financial markets, including help for the vast money markets, where investors park their cash, and the commercial paper market, where most U.S. corporations borrow to finance daily operations. Commentators searched the thesaurus for superlatives to describe how new all this was. A Bloomberg TV announcer said that the Fed was "throwing the kitchen sink and more, all the stuff under the stove and in the closet, at the markets."

With little yet known about the virus, relatively few people dared venture out to shop for anything more than necessities. Most restaurants and bars were closed anyway. It was no party, beyond the much-criticized college students who massed by the thousands for spring break in Florida, in defiance of social-distancing rules. Yet for much of the population, it was weirdly not a downer, either. Many professionals, working from home under lockdowns, admitted at least to friends that they were having a fine pandemic.

From their beginnings, welfare states had always targeted benefits to the poor, or to those who had paid into pension programs, or who met certain conditions, like holding a job. As Covid spread, all those conditions were shelved, in the interest of getting quick approval. If every member of society is a beneficiary, fewer will be dissenters, and politicians were more than willing to spread the benefits around. The poor did get help. Yes, poverty fell. Food insecurity fell in parts of Europe. Forecasters who had expected an "eviction 'tsunami'" were surprised when eviction rates fell instead, under order from a federal moratorium. But the middle and upper classes fared at least as well.

In rich countries, disposable income actually rose during the 2020 recession, thanks to government support. In Europe, governments paid laid off workers a portion of the previous income, as if they had gone on pension. In the United States, cash support came via direct deposit to bank accounts or by cash card in the mail to most of the adult population—170 million recipients in all. Government dollars were keeping millions out of poverty—and were also dropping, unsolicited, into the mailboxes of college grads working their first corporate jobs and doing better than just fine. Pandemic Oversight, an independent watchdog established by Congress to track relief spending, reports that of about $810 billion delivered as cash benefits, more than $110 billion went to recipients making $100,000 to $200,000 a year. By one count, recipients in this group got on average more than $5,000 each. Checks amounting to more than $660 million went to Americans making more than $200,000.

Under lockdown, recipients found it hard to spend all this cash, so a big chunk went to savings. Bank deposits swelled by $3.5 trillion at the peak. Savings hit multi-decade highs. Credit scores improved across the board, for all income levels. Another big chunk went into buying stocks and bonds or houses—home prices soared. Americans making less than $75,000 a year qualified for the biggest relief checks, and day trading in this income group spiked by more than 50 percent.

The knowledge that even sinking demons would not be allowed to fail magnified the already inflated asset values to new, often absurd heights. Online personalities hyped everything from cryptocurrencies to the "meme stocks" of dying theater chains and heavily indebted video game retailers. The founder of Barstool Sports somehow repackaged himself as an investment guru and screamed at his listeners to "Get on board. BUY! Everyone makes money. Everyone makes money. Buy. Buy. Buy."

Though stocks had been booming in a weak economy for a decade, this odd couple got odder in 2020. The worst downturn since World War II ushered in the best twelve-month run for the U.S. stock market. "Fundamentally we have now socialized credit risk. And we have forever changed the nature of how our economy functions," warned Scott

Minerd, who as CIO at Guggenheim Investments was one of the largest players in global bond markets. "The Fed has made it clear that prudent investing will not be tolerated."

At the peak, household net worth had risen by $35 trillion on higher home and stock and bond prices. Surveys of business and consumer confidence, far from plunging, were skyrocketing by 2021.

In Silicon Valley, the boom in online sales and services inspired a hiring boom, even if there was no work for the new hires. The aim was to hoard talent, and rising profits made it easy to raise salaries. Software executive Thomas Siebel told the *Wall Street Journal* that "People were job-hopping from jobs where they were doing nothing, working from home to another where they were doing nothing, working from home, and got paid 15 percent more."

Again, no one questioned the need for government stimulus during a severe global recession. I certainly didn't. The legitimate questions were of balance and scale, of spending with no filter and far in excess of the sums required to make up for any weakness in demand, the accumulating risk of ill-advised habits internalized over decades. Going into the pandemic, Fed officials had made clear how they weighed the risks—they would err on the side of doing too much rather than too little, of haste rather than calm. "Get in the boats and go," Powell urged Fed staff, quoting the orders of British officers during the evacuation of Dunkirk. Dropping the traditional reluctance of central bankers to offer unsolicited public advice to elected leaders, Powell also called on the Trump administration to mobilize "the great fiscal power of the United States."

Deliberately erring on the side of excess would have consequences, too. The U.S. government issued more new debt in the first twelve months of the pandemic than it had in the first two centuries after its founding in 1776, much of it in Fed loans financed by the Treasury. The same basic escalation—governments and central banks working together to dose all pain—was visible across the capitalist world, smashing the stimulus records set in 2008. The United States would unleash total monetary and fiscal stimulus amounting to 25 percent of GDP, or 50 percent more than in 2008; Britain would spend in excess of three times more, the European Union would spend in excess of four times more, and Japan would spend five times more, a total of 44 percent of GDP. Eventually even many defenders of big government would concede that the trillions in new spending had been "too large, too broad, and too long-lasting."

THE AUGUST REVOLUTION

Two years before the pandemic hit, the Fed had launched a study of how to respond to the next crisis and conducted town hall meetings around the country—the "Fed Listens" tour—absorbing the worries of working and minority communities left out of the disappointing recovery. Though the Fed can create unlimited sums of money, its officials know very well they cannot guide that money to underserved communities. Congress could, but it was paralyzed by its divisions. The Fed decided it would have to act anyway, even if its tools are too crude for the task.

Powell announced the conclusion of its listening tour in August 2020. Responding to the growing anger over rising inequality and limited job opportunities, the Fed would turn its old priorities upside down. Instead of trying to identify moments when the economy was producing too few jobs or too many, it would worry only about too few jobs. Recognizing that tight labor markets mean more jobs and higher wages "particularly for many in low- and middle-income communities," it would respond accordingly. In effect, the Fed was saying there was no such thing as excess in labor markets, only "shortfalls," which would reinforce the Fed bias toward keeping rates lower for longer.

In historical context, the August revolution was just another step in "the inescapable logic of the last four decades," as "societies insisted on growth that could no longer be justified by underlying productivity growth," wrote analysts at Macquarie Research. Easy money had "hooked" households and corporations on rising asset prices, leaving them intolerant of what had once been "healthy" market corrections. With rising debt and market bubbles now "at the core of modern economies," central banks had become "slaves of the system they created, albeit at our urging."

Going back to its founding, the Fed had seen its role in society expand dramatically, from fighting inflation to ensuring full employment and stabilizing financial markets at home and abroad. Though conservatives worried that "mission creep" at the Fed was further extending the reach of unelected central bankers, progressives were pushing it to fight new causes. In Congress, they urged the Fed to take even more radical steps to generate growth in the economy and jobs, and to fight racial inequality and climate change as well. Some had voted against the renomination of Chairman Powell, for refusing to deny corporate bailouts to oil companies. The politicization of economics was complete.

JUST A MOMENT, OR A LANDMARK MOMENT?

Asked in 2020 whether they had any doubts about creating so much money, central banks resorted to the same old line: not to worry, their bond-buying experiments in the 2010s had not reignited consumer price inflation, so there was no reason to think a similar buying spree would trigger inflation now.

But there was. The circumstances that had constrained inflation in consumer goods and services for the last half century were shifting.

The working-age population had started to shrink in Japan in the early 1990s, and now the depopulation trend was spreading across Asia to Europe and beyond. The farther it reached, the more upward pressure it put on wages.

At the same time, many countries had started to turn inward, throwing up barriers to trade after the crisis of 2008, and this new hostility to globalization and outsiders in general grew in the pandemic. By 2020, the leaders of China and India, among other big beneficiaries of globalization, were singing the praises of "self reliance" rather than open borders. With a shrinking world labor force, and less international competition, the forces that had contained consumer price inflation were melting away. For the first time since Johnson and Nixon, critics warned, central banks were creating money to help finance runaway government spending, and the risk of inflation was rising.

In late 2020, economists Michael Bordo and Mickey Levy looked back two hundred years and found that for most of that period a link between government deficits and inflation appeared only during major wars, particularly World War II. In the 1960s, that link reappeared in a new way, as governments in the United States and the United Kingdom put pressure on central banks to finance rising deficits even in peacetime. Now, they warned, given the scale of government spending during the pandemic, the risk of deficit-driven inflation was back. That warning proved timely when inflation returned with a vengeance in 2021.

If the pandemic was just an unusually ripe moment for big-government schemes, perhaps it would pass without changing much. The chatter among the American elite, however, suggested a ruling class more confident than ever in its ability to manage and control economic growth.

Rather than question why Washington would mail cash cards to most Americans, including the gainfully employed, when government lockdowns had just thrown forty million less fortunate Americans out of work, millennial columnists were hailing these programs as the precursor of a universal basic income. Never mind that even a back-of-the-envelope calculation shows proposals for a $1,000-per-month universal basic income would bust the U.S. budget. One commentator hailed Biden programs that provided cash-like benefits with no conditions as progress in "the quiet revolution of giving people money."

Liberal economists mock as puritanical any suggestion that generous government support can erode the work ethic, yet as the pandemic rolled on, so did the mainstreaming of an anti-work ethic. In a 2022 poll, one in eight Americans said they planned "no return" to pre-pandemic activity, including work. No doubt some of this had to do with lingering fear of infection and burnout during the pandemic, but attitudes to work had changed. As the number of Americans choosing to work part-time surged over the course of the year, a new buzz phrase emerged: "25 hours is the new 35." Social media began to celebrate "quiet quitting" and "acting your wage," meaning do what you are paid for, and no more. Wicked Clothes, a trendy designer for twentysomethings, launched a line of T-shirts with slogans like "Work is TRASH" and "Summon Someone Else."

In early 2023, America's most-read newspaper, the *New York Times*, began embracing the new ethic. One op-ed traced Paris protests pushing for a "right to laziness"—subsidized by a universal basic income—to a venerable French intellectual tradition that casts "a certain kind of laziness" as "focused calm or even spiritual elevation." A follow-up piece recast the traditional American values of independence and self-reliance—particularly the "strain" that frowns on accepting state aid—as the nation's "most toxic myth." Liberal think tanks joined in, analyzing the pandemic relief programs as models for a permanent campaign against economic hardship in all its forms.

Capitalist societies just seemed exhausted, eager for government relief even if it was not exactly required by Covid. Together Trump and Biden had rolled out more than $10 trillion in spending, all but the first $2 trillion under Trump after the recession of early 2020 was over. Though the Biden team positioned some of their spending as pandemic relief, they presented their new industrial policy as a revival of the American ambition that put a man on the moon. Many commentators cheered. While we are spending trillions anyway, one wrote, how about "Let's Launch a Moonshot for Meatless Meat."

The relief spending bills also earmarked hundreds of millions for state projects—a history museum in Texas, prisons in Alabama, water conservation in Utah—that had nothing to do with the pandemic. Long reluctant to support state and local debt, which would involve highly political decisions over who gets help, the Fed, too, gave in to pressure from distressed cities like Detroit, offering support to state and municipal bond markets for the first time.

Americans get that there are risks involved in spending beyond one's means; the number who say cutting deficits is a top priority has fluctuated between 20 and 70 percent in recent decades, rising sensibly enough in good times. And not everyone was indifferent to the excesses of the pandemic rescues, warning that the government was spending far more than needed to cover losses, and that there would be consequences. Former Treasury secretary Larry Summers called the rescues "the least responsible macroeconomic policy we've had in the last 40 years," inspired by intransigent Democrats and "completely unreasonable" Republicans.

Summers warned that stimulus on a level appropriate to a world war, not a recession, could "set off inflation pressures of a kind we have not seen in a generation." But Summers was born in the 1950s, not the 1980s, and he was out of step with a zeitgeist that dismisses concern about deficits and debt as "pining . . . for the swashbuckling days of nineteenth-century free market capitalism," or the kind of penny-wise moralizing one might have heard from Calvin Coolidge in the 1920s, as if times had not changed. Capitalism was not debt-soaked and addicted to borrowing then, but it is now.

Even as inflation made its reappearance worldwide in late 2022, forcing central banks to raise interest rates and thus disrupt the flow of easy money, the underlying impulse to spend did not abate. Governments had assumed vast new powers to borrow, to rescue, even to shut down businesses during the pandemic. And having been exercised once, these powers are likely to be reintroduced and expanded on in future crises as if they are nothing new.

===

SEVEN

BEYOND BORROWING AND SPENDING

Conventional histories of the "era of small government" since Reagan and Thatcher look past the big-picture trends in spending and deficits to focus on more specific ways the state shapes the economy. Though each narrator chooses a different mix of policies, the core building blocks include the moments when leaders cut public welfare or investment or jobs, sold off public companies, or pushed deregulation. Yet none of these efforts changed the basic direction of government, either.

The state in nearly all its manifestations is more interventionist than it was in 1980. The welfare state, measured by social spending as a share of the economy, has expanded steadily. The regulatory state, measured by the sheer number and restrictiveness of new rules, has expanded steadily. Even when the biggest wars were over, smaller wars and new crises helped to drive the growth of the national security state. Dramatically and for the most part secretly expanded during World War II, its existence was revealed and formalized in the 1947 law creating the National Security Council and the CIA.

Since then, the number of security agencies has multiplied to eighteen—they include the intelligence arms of the Coast Guard, the Air Force, and the Space Force. A major expansion came after the terror attacks on New York and Washington in 2001, when the Bush administration created the Department of Homeland Security and the Transportation Security Agency. The TSA alone now has some sixty thousand full-time employees, accounting for roughly 15 percent of the government's regulatory staff. The Immigration and Naturalization Service was divided into three agencies with expanded budgets, including ICE, the customs enforcement arm that aims to block criminals and terrorists at the border. At U.S. airports, incoming tourists and travelers began facing two- to four-hour waits to get through immigration checks, a bureaucratic welcome that continues to chill America's reputation. Classified until 2007, the intel budget grew by nearly half to $90 billion in 2022. "National security," a winning argument for new spending at least since Eisenhower used it to rally support for national highways during the Cold War, was rolled out anew by Biden to build support for American industries competing with China.

"THERE IS NO EVIDENCE THAT THE UNITED STATES HAS BECOME STINGIER OVER TIME"

Reagan is remembered for his controversial critiques of "welfare queens," or women supposedly living comfortably on benefit checks. But cutting the safety net out from under them was not his primary concern. He was the kind of reformer who wanted to shake things up, who believed less in order—protecting the free market by encasing it in rules—than in freedom, unshackling people from rules entirely. In this respect Reagan, like Barry Goldwater and other "conservatives" before him, shared something essential with the new left radicals of the 1960s who would eventually become centrist neoliberals of the Democratic Party in the 1990s: a desire to free America from what they saw as an "organized and bureaucratized society," as Gary Gerstle writes, dominated by big corporations, unions, and government, which were "suffocating the human spirit."

Reagan's quarrel with the growing welfare state was less that it placed a floor under the poor than that it placed a "ceiling above which no one shall be permitted to climb." He said this in a 1957 speech, and later as president translated the sentiment into economic policy, by cutting taxes on the rich without fully funding them with cuts to welfare spending. Reagan did manage to slow the big-government boom that began with Kennedy and Johnson, but he did not reverse it. Government spending accounted for 21 percent of the economy, and welfare accounted for about 45 percent of government spending, when Reagan took office and when he left.

Sounding much like Reagan, Clinton declared that "we have to end welfare as a way of life." His "workfare" reforms did impose work requirements as a condition for receiving payments; they did not turn the tanker of the welfare state. While Clinton did cut welfare slightly as a share of GDP, he was merely rolling back the increases approved under his predecessor, George H. W. Bush. Including just the major entitlement programs, Medicaid, Medicare, and Social Security, welfare spending was 9 percent of GDP in 1981, and the same share in 2001. Then, under George W. Bush, welfare spending started to grow again to 12 percent of GDP by 2019, spiking to 17 percent during the pandemic. A similar trend is visible in spending on unemployment benefits, which have been dead flat at around 4 percent of GDP, with spikes to new record highs during each of the last three crises, in 2001, 2008, and 2020. While it is of course normal for unemployment payments to rise in recessions, the string of record highs reflected the momentum of the welfare state more than the severity of the downturns.

Over that time, welfare was becoming a key source of support for the poorest 20 percent of Americans. Direct government benefits include food stamps, supplemental income payments for Medicaid recipients, and school lunch programs. By the eve of the pandemic, these direct benefits had more than doubled to 68 percent of total income for the bottom 20 percent. Medicaid benefits accounted for the largest share of the increase.

In 2022, former Senator Phil Gramm and the economists Bob Ekelund and John Early came out with a provocative book titled *The Myth of American Inequality*. They calculated that government benefits paid to families in the bottom 20 percent of the income curve have risen to $45,000 a year, up from $9,700 in the mid-1960s. The book was widely ignored outside conservative circles, and did not help broaden its appeal by sounding at times like a blast from the nineteenth century—for example, in holding up Scrooge, the Charles Dickens character, as a model of penny-pinching capitalist virtue. Yet young progressives, studying the same data, do not challenge its basic conclusion about government support for the poor: the welfare state has been expanding for decades.

Pulitzer Prize–winning sociologist Matthew Desmond's *Poverty, by America* is a critique of U.S. failures. He confesses that when he started his research, he "bought into the idea, popular among progressives" that the persistence of poverty could be pinned on reduced welfare spending since Reagan, "but I was wrong." Reagan never made lasting cuts to the welfare state, and since then spending on the thirteen largest means-tested programs—those reserved for the poor—has by his count more than tripled to $3,400 per person. "'Neoliberalism' is now part of the left's lexicon, but I looked in vain to find it in the plain print of federal budgets, at least as far as aid to the poor was concerned," writes Desmond. "There is no evidence that the United States has become stingier over time. The opposite is true."

America's reputation as an especially heartless capitalist society doesn't fare well in comparison with the other ones, either. Since 1980, welfare spending has increased in twenty-one of the twenty-three rich capitalist economies tracked by the Organization for Economic Cooperation and Development (OECD) and has increased significantly faster than average in the United States. Today the United States spends about 20 percent of GDP on social benefits—as much as Japan and the United Kingdom, and closing in on the average in the rest of Europe.

By rank, the United States still falls among the less generous welfare states, when welfare is measured as benefits delivered essentially as checks from the government. When the OECD researchers include health and pension benefits mandated or subsidized by government but delivered by private employers, then "total social spending" in the United States amounts to 30 percent of GDP. By that measure the American welfare state is the second most generous in the world, behind only the French.

The story outlined by conservative think tanks like the Fraser Institute or the Tax Foundation does not differ materially from that of French economist Thomas Piketty, whose painstakingly assembled historical data is considered state-of-the-art. His story is worth focusing on, since these issues are so intensely politicized that the left won't listen to data from the right, and vice versa. Piketty is an intellectual leader of the left and his mission is hardly to shoot down progressive narratives. His data, however, does more to undermine than support the idea that the decades after Reagan and Thatcher were an era of shrinking government.

Piketty writes that one of the main reasons that European empires started to grow faster than Asian empires was the rise of an effective state. Early in the seventeenth century, no global power collected more than 3 percent of national income in taxes, including "obligatory levies of all kinds." Over the next two centuries, the reach of the state grew not at all in China and the Ottoman Empire, while tripling or more in England, France, and Prussia.

When all states were weak and disorganized, he writes, balance prevailed. When a more centralized European state started to emerge, Europe came to dominate: a state that could collect taxes could build a stronger economy—and expand its empire, through military conquest. Until the early twentieth century, however, the role of the state would be confined largely to basics, including police, courts, and other supports for the rule of law, as well as roads, bridges, and other infrastructure that allow commerce to flourish.

Though its roots have been traced to Germany under Bismarck in the 1860s, the expansion of the European welfare state begins to show up in taxing and spending data only around 1910. This turning point coincides with the rise of labor parties in Europe, and the Progressive movement in the United States. Graduated income taxes appear at this point "more or less everywhere within the space of a few years." By 1910, tax receipts had risen from 3 percent to 10 percent of national income in the major European powers—the United Kingdom, Germany, France, and Sweden. Then the tax collection rises to 47 percent on average by 1980, where they remain today.

The growth of government between 1910 and 1980 "is explained almost entirely" by what Piketty calls "the welfare state's spectacular rise to power." Spending on basics like police and roads shrinks as a share of the total, while welfare spending grows, and what Piketty doesn't mention but his data also shows is that this trend never reverses after 1980, in the major European powers. Spending on the basics falls a few points, to 10 percent; spending on welfare, including pensions, health, education, housing, and income subsidies, rises a few points, to 37 percent of the total.

Far from questioning these trends, of course, he argues that an even bigger welfare state would not only help fix inequality, it could also help revive growth. The economic boom in the decades after World War II came when top personal tax rates were 70 percent or higher in advanced capitalist countries, proving that "virtually confiscatory tax rates have been an immense historical success."

As top personal tax rates fell after 1980, Piketty points out, per capita GDP growth slowed by more than half, to barely 1 percent—but this connection is thin at best. Surely the growth slump since 1980 is less plausibly explained by one narrow slice of the tax code, as it appears on paper, than by the growing and very real burden of government, in all its forms. Since the early 1960s, few Americans have ever paid the top rate, and the richest 1 percent have paid more than 30 percent of their income in taxes in only one year, during the dot-com bubble. The dodges are as intricate as the tax code, including especially complex loopholes for income from small businesses and investments. Since confiscatory taxes have never been collected, at least not in the United States, it's hard to say they are a proven success. The welfare state has been built mainly by piling on debt, not taxes.

The historic scale of big government's recent advance is perhaps best illustrated by the United Kingdom, for which data goes back the furthest, to the late seventeenth century. In peacetime, UK government spending hovered close to 10 percent of GDP for more than two centuries before stepping up to 25 percent after World War I, and to 35 percent after World War II. Major spikes to more than 40 percent of GDP came only during the two world wars, the global financial crisis of 2008, and then the pandemic of 2020—and in all four crises the rise in spending was not matched by rising revenues. Instead, the United Kingdom was digging itself deeper into debt. "Capitalism as we know it has failed," wrote Nick Timothy, chief of staff to Prime Minister Theresa May, in 2023. "The government and the country became addicted to cheap credit . . . hurting households with less, helping those with more, and making it harder for young people to get on to the property ladder."

Current welfare spending is also dwarfed by the promises of future benefits. Beloved of American voters, these guarantees of pension, health, and income benefits are virtually untouchable by Congress, which has chosen to ignore the numbers. Most of the spending commitments made by Social Security and Medicare are not covered by future taxes, making them "unfunded liabilities." Technically, these programs are insolvent. Their sorry financial condition inspires only occasional bouts of urgency, since the commitments are calculated over the next seventy-five years.

For a variety of reasons, including the aging of the population, these unfunded liabilities have risen much faster than the public debt. Since 2000, U.S. government debt rose from $3 trillion to $22 trillion, while the unfunded liabilities for Medicare, Social Security, and other government pensions increased from $21 trillion to $71 trillion. As the government's debts rose by roughly $20 trillion, its unfunded promises of future benefits rose by $50 trillion. The tax dollars already committed to backstop our lives—through contingent liabilities like mortgage support, or unfunded liabilities like Medicare—are grossly understated by current debt and deficit figures.

The safety net has grown more dysfunctional as government extends its guarantees to the super-rich in the financial markets, but the broader issue is that politicians are socializing all manner of risks for everyone, refusing to say no to anyone, and running up debts whether the economy is struggling or not.

PUBLIC INVESTMENT, PUBLIC JOBS, AND PUBLIC COMPANIES

From the *New York Times* to *Bloomberg* and *Foreign Policy*, many commentators greeted the administration's "modern American industrial strategy" as a belated correction after "decades of downward drift" in U.S. public investment. The White House encouraged this spin, claiming it was reviving the ambition that "had energized the American project" for much of its history, building the national highways after World War II and landing a man on the moon in the 1960s, but had collapsed since. In 2021, Biden told Congress that in recent decades public investment in research and development had fallen by half, and as a result the United States was "falling behind in competition with the rest of the world."

While there is a case to be made for raising U.S. public investment in a carefully targeted way, this claim of "falling behind" is not it. Public investment did rise after World War II, peaking at about 7 percent of GDP in the 1970s. By 1980, it had fallen back to its long-term trend— around 3 percent of GDP. It has remained there ever since. Meanwhile, in other big, developed economies, public investment was indeed falling, from 5.5 percent to 4 percent of GDP on average. The United States was not drifting downward—its closest competitors were drifting back to its level. As for "falling behind" less developed countries like China, those nations almost by definition invest at a higher rate, because they have a greater need for new roads and bridges.

Much of what the administration was packaging as "infrastructure" investment, moreover, would in fact go to social programs like health care, education, and childcare. Presenting planned increases in social spending as a strategic response to China's spending on roads, 5G networks, and other forms of infrastructure, traditionally defined, was patriotic marketing of a misleading kind. Though public spending can pay for itself in theory if it comes in the form of investments that lift productivity, the record of the last four decades is that deficit spending has provided no such lift.

Fellow Democrat and former Obama economic adviser Steven Rattner warned that in pursuing the biggest expansion of government since at least the 1960s, Biden was showing "disdain" for private business, leaving bureaucrats with at best "mixed" commercial experience to invest hundreds of billions of dollars, diving headlong into "the quagmire of government picking winners and losers."

The same goes for the supposed gutting of public sector jobs, starting with Ronald Reagan. That story often begins in 1981 with Reagan firing more than eleven thousand striking air traffic controllers—as if a much broader culling of the federal workforce had followed. The reality is that the number of government employees, including local, state, and federal, rose by more than a million during the Reagan years to nearly 18 million, and has since climbed to 23 million. It's true that if you look at full-time government jobs as a share of all jobs in the United States, that share has fallen from around 18 percent in the early Reagan years to 15 percent now. But that misses the growing army of private contractors on the public payroll.

These contractors work throughout the public sector, from the Pentagon to prisons. In late 2020, a Brookings Institution paper argued that despite his anti-state rhetoric, Trump had "opened the contract and grant spigots," adding some 2 million employees to the federal payroll. By the end of his term "the true size of government" was "nearing a record high."

These debates are heavily partisan; liberals cast private contractors as greedy corner-cutters; conservatives cast public employees as lazy incompetents. In the big picture, however, it makes little difference whether the state pays workers as employees or contractors—both impact spending and deficits the same way. Both sets of workers operate in a thicket of special rules controlling government workplaces. If you find that hard to believe, ask any contractor who has worked for the government just how maddening it can be.

The one way in which government has clearly retreated is as an owner of airlines, utilities, and other public companies. As early as the 1950s, in the name of "denationalization," the United Kingdom sold off its interest in steel companies and Germany sold a majority stake in Volkswagen. These sales gained steam in the 1980s, spearheaded by Margaret Thatcher, who saw them as a way to reverse "the corrosive and corrupting effects of socialism" and popularized the term "privatization." Among her high-profile sales: British Petroleum, British Airways, British Telecom, and Rolls-Royce.

Over the next three decades, from Europe to Latin America, governments in more than one hundred countries followed the Thatcher lead, selling thousands of public companies for an estimated $3.3 trillion.

Sales of public firms peaked, naturally enough, in countries where the government had the most to sell. France in the early 1990s held a majority stake in some three thousand companies, many large; that number fell to about fifteen hundred, mainly small, by 2015. Over the same period, Canada sold off more than fifty major enterprises, including electric utilities, a railway, an airline, and the air traffic control system. As of 2010, outside the United States, recently privatized companies accounted for half the value of global stock markets.

By then, however, the campaign was losing steam. Fierce resistance from public unions and other special interests was starting to slow privatization. If governments were still selling, they were parting with only minority stakes. Germany, Australia, and Japan all sold minority shares—in no case more than a third—in their national telecom monopolies.

In other instances, political resistance prevented even a partial sale; instead, the government was forced to let the state company "operate until it was essentially bankrupt," according to an OECD study. When the losses became too large to ignore, the government went out and found a private investor—in some cases foreign—to buy a stake in the company at a fire-sale price. Efforts to sell the state airlines in Italy and Greece—Alitalia and Olympic—fell into this category, which I have described elsewhere as "privatization by malign neglect."

The unexpected twist: by the 2010s many of the industries widely privatized in Europe—seaports and airports, postal and passenger rail services, electric utilities—were still state-owned in the United States. Though the United States had maintained its reputation as the land of limited government, and had started out with relatively few publicly owned companies, resistance to selling them would prove at least as fierce as in Europe—maybe more so.

The Reagan administration tried but failed to sell off major state enterprises including the U.S. Postal Service, Amtrak, the air traf-

fic control system, public lands, and the Tennessee Valley Authority (TVA)—the federally owned electric power company that dates
to the Depression and serves parts of seven southern states. Reagan
succeeded in offloading only smaller assets, the most important of
which was Conrail, the cargo carrier, for $1.7 billion. The next Dem-
ocratic president, Bill Clinton, managed to sell off bigger assets, most
significantly the Elk Hills Naval Petroleum Reserve, which sold for
$3.7 billion in 1998. But many of the biggest ones, including the
postal service, Amtrak, air traffic control, and the TVA, are still government enterprises.

Clinton also oversaw a law-and-order crackdown that vastly expanded the prison system, which came to house the world's largest
inmate population. Prisons sprang up all over the country, many operated by private contractors, and so somehow the incarceration angle
got stirred into confused narratives about the supposed retreat of the
state. Every prison, whether publicly or privately owned, is created, sanc-
tioned, regulated, and paid for by the state. Welcomed at the time in
both parties, prison expansion was the ultimate state encroachment on
personal freedom—not a triumph for the free market. The United States
was arguably the major capitalist economy where privatization did the
least to limit the government's reach into private lives.

THE RED TAPE FACTORY

Though it dates to the late nineteenth century, the regulatory state began to
grow in earnest during the New Deal. Early on, the focus was on economic
regulation, designed to manage swings in the price or supply of goods in
specific industries. By the mid-1960s, rising wealth allowed the United

States to turn its attention to social regulation, aimed at improving the quality of life for the growing middle classes. Within the next fifteen years, Congress passed more than ninety statutes to protect consumer health and safety, limit pollution, or otherwise defend the environment. Typically "much more complicated" than economic regulations, wrote Harvard law professor Robert C. Clark, social regulations addressed "areas that previous generations might have considered matters of secondary concern."

Though standard histories of neoliberalism since 1980 cast Democratic and Republican presidents as equally committed to shrinking the regulatory state, it would be more accurate to say neither party got much done. First published in the Depression, the Code of Federal Regulations started issuing yearly updates in the 1960s, and has since grown more than eightfold to 180,000 pages in 240 volumes.

Under Nixon, his economic adviser Herb Stein would later recall, "probably more new regulation was imposed on the economy than in any other presidency since the New Deal." Often acting to defend his flank from liberal critics, Nixon not only increased Social Security, Medicare, and Medicaid benefits but also extended new regulations to protect job safety, clean air and water, marine mammals, and more.

By the late seventies, the rise of the regulatory state was provoking an intellectual backlash from an unexpected alliance: University of Chicago conservatives and pro-consumer liberals. These groups didn't talk much or attend each other's conferences, yet they pushed in the same direction. The conservatives attacked regulation for distorting prices, disrupting supply, and undermining free market efficiency. The liberals largely agreed but focused on how the costs of coping with regulations raise consumer prices and thus hurt the average American. Still, the rhetoric didn't produce much action.

Jimmy Carter built on the new environmental and consumer agencies that Nixon had founded. Dozens of "Nader's Raiders"—disciples of consumer advocate Ralph Nader—would serve in Carter's administration. Spurred by the activists, Carter cut regulations to lower prices for airlines, trucking, rail, and phone service; he also added regulations and agencies to protect consumers in those industries. During his campaign, Carter promised repeatedly to cut what he said were nineteen hundred federal agencies to two hundred, but when he took office his aides told the press to stop trying to hold him to those cuts—counting agencies was a silly "numbers game." Carter ended up creating the Departments of Education and Energy, and helped turn Washington into a hothouse for attorneys.

America has more lawyers per capita than any other country, a quirk often attributed to a combative culture. But the lawyer population took off as corporate regulations multiplied—growing by about thirty thousand per decade before 1970 and accelerating to one hundred thousand per decade ever since. At the end of Carter's presidency in 1980, private lobbyists outnumbered federal employees in Washington for the first time.

Under Carter, the White House issued an executive order that required regulators to conduct cost-benefit analyses before imposing new rules, hoping to avoid carelessly inflicting significant costs on businesses. As one head of the White House office in charge of these analyses would put it, many decades later, the process did less to streamline costs than to "perpetuate puffery" from regulators seeking to justify new rules, by playing up their benefits.

Reagan did try to reverse direction, but his efforts foundered when it came to popular environmental and consumer regulations. Reagan's Interior secretary, James Watt, an acerbic Wyoming lawyer who vowed to "undo 50 years of bad government" and open public lands to oil drilling, quickly became his most controversial cabinet member. Critics said that putting Watt in charge of federal lands was "like asking

Dracula to guard the blood bank," and drove him out of office after three years.

Overall, the growth rate of the bureaucracy did slow. The number of new rules published in the Code of Regulations fell from more than seven thousand a year under Ford and Carter to more than five thousand a year under Reagan, four thousand under George H. W. Bush and Clinton, and three to four thousand ever since. Since 1996, the bureaucracy has issued more than three thousand new rules every year but one (2019), so a chart on the cumulative growth in red tape looks like a set of stairs, climbing upward.

In the end, writes scholar Adam White, even ardent deregulators like Reagan and Trump came to recognize that the administrative state "benefits from—indeed, *requires*—Hamiltonian 'energy in the executive.'" They aimed as much to reassert presidential control over the bureaucracy as to cut it back, which was pretty near impossible, anyway. Cutting or changing a regulation requires the same laborious process of public comment and review as adding a new one. The way the system works is that to eliminate rules, agencies need to overwrite them with new rules. As the U.S. government was adding more than three thousand final rules a year over the last three decades, it withdrew roughly twenty rules from the code of regulations.

Though Clinton and Obama were often cast by progressive critics as deregulators, they both added about 25,000 rules to the code, over the course of two-term presidencies. Even their landmark efforts at deregulation were in reality a mixed bag of less and more government. Clinton, for example, is best remembered for the deregulation of finance and telecommunications, but his administration also tightened regulations on the tobacco industry, elementary and high schools, family and medical leave, and much more. His signature Telecommunications Act of 1996 did open market access to phone lines for all internet companies, and thus set the stage for the rise of giants like Google and Amazon. On the other hand, it subsidized universal service to homes, schools, and public spaces through a tax on providers.

Every new page of regulatory law written by Congress generates many more written by the bureaucracy. The U.S. tax code includes nearly seven thousand pages of laws written by Congress, and another sixty-eight thousand pages written by the Internal Revenue Service. The result is a complex maze in which sophisticated dodgers find it easy to hide. In contrast, the codes of nations like Singapore and Estonia—which has a flat tax of 20 percent for individuals and corporations—have been called "pure genius." They are simple and raise sufficient revenue for government priorities without twisting individual economic decisions. They are also small exceptions to the rule of increasingly complex regulatory codes.

Scholars of the regulatory state try to bring some nuance to the crude page counts by homing in on the impact of final rules. One way is to assess "the restrictive tenor" of new regulation by counting words like "ban" and "prohibit." In the mid-1970s, U.S. industries faced on average one thousand "restrictive" regulations; by the mid-2010s, that number was up to five thousand.

No matter how the code is parsed, it has grown in scale and impact over time, if not always at the same pace. Considering only rules with an "economically significant" impact—which impose more than $100 million in costs on business, or on state and local government—shows the same upward trend. The regulators issued nearly three hundred significant new rules a year under the last three Republican presidents, including Trump; and they issued nearly four hundred under the two Democrats, Obama and Biden.

Trump did attempt to change course. He came into office promising what one adviser called "the deconstruction of the administrative state," and issued a controversial order, requiring the removal of two rules for every new one. His effort was not terribly realistic, since it is hard to cite any case of a bureaucracy downsizing itself. And it was undone in the end by Trump's own "affinity" for certain kinds of regulation—like trade tariffs or restrictions on tech and trusts. A flurry of regulations during his final year in office put his administration's output of new rules on par with his predecessors'.

On his first day in office, Biden gave the regulators another big push forward. He scrapped the controversial "one in, two out" order, along with the attempt to contain regulatory costs established by Carter. Balanced cost-benefit analysis was out. Instead supervisors were directed to search for opportunities to write regulations "that are likely to yield significant benefits," even if those benefits "are difficult or impossible to quantify." Regulators were to avoid "harmful deregulation." This executive order put into action the progressive view that capitalism has gone wrong for lack of rules, so the answer is to write more of them. Biden was setting the stage for the "Regulatory Roaring 20s," writes Clyde Wayne Crews Jr. in "Ten Thousand Commandments," an annual analysis of red-tape trends from the Competitive Enterprise Institute.

The impact of regulations is perhaps best measured by the total costs it imposes on the economy. And in the first two years under Biden, new regulations added an annual average of around $160 billion in economic costs and 110 million hours of paperwork, for impacted businesses as well as state and local governments. By comparison, new rules added an annual average of $16 billion in costs and 82 million paperwork hours under Trump, $108 billion and 72 million hours under Obama, and $67 billion and 58 million hours under George W. Bush.

In short, Biden increased regulatory costs ten times faster than Trump. Though government has grown bigger under every president, the latest president was growing it at an exceptional pace.

A "GLOBAL REGULATORY HEGEMON"

Meanwhile, the regulatory state was extending its reach even more deeply into the economies of Europe. In his 1996 book *Freer Markets, More Rules*, UC Berkeley political scientist Steven Vogel argued that the deregulatory revolt, supposedly dating to the United Kingdom under Thatcher, was largely a myth. It never happened in the United States, Japan, Europe, or the United Kingdom. In a search of the key British regulatory agencies, from finance to competition, he found that only three of fifteen predated Thatcher. The other twelve, from the Office of Rail Regulation to the Radio Authority, were established after 1980.

Scanning the results of the deregulatory revolt that was believed to have swept the capitalist world, from the mid-1970s through the mid-1990s, Vogel wrote that "in most cases of deregulation, governments have combined liberalization with reregulation, the reformulation of old rules and the creation of new ones. Hence we have wound up with freer markets and more rules." In Margaret Thatcher's "Big Bang" reform of the British financial system in 1986, for example, the government opened the London Stock Exchange to outside owners and eliminated fixed commissions on stock sales, but also passed a new Financial Services Act creating a web of red tape "more complex and burdensome than what it replaced."

That same year, the nations of Europe began moving to create a single market for goods and services, and a new continental government with what Columbia Law School professor Anu Bradford calls "vast power" to regulate those markets. Since then this new regional layer of government, led by the European Commission in Brussels, has expanded steadily, adding staff at a pace of 5 percent a year. It has hired mainly true believers in the project of unifying Europe—multilingual technocrats who have been educated in more than one country and tend to identify above all as European, not German, French, or any specific nationality. In a federation of societies that "have structured their economies so as to allocate more rights to the state as opposed to the individual," the Eurocrats would extend this trust in the state to the creation of a regional government. And in part because the European Union lacks the power to tax and spend directly, its energies have been channeled into the construction of what scholar Giandomenico Majone called "an almost pure regulatory state," which by the late nineties was issuing new rules at an "almost exponential" pace.

Nonetheless, critics of neoliberalism were by that decade describing deregulation campaigns as a worldwide "race to the bottom." Companies were said to be racing to countries with loose regulations, which put pressure on other countries to lower their own standards. Those critics could cast even the creation of the European Union in 1993 "as an achievement for the deregulatory impulse," on the grounds that the European Union opened national borders to the free movement of goods and people.

Clearly, the idea that the world's first continent-wide state can be called a victory for small-government ideologues will astonish the one-third minority of EU citizens who hold an unfavorable view of the union, and the majority who can't say they "trust" it. They are leery of government by technocrats in Brussels, who have exclusive authority to set tariffs and other rules related to the single market, share authority with national regulators over issues from the environment to consumer protections, and have quietly extended their reach into other fields, from transport to social policy. These Europeans would prefer not to have a central European authority telling them to funnel financial support to poorer neighbors, or issuing detailed regulations on how to make and package their local cheese and wine. No doubt the motives behind the British vote to leave the European Union were complex, and polls show most Brits came to regret it. On one level, however, Brexit was an impulsive eruption of frustration with European red tape.

The fact that most Europeans now live under two central governments—one national, one continental—creates a lot of confusion. In his book *The Great Reversal*, Thomas Philippon argues that after 2000, European national governments started to deregulate as the United States continued to regulate, and thus Europe "of all places" replaced the United States as "the land of free markets." That conclusion is based on an OECD index of national regulations, which does show a remarkable shift: seventeen of the nineteen leading EU member states were more densely regulated than the United States in 1998; fifteen years later, only two were. As Philippon also points out, that index tracks only national regulation in consumer goods and services, leaving out parts of the regulatory codes that cover everything from taxes to labor rules.

There is plenty of evidence that these national codes are getting more onerous in the large European economies. By 2023, more than a quarter of Germany's medium-sized businesses were considering shutting down or moving abroad, citing "too much red tape and higher taxes." France had suffered an exodus of millionaires fed up with high taxes, and it had developed a strange bulge in the number of companies with just under fifty employees—the point at which its tough labor regulations kick in. Many of these companies demonstrate an equally unusual habit, applying for patents only if those patents promise "radical" and not merely "incremental" improvements. In short, they appear to be looking only for patent breakthroughs that could make them many times larger, and large enough to make the cost of French labor regulation worth bearing.

Far from a race to the least regulated havens, companies are racing to meet the high regulatory standards set by the largest, richest, most demanding state and national governments. In the United States, where all automakers must, for example, meet the emission standards set by the largest state, this has been called "The California Effect." Even so, U.S. rules are still much looser than European rules, which are settling at the strict bar set by its richest and most interventionist countries, led by Germany and France. In Euro-jargon, the continent's rules "are harmonizing up" to the strictest national standards, not "harmonizing down" to the loosest. National regulators appear to be ceding authority for writing rules to the European Commission and serving as its enforcer instead.

Any global company that wants to do business in Europe—which is all of them—must build its goods or craft its services to meet those high EU standards. And those companies, in turn, press their national governments to "harmonize up" to Europe's standards. Anu Bradford coined "the Brussels Effect" to describe this trend, as European rules now shape industrial production and processes the world over, including how honey is made in Brazil, how milk is produced in China, how plastic toys are manufactured in Japan, and the degree of privacy enjoyed by internet users worldwide. Quietly, Europe has become "the global regulatory hegemon." Though Bradford views this as a hidden strength, proof that Europe remains far more geopolitically "relevant" than its critics suggest, she ends up sounding agnostic on whether an expanding Eurocracy does more to help or harm the economy. That question "may not even matter," she says, because like it or not, individuals, corporations, and governments "can do little to rein in the Brussels Effect." The same can be said of bureaucracies worldwide, which have been expanding for the last century.

=========

EIGHT

WHACK-A-MOLE

C entral bankers often say that the best way to contain the excesses generated by easy money is not less easy money. It is stricter rules—"macroprudential regulation," they call it. But when governments and central banks are pumping more money into financial markets than they can handle, the practical impact of new rules is to redirect the flow of money, not restrain it.

The first human laws date to 1750 BC and the Code of Hammurabi, who was the king of Babylon. His code was concerned largely with the regulation of commerce and interest rates, and the game of dodging the rules started when the king put down his pen. Caps on the maximum rate creditors could charge were evaded by charging the max each month rather than each year. Even the Vatican was never powerful enough to prevent lenders dodging its moral injunctions against usury, because finance will always find a way.

The result is a game of whack-a-mole. Authorities smack the regulatory gavel down on one hole, only to see the mole pop up from another, which is why crises rarely emerge in the same corner of the financial markets twice in a row.

The story of the first major U.S. crisis after 1980, which struck the savings and loan industry, is often recounted as a case of "Where Deregulation Went Wrong," to quote one book title. But the same histories show how regulation set the stage. Into the 1970s, banks were governed by Depression-era regulations that had effectively killed off the freewheeling financial speculation conducted by banks in the 1920s. The key was Regulation Q of the Glass-Steagall Act, which limited how aggressively banks could compete for customers by capping the interest rates they could offer on standard checking or savings accounts.

To get around Regulation Q, bankers led by Citibank CEO Walter Wriston invented new products including commercial paper, junk bonds, and certificates of deposit, starting in the 1960s. To customers, these offerings looked like bank accounts, only better, because they paid a higher rate of interest. Deposits flowed in, forming the pool of capital that began to fund the Wall Street revival of the 1980s.

In this environment, the old S&Ls were doomed. The Roosevelt administration had created them during the Depression to encourage homeownership by providing low-cost mortgages, as we have seen. The S&Ls were protected from competition and supervised by the Federal Home Loan Bank Board, which was itself subject to voluminous rules, including limits on pay for its examiners, who developed a reputation as "low paid, heavy drinking specialists in trivial details." Working according to rhythms set by regulation, S&L executives lived by the 3-6-3 rule: borrow at 3 percent, lend at 6 percent, on the golf course by 3:00 p.m.

Sleepy S&Ls could survive in a period when home prices were rising steadily and mortgage defaults were rare. They could not, however, weather the Volcker shock, which brought higher interest rates, rising defaults, and the new options invented by bankers like Wriston. The S&Ls started losing deposits to the innovators, and losing money as their borrowing costs went up while the interest they were allowed to charge on mortgages remained fixed. By the early 1980s, the industry was losing hundreds of millions of dollars a year.

This was the backdrop to "deregulation" of the thrifts, first by Jimmy Carter in 1980, then by Reagan in 1982. The aim was to rationalize a government-created ecosystem in which S&Ls could no longer survive. The new rules did allow much that had been forbidden, for example allowing S&Ls to diversify from residential into commercial property. Suddenly, S&Ls became the most aggressive commercial real estate speculators, because they now operated under looser rules than commercial banks. Smelling opportunity, everyone from dentists to developers to politicians began to open or partner with S&Ls, pushing sometimes shady deals that ultimately melted down in the financial scandals of the eighties and nineties.

Regulation was not in retreat, it was in uneven evolution—easing faster for S&Ls than for banks. At the same time, government was increasing its support, most importantly by guaranteeing S&L deposits up to $100,000. The previous limit was just $40,000. Thus freed to pursue new ventures, with more ample insurance against losses, the old thrifts indulged in a wild party of capital misallocation. An industry built to provide affordable mortgages became a haven for speculators in casinos, ski resorts, fast-food franchises, windmill farms, and more.

While deregulation of the airlines and the trucking industry had given power to "market forces," deregulation of S&Ls played out very differently, according to the White House commission assigned to trace the origins of the crisis. In this case, the power was given to government, which through a combination of looser rules, less supervision, and more state insurance invited S&Ls to ignore market forces, and "doomed" the industry to collapse. The biggest mistake, the commissioners wrote, was generous government insurance for risk-takers, which explains why "so many crooks" flocked to the S&L industry.

During the S&L crisis, Boston College professor Edward J. Kane first identified "zombies" infecting the capitalist system, applying the term to "zombie thrifts" that were insolvent but kept alive by regulators looking the other way. There were one hundred zombie thrifts on government support in Texas alone, the epicenter of scandals that spread deep into Arizona and California. The Keating Five, a circle of U.S. senators who tried to aid a failing California thrift that had contributed to their campaigns, came to symbolize the era. In the late 1980s and early 1990s, the government finally reversed course and created an agency to "resolve" or shut down the money losers.

This turn in the tale is often spun as the moment government realized deregulation had failed, and retook control. That's a take only statists could love. A confident government had set the stage for the crisis, by setting rules that made it difficult for the thrifts to survive the 1970s. It helped turn the crisis into a mania, by loosening rules for S&Ls but not other lenders, while also guaranteeing larger deposits. Government support did at least as much to fuel the crisis as deregulation had. Finally, the crisis began to ease only when regulators stopped trying to prop up S&Ls, and allowed or encouraged them to fold. Blaming the crisis entirely on smaller government and deregulation thus oversimplifies a story in which government was deeply involved every step of the way.

RACING AROUND THE RULES

As the dot-com boom gained momentum in the 1990s, some of the most apparently successful companies of the age, including Enron and World-

Com, were building their images on what turned out to be murky or just plain fraudulent governance and accounting practices. After these companies imploded and their rather shocking secrets were revealed by the bust of 2001, Congress passed the Sarbanes-Oxley Act, commonly known as SOX, aiming to bring light to corporate accounting, hold executives criminally responsible for fudging the numbers, and reward whistleblowers for reporting this kind of fraud before it became a systemic crisis.

No doubt many of the new SOX rules made sense in themselves; together their effect was to scare many companies and their top executives out of public markets entirely. Private firms delayed going public or decided not to, and public companies went private at least in part to avoid the new rules and the related compliance costs. By most accounts, SOX effectively shut down many small companies that could not afford to meet its reporting requirements and killed others in the cradle. Today one of the most visible legacies of SOX is the multiplying class of corporate "unicorns"—privately held companies with an estimated value of more than $1 billion, which now number around 1,200 in the United States.

As the dot-com mania gave way to the housing mania after 2001, credit was growing much faster than the economy in many countries. And the credit moles were moving to new holes. Governments tried to slow the bubble with rules—for example, by capping mortgage loans at a certain share of the borrower's income—as the United States did in early 2014. To cope, banks shifted their focus away from homebuyers and began lending more to corporations, including risky ones. They lowered lending standards for big business but not for small entrepreneurs (who often put up their homes as collateral). Surely regulators trying to protect homeowners never intended to disadvantage small business owners, but they did.

In the 2000s, the budgets of the financial regulatory agencies were growing, by their own accounts, and the costs imposed on the economy by new financial regulation were growing as well. In 1999, for example, Congress had repealed much of Glass-Steagall, the Depression-era law that forced banks to be very conservative—and prevented them from speculating with depositors' money. In its 145 pages, the act of repeal lifted some restrictions and added many others, including tighter oversight of bank holding companies, a ban on new thrift-holding companies, even a requirement that banks must post fees on cash machines twice— on the machine and on the screen. With the easy money era kicking into gear, financial entrepreneurs were designing new investment products that would allow them to employ easy money with the least regulatory resistance. Hence the explosion in opaque new debt products—CDOs and the rest—that made it so difficult to see the credit meltdown coming in 2008.

The game was getting faster owing to globalization, which gave the lenders new and larger credit markets to serve. By the 2000s, capital had begun flowing to markets where regulations were relatively light. When new rules restrained corporate lending by domestic banks in the United Kingdom, foreign banks filled the breach. When new rules limited lending by the foreign branches of big American banks, those banks started lending directly to overseas borrowers instead. The permutations were virtually endless.

NOTHING SHADOWY ABOUT SHADOW BANKS

By 2008, the American financial system had been transformed, as the action shifted from heavily regulated banks to "shadow banks." In most cases, they are neither shadowy, nor banks. Instead they are household names in other branches of finance, from insurance companies to pension funds and hedge funds. Their customers were hardly under the radar, either: they included much of corporate America.

The big advantage of shadow banks is that they don't have to comply with regulations that dictate how much capital banks have to have on hand, and the kinds of products they can offer. The downside: their depositors aren't insured by the federal government. By the time the crisis hit in 2008, shadow banks were at the heart of it—they held higher deposits and loaned more money in a wider variety of innovative new forms than traditional banks.

This is not a murky corner of finance. Increasingly, it is finance.

At the heart of the 2008 crisis was a breed of debt products called derivatives—contracts that are based on or derived from the price of some other asset. As this market exploded in the 2000s, the variety of assets one could bet on through derivatives grew bewilderingly complex, from stocks to bonds, platinum to weather patterns. A small share went to Main Street businesses like farms or carmakers, which used derivatives to protect themselves from the unexpected—say, spikes in steel prices or drought. But 90 percent of derivatives were purchased by financial firms betting one way or another on the financial markets. The over-the-counter market for derivatives—in which deals are done directly between seller and buyer, not on a regulated public exchange—grew eightfold in the decade, to more than $680 trillion on the eve of the crisis. Over the same period, the world economy doubled in size, to $64 trillion.

The subsequent meltdown in derivates is widely blamed on deregulation of the over-the-counter market, but why did that market come into being? Because financial entrepreneurs will always find a way to work around the latest regulatory regime, like the one that emerged from the 1999 repeal of Glass-Steagall. If new rules put one financial market under intense scrutiny, then firms "create a new market that's opaque to replace the one that's rendered transparent," writes the author of *Zombie Banks*, Yalman Onaran. As new reporting requirements brought more of this trading into the light, new derivatives were invented to trade the same debts without reporting them.

After the housing boom went bust in 2008, regulators, as usual, set about trying to prevent the last crisis. Congress passed the Dodd-Frank Act, which was 848 pages. To clarify what Congress had said, the regulatory agencies added another four hundred rules, each of which became its own "regulatory quagmire." By comparison, Glass-Steagall was less than forty pages, and this tendency to write more complex legislation "may only have created more loopholes for banks to exploit," argues author Philip Coggan in *More: The 10,000-Year Rise of the World Economy*. Dodd-Frank was supposed to end taxpayer bailouts for banks deemed too big to fail; instead its intricacies created a business environment in which smaller banks would struggle.

Much of the new regulation focused on limiting the type of loans that had triggered the 2008 crisis, to wit, mortgage loans from big banks to poorly qualified or "subprime" borrowers. But with easy money still encouraging reckless lending, the action simply shifted even further from the big Wall Street banks to the shadow banks, whose share of the mortgage market rose over the next decade from 10 percent to more than 50 percent. As the new rules slowed the growth in mortgages, shadow banks moved on to other forms of consumer lending, including college and car loans. The game played on, spurred by the Fed's new role as a major buyer in the markets.

In a 2018 review of regulations imposed after the crisis of 2008, Fed researchers found a "vicious circle," in which complex rules force firms to become more complex themselves, thereby requiring more intricate rules. This circle of growing bewilderment plays to the advantage of the biggest institutions, which pay more and draw more "top talents" and can therefore stay one step ahead of this game. When the tangle of post-2008 regulation fueled the rise of shadow banks, the big banks did not protest much, because they could profit by funding the investments made by the shadow banks. "Thus the tendency to make regulation complex can backfire. The vicious circle among the complexity of financial regulations, financial innovations, and governance structure of financial institutions needs to be stopped," the Fed researchers concluded.

At the same time, the Fed governors were deliberately encouraging investors to move beyond safe Treasuries and take more risk—whether in private markets or public ones. Prices were rising fast for stocks and bonds in the public markets, but even faster for their equivalents—equity and debt—in the private markets. With prices for all kinds of assets going up so rapidly, financial engineering offered higher potential profits than plain old engineering. Why invest in research and development or new factories that could take years or decades to pay off, if a new debt offering or stock buyback promised higher rewards, sooner?

It was perfectly rational for investors to move into private markets, where they could put the money flowing out of central banks to work with less oversight. The leveraged buyouts that had been invented during the Wall Street boom of the 1980s had developed a bad name, and had been repackaged as "private equity," or just PE. In the classic version of these deals, a PE firm raises money from investors to create a buyout fund, then creates a shell company that borrows against that fund to buy a targeted company. Then the PE firm merges the shell company with the target company, and the debt ends up on the books of the target company. If that sounds like three card monte, it is not. In many cases, well-established PE firms are welcomed as saviors; by virtue of their own good credit, they can actually lower the borrowing costs of the companies they purchase, with the intent of building them into solid enterprises.

There is, however, nothing that too much money cannot spoil. As central banks pushed interest rates to zero and below, new players were drawn to the PE industry, many borrowing without care and purchasing companies with the intent to cut costs and payroll and flip them quickly. Between 2000 and 2022, the number of PE firms rose from fewer than three thousand to nearly fifteen thousand, and the amount of money they manage rose by more than 1,000 percent, to $9.8 trillion. By the end of that period, the typical U.S. company managed by a private equity firm had debt five and a half times higher than its annual earnings—or twice the level that a ratings agency would consider "junk." That was up from just three and a half times annual earnings before the crisis of 2008. The share of deals using the heaviest debt (more than five times earnings) had nearly tripled, to two-thirds—in other words, the riskiest deals were now the most common kind.

Thousands of companies were resold or refinanced not once but multiple times, adding to their debt burden each time. With so many company owners and CEOs focused on reengineering existing debts, capitalism became a system for extending old lives, not creating new ones. Since a PE fund will often buy a dozen companies with the intent of finding one huge hit, some of these funds became covers under which one big success supported a host of duds. "The world has moved on. We must think of western financial systems as essentially capital redistribution mechanisms, dominated by these giant pools of money that are used to refinance existing positions, rather than raising new money," writes investor Michael Howell. "New capital spending has itself become eclipsed by the need to roll over huge debt burdens."

Lenders of all kinds—banks and shadow banks—were all in. They had the same incentives to take more risk as other players in the markets, and nothing highlighted the blind search for higher returns more clearly than the market for private lenders, which nearly quintupled after the crisis of 2008 to more than $10 trillion, providing a comfortable haven for both borrowers and creditors seeking to avoid regulators. As Karen Petrou, cofounder of Federal Financial Analytics, a Washington, DC, consulting firm, writes of the private-lending market: "the less costly the rules, the more likely the activity will find its way there." Again, though, the explosion in private-lending "activity" was inspired in the first instance by the easy money, and the expectation of bailouts if bets went bad, not looser rules.

Over time, lenders dropped any pretense of seriously vetting corporate borrowers. Quite the opposite, they were "incentivized not to look," writes Chris Leonard. By 2022, nearly 100 percent of the loans private funds use to finance buyouts were "covenant lite," meaning largely free of conditions, up from near zero percent a decade earlier. Lenders no longer seemed to care if corporate borrowers were exposed for fraud or incompetence, said junk bond investigator Vicki Bryan: with Fed purchases reinforcing an artificial bottom for bond prices, "you can't lose in this market. And if you can't lose, it's not really a market."

One particularly fearless corner of the private-lending world was occupied by business development companies, or BDCs. Created by Congress in the 1980s, BDCs got tax breaks to lend to businesses that were too small and risky to obtain a loan from banks. They charged super-high rates but never took off until after 2010, as round after round of Fed bond buying kept flushing easy money into the system. Over the next decade, the number of BDCs doubled to nearly one hundred. The assets they managed quadrupled to around $100 billion, as some of the world's biggest asset managers flocked to their promise of 7 to 8 percent returns on private loans to small, fragile companies. As one investor told me in 2021: "Swing a stick in Manhattan these days and you are going to hit someone involved in private lending."

Even if investors were pouring money into private markets to avoid regulation, they still expected government help in a crisis. The peared, in comparison to

Depression-era bargain was that banks that lived by the new regulations (such as capital requirements) would be eligible for deposit insurance and emergency lending in a crisis. Shadow banks would get no such protection. But there was that escape hatch, in the clause that allowed the government to protect firms of all kinds in extreme situations. So it was that in 2008, writes Ben Bernanke, the government dusted off this Depression-era rescue clause and "shadow banks would find themselves protected by the government safety net after all."

Trying to control global flows of money by regulating banks has grown more difficult over time, as more lending takes place outside the banking system. The share of new lending that originates in non-banks ranges from a low of 20 percent in New Zealand to a high of 80 percent in the United States. Yet as late as the fall of 2019, Fed officials were saying that the economy was in a "real good place," based in large part on how sturdy the finances of the big banks appeared, in comparison to 2008. The lending action had shifted to shadow banks, but the Fed did not mention them.

Having originated in the United States and risen to dominance in the 2000s, the shadow banks spread worldwide in the 2010s. The assets under their control rose from $30 trillion to $63 trillion, and in recent years have grown fastest in parts of Europe and Asia. China is a middle-income country, and with less wealth it is less able to shoulder rising debt than a high-income country. Yet its shadow-banking sector, at around 60 percent of GDP, is one of the world's largest. In Europe, the hotbeds include financial centers like Ireland and Luxembourg, where the assets of shadow banks, particularly pension funds and insurers, have been expanding at an 8 to 10 percent annual pace.

Even today, central bankers keep saying that the way to prevent debt crises is to guide the rising flow of easy money with macroprudential rules. They keep issuing ever more complex rules to achieve that goal, without success. Rules alone will never be able to contain speculative excesses in the financial markets so long as the bias of policymakers is to spend and create more money than needed to ease a crisis. Rewriting the rules can determine which corner of the markets are most or least prone to excess, but can do nothing to rationalize markets distorted by too much easy money. Even as the return of consumer price inflation forced the Fed to tighten sharply in 2022, only the next crisis would show whether the underlying bias—better to err on the side of excess—was gone.

THE BLUNT INSTRUMENT

Today the basic government approach is to let bubbles inflate and pop, then mop up the mess, then try to regulate away the worst excesses that led to the bubble in the first place. The mainstream defense of this strategy is that, yes, if central banks can anticipate bubbles, particularly the most dangerous ones—housing bubbles fueled by debt—and if they have tools to deflate those bubbles without triggering a recession, they should act. "But those are two very big *ifs*," warns Alan Blinder. For example, he argues that the housing bubble from 2000 to 2006 was not widely spotted until 2005—which was too late. And a sharp tightening earlier on "might . . . have broken the economy's back before it burst the house-price bubble." The takeaway, he says, is that central banks should use regulation and not tighter monetary policy to defuse housing bubbles "because blunt instruments cause collateral damage."

Unfortunately, easy monetary policy is as blunt an instrument as tight monetary policy, and it has been causing collateral damage to society for at least two decades now. True, it is not easy to spot bubbles in real time, but a growing body of research outlines practical warning signs, particularly the pace of increase in debt, and in asset prices. A 2018 Harvard Business School study of forty stock bubbles that have hit specific U.S. industries since the crash of 1929 found that, if prices rise by 150 percent or more within two years, "a crash is nearly certain."

While tighter monetary policy might have triggered a recession some months earlier, easy money most certainly did set the stage for the market collapse and the Great Recession that began in December 2007 and lasted more than a year. The extended damage caused by that bubble was almost certainly worse, as a result of its being allowed—encouraged—to inflate for so long. And while regulation does need to be carefully calibrated, tweaking the rules can redirect but cannot contain a sea of near-zero-interest loans that amounts to trillions upon trillions of dollars, and sloshes through markets worldwide.

Over the past four decades, as financial markets grew to more than four times the size of the global economy, feedback loops shifted. Markets, which used to reflect economic trends, are now big enough to drive those trends. The next financial crises are thus likely to arise in new areas of the markets, where growth has been explosive, and regulators haven't yet arrived. In tightly interconnected markets, an explosion in one corner can quickly wash across the whole—as the relatively small market for subprime loans proved in 2008.

Histories of the last four decades tend to cast neoliberalism as a faith-based belief that less government, including lighter and fewer regulations, is in every case better. Yet from its beginnings, a dominant strain of neoliberalism—perhaps the dominant strain—has been built on a paradox: "government intervention was necessary to free individuals from the encroachments of government," as historian Gary Gerstle has put it.

Stretching back to the nineteenth century, neoliberals and their classical predecessors had believed that free markets need a baseline of order to function and would need to be "encased" in rules protecting property and the free exchange of goods, money, and credit. Those rules, moreover, would have to be adapted constantly over time. This is what the small-government narrative misses: in attempting to adapt over time, always seeking to contain the excesses that fueled the last crisis, the rules encasing the markets have only grown thicker and more complex, whether each new wave is promoted as deregulation or stricter regulation.

NINE

WHY STATES RARELY SHRINK

S o how could so many smart people have come to believe they were living in "an era of small government"? Perhaps the main reason this myth could sink such deep roots is the financialization of capitalism. Global financial markets—for stocks, bonds, and a fast-expanding array of more exotic debt assets—were for decades growing much faster than the economy. So government must have been retreating. The private sphere swells, the public sphere retreats. It sounds sort of right in a yin-yang way. The reality is that financial markets expanded alongside government, energized by the easy money culture.

This image of retreating government also seemed to match the post-1980 rise in international flows of people, money, or trade, summed up as "globalization." Forgotten was the fact that an earlier era of globalization, in the period around 1900, had by some measures generated even faster flows of people, money, and trade, and just as much hype. Some writers even declared war obsolete, since so many people now had so much to gain from peaceful commerce. That illusion was shattered by the outbreak of World War I in 1914. Yet as the next round of globalization picked up pace in the 1980s and '90s, once again leaders cast it as an unstoppable force—like the passage from summer to fall, said British prime minister Tony Blair.

Governments proved to be more than a match for globalization. In 1991, the Soviet Union fell under the weight of its internal contradictions. Communism crumbled. Scholar Francis Fukuyama declared this moment "the end of history," implying that the long struggle over the role of the state was settled. Markets would lead, the state would stand aside. No country inspired more excitement than China, where the embrace of free market principles by a one-party Communist state seemed to confirm that history could move in only one direction. China was prospering, and its rising middle class would put more pressure on the authorities to grant political freedom alongside widening economic freedoms. President Clinton captured the mood when he said that China "is speeding a process that is removing government from vast areas of people's lives," and by welcoming it into global markets, the rest of the world "will move China faster and further in the right direction."

The excitement around China hit a crescendo soon after its economy navigated the crisis of 2008 relatively unscathed, particularly compared to the United States. Americans began studying the achievements of Chinese state capitalism and what "the U.S. must learn from" it, as the *Atlantic* magazine put it in 2012. When Xi Jinping came to power the following year, one columnist predicted that he would accelerate economic reforms and allow some political reforms—since democratic capitalism was the future. After all, "how can mighty China be more backward than Myanmar?" Xi, it was said, might even remove Mao's tomb from Tiananmen Square.

The West was not really listening to Xi, who was saying publicly that he intended to reimpose state control and Maoist values in all facets of economic life. The depth of his commitment became clear a decade later, when he brushed aside term limits to claim a third stint as paramount leader.

Outsiders were also underestimating the statist convictions of Russia. After Vladimir Putin emerged from the dust of the Soviet collapse as leader of Russia in 1999, he would make visits to New York pitching investors on his ambition to turn his tattered nation into "a normal European country." His audiences took that to mean a capitalist democracy and believed him. Yet by the early 2010s, Putin was in his second decade in power, now an unabashed dictator reasserting control over the limping economy, choosing which of his cronies would benefit most from Kremlin largesse, creating a "Fortress Russia" impervious to foreign creditors. By early 2022, when Putin launched the invasion of Ukraine, the most-read book in Russia was George Orwell's *1984*, suggesting that his portrait of the state as Big Brother strikes a chord.

To be sure, developments in the rest of the emerging world, outside China and Russia, were very different. Since 1980 the state has staged a more linear and genuine retreat in formerly socialist economies from India to Eastern Europe. In these nations the state does play a smaller economic role—often much smaller—than it did forty years ago. Eastern Europe and particularly its largest economy, Poland, eagerly embraced an old-school American-style entrepreneurial culture and worked deliberately to distance itself from socialist control.

The retreat of government in much of the emerging world thus may have encouraged the misperception that the state had been pulling back everywhere. The big picture was more layered, with the state advancing steadily in advanced capitalist countries, retreating in many less advanced economies, and by the 2010s making an aggressive comeback in

China and Russia. History as a running contest over the proper role of government was not ending, not with the clarity that Fukuyama implied.

As globalization took off in the 1980s, so did its supposedly most uncontrollable offspring, the internet. Floating in cyberspace, seemingly beyond reach of regulators or censors, internet data was said to pose a greater threat to government than government posed to it. "Information wants to be free," the cyber gurus said, and would, like water, find and widen the cracks in any system built to contain it. Bill Clinton again caught the mood when he said that information was "going to liberate Americans and bring them together," giving every person "the opportunity to make the most of his or her life."

Clinton's optimism seemed indisputable at the time; now it seems naive. In autocratic and democratic nations alike, big tech firms have demonstrated that data has no desires. It is just a commodity, albeit a valuable one—"the new oil"—but even more susceptible to direction and subtle manipulation than oil, with algorithms playing the role of pipelines. Its corporate and government masters exercise enormous power over people's minds.

Over the last two decades, governments from Russia to China and beyond have shown that data can be channeled, policed, and controlled. In 2019, James Griffiths published his cautionary book on *The Great Firewall of China* and the disturbing model it offers for "how to build and control an alternative version of the internet." The rise of advanced surveillance states has raised legitimate concern in the West about the ways the internet can be used to control, not liberate. Nonetheless, the continued global boom in data traffic seems only to have reconfirmed the one-dimensional narrative about governments-in-retreat leaving markets—including the market for information—to run wild.

By 2020, when so many commentators welcomed the end of the era of "small government," it had been over for many years. On this recent scholarship agrees. Gary Gerstle says this order began "coming apart" with the crisis of 2008 and the subsequent rise of leaders like Trump and Sanders, who were openly hostile to the free market. In *Slouching Towards Utopia*, Brad DeLong says that "a long century" of growing global prosperity ended definitively in 2010, when growth and productivity fell off a cliff. In short, Reagan's attempt to revive capitalism by reversing the rise of government had exhausted itself long before 2020.

THE LAWS OF GOVERNMENT GROWTH

As early as 1890, the economist Adolph Wagner, marshaling evidence from his home country, Germany, formulated "the law of expanding state activity." Government spending not only tends to rise, it tends to rise faster than a nation's average income. At the time, Germany under Bismarck had been building the first welfare state, and the same connection has since been established in other economies—advanced and developing. As the economy grows and incomes rise, the state generally takes an increasing share, which it redistributes as public services.

Others have tied the steady expansion of government to the rise of democracy. The richer voters get, the more they expect in public services and protection. Before World War I, democracies did not exist outside the British Empire, the United States, Canada, and Australia, plus a handful of countries in northern Europe. Everywhere else authoritarians ruled. Most of the major combatants in the Great War were monarchies of more or less absolute forms: Russian, Austrian, Ottoman. After the war ended in 1918, the number of democracies began to rise as the monarchs crumbled. The greatest increases came in two leaps, after World War II, then after the fall of communism in 1989. During the first leap, the welfare state was creating new expectations in Western democracies.

During the second, the age of easy money consolidated its grip, as political leaders looked past mounting deficits and debts in order to meet the rising expectations.

Democracies were also deepening, by extending the right to vote. For much of the nineteenth century, demands for "universal" suffrage generally meant extending the right from white male property holders to all white men. In the 1890s, New Zealand was the first to grant the vote to women, with the United States following only in 1920, the United Kingdom in 1928. And still many groups were shut out of democratic politics. The United States guaranteed black Americans access to the ballot only in 1965. Gradually the power of the vote was shifting from the wealthy establishment, which had little pressing need for government support, to groups that did.

Once created, new government agencies and powers tend to take on a life of their own. Programs and agencies established during tumultuous times, from the New Deal and the Great Society through the oil shocks of the 1970s and the global financial crisis, rarely if ever get shelved when good times return. Former British central banker Andrew Haldane once compared an expanded government safety net to plastic wrap, once it is stretched, it stays that way.

It is possible to find examples of agencies that have shut down, but they are rare and often very old, dating back to the Depression. Some of the major emergency relief agencies created by FDR—the Works Progress Administration, the Civilian Conservation Corps—no longer exist. Yet, when agencies disappeared, it generally meant that they had been renamed or merged or had even split into multiple agencies. After the Reconstruction Finance Corporation closed in the 1950s, many of its lending functions were scattered to other arms of the bureaucracy, including the Small Business Administration.

The old pattern repeats—government grows in crisis, and never retreats. Every new agency develops a circle of supporters—its own staff, clients in the public, backers in Congress—who defend its turf. Nixon had a grand plan to reorganize government and streamline the twelve major departments into eight, but no departments got cut. Congress approved only the parts of the Nixon plan that created agencies, including the Environmental Protection Agency and the Occupational Safety and Health Administration. Carter did not cut the number of federal agencies, despite his repeated campaign promises on that score. Ronald Reagan would try to eliminate the two big agencies created by Nixon as well as the Department of Energy, created by Carter, and again Congress turned him down.

A more activist state is increasingly expensive, requiring more bureaucracy and a larger population of bureaucrats. Since 1980, spending by the dozens of U.S. regulatory agencies has risen from $20 to $70 billion in constant dollars, and staffing has nearly doubled to 280,000, according to data from George Washington University. This expansion unfolded under every president, with the partial exception of Reagan, who cut back the federal bureaucracy in his early years but saw it regain its old staffing and funding levels by the end of his second term. He is also the only president in the last half century who did not issue a burst of "midnight regulations" during his final month in office.

Over time, the public comes to expect the services they have, and more. This process of mushrooming expectations peaked during the pandemic, when the government paid most of the country to stay home, and that extreme is also a precedent. By mid-2023, liberal commentators were noting with regret that while the United States had quickly erected a "European welfare state" as the virus raged, most of the emergency programs, from expanded unemployment, health, and childcare benefits to free school lunches and the ban on evictions and foreclosures, had expired or were scheduled to shut down soon.

"It's Largely Over," concluded a *New York Times* headline. Much remained, however, including food, housing, and rental assistance, and the momentum of these programs was, as usual, hard to slow. Into the fall of 2023, the government was still laying out up to $20 billion a month just for tax credits to help companies retain and insure employees during the pandemic, which was, of course, long over. Whatever the fate of any one subsidy, the basic promise of the state had grown into a sweeping pledge to ensure constant growth in the economy.

CHASING THE MIRACLE

Perhaps the least well understood reason why government tends only to grow is that the thinking of policymakers is still rooted in an era of miracle growth, which grinded to a halt at least fifteen years ago.

Historically, about half of economic growth is attributable to population growth, which political leaders can contain—witness China's now scrapped one-child policy—but can do little to promote. Many governments have tried paying families "baby bonuses," dating back as far as the late 1980s in Singapore and Canada, without reversing the decline in birth rates. The decision on whether to have more children may be one of the few personal choices still beyond government reach.

The other half of growth can be attributed to productivity, more output per worker, which governments have been doing more to stifle than encourage.

The miracle era took off after World War II, and the most obvious driver was the postwar baby boom. Worldwide, the rate of economic growth came close to doubling to 4 percent, up from just 2.4 percent in the first half of the twentieth century, which was itself up from 1 percent in the nineteenth century, and one-third of 1 percent in the eighteenth century. These global averages do not exclude regions that were left behind during the late twentieth-century boom: East European states under Soviet Communism, landlocked regions of Central Asia and Africa.

Though population growth took off in similar stages, accelerating to nearly 2 percent in the late twentieth century, the economy was growing twice as fast. As the world population doubled to 6 billion between 1960 and 2000, world economic output rose nearly fivefold, to $31 trillion. The added boost came from productivity. Capital was flowing into useful plants and equipment, at least in the immediate postwar decades. Each worker was producing more. Productivity growth, like population growth, also doubled to around 2 percent in this period. The living standard of the average person more than doubled. "The entire human race is getting rich at historically unprecedented rates," wrote Nobel laureate Robert Lucas in 2004.

Not surprisingly, political leaders would take full credit for this "miracle." As we have seen, presidents, Treasury secretaries, and central bankers had started to cast themselves as masters of the business cycle since at least the 1930s, and have done so with growing confidence ever since. But governments did not have much to do with sustaining the postwar miracle—certainly not in its later stages.

In the 1980s, the first cracks appeared as both population and productivity growth started to slow. The feminist movement of the 1960s and '70s had given women wider choices on how to live their lives. Many women chose not to have kids, or not to have as many. As birth rates fell, population growth started to decline. With a lag, as it takes time for babies to grow into working adults, growth in the world's working population (age sixteen to sixty-five) started to slow, and to slow with a vengeance after the global financial crisis, from the 2 percent average of earlier decades to around 1 percent after 2008.

The impact of population growth on economic growth is simple, one-to-one: the 1 percentage point decline in working-age population growth slowed the global economy by roughly 1 percentage point. And that in turn was enough to reduce the "miracle" growth rate of 4 percent to 3 percent, which is a huge hit—a 25 percent decline.

At the same time, productivity growth was slowing, too. As governments and central banks poured more capital into the markets than investors could deploy effectively, less of that capital went into the kind of investments that raise output per worker—like new factories, or new factory equipment. Instead, much of the money went into stocks or bonds or newly created debt products. Productivity growth had already started to slow by the 1980s.

Yet the miracle economic growth rates would last another three decades, until the crisis of 2008, sustained by two new and in some ways insidious forces. The more troubling of the two was a debt boom. The world's total debts, including borrowing by households, corporations, and governments, had been drifting downward since World War II, from 140 percent of global GDP in 1950 to less than 100 percent by 1980. Then that trend started to reverse in the early stages of the easy money era, and a worldwide debt boom began.

Between 1980 and 2008, the world saw a unique phase of economic growth turbocharged by debt. The world economy grew rapidly, but total debt grew even faster, more than tripling to 300 percent of GDP by 2008, and rising in developed and developing nations alike. In the United States, the epicenter of this debt-fueled boom, the economy grew fourfold between 1980 and 2008, and total debt grew more than elevenfold.

As governments continued to borrow and spend, backed by central banks unleashing trillions in new credit, some of this easy money did find its way to productive forms of investment, helping to keep the mir-

acle alive. Unfortunately, a growing share did not. In developed economies on average, by 2022 it was taking $3 to $5 of debt to generate $1 of
economic growth—triple the level of the 1970s. The miracle had a rotten,
indebted core.

The second growth-booster was globalization, a far less troubling development, since it did promote productivity growth. After opening to
the world in the early 1980s, China began to open even faster in the subsequent decades and was welcomed for many years by the West. Other
emerging nations followed. Trade doubled as a share of global GDP, to
60 percent at its peak, which was also reached in the financial crisis of
2008. Capital flows rose even faster, increasing more than eightfold, from
2 percent in 1980 to 17 percent of global GDP on the eve of the crisis.

By making it increasingly easy to price-shop from suppliers worldwide, whether for goods or loans, globalization helped spur competition
and growth. Political leaders encouraged the action by flying around the
world, corporate leaders in tow, cutting free trade and financing deals.
Globalization was making it easier to arrange debt financing, and the
burden of debt was not yet slowing global economic growth.

At its optimistic peak, in the 1990s, this era of globalization revived
the hopes that swirled around its predecessor in the early twentieth century that in an increasingly connected world, violent conflicts between
major powers would disappear, because all sides were profiting so richly
from peace. By 2000, according to Oxford University professor Max
Roser, the average number of war deaths per 100,000 humans was down
to just two a year, at or near an all time low since the year 1400.

The problems that follow from soaking capitalism in so much debt
would start to become visible after 2000, and became crystal clear after
those debts melted down in 2008. The resulting recession, deepened and
prolonged by all the debt gumming up the world's financial arteries, was
the worst since World War II.

After the crisis, globalization stalled as nations turned inward. Trade peaked and started to fall as a share of global GDP. Capital flows plummeted back into the low single digits as a share of GDP, and as these flows diminished, weaknesses were exposed. Flattened borrowers were forced to start paying down debts, and total debt started to level off sharply as a share of global GDP.

The growth boost from globalization was over. The growth boost from rising debt was losing its pop. And it mattered greatly who those suddenly chastened borrowers were. Households were trying to lower their debt burdens, and so were banks and other financial corporations. Other types of companies were still amassing new debts, rapidly in some corners of the private market, but on average nowhere near as fast as governments were.

Thus the big picture: the new restraint of private households and some corporate borrowers was completely offset by governments, led by presidents and prime ministers who felt obliged to sustain the miracle growth rates of earlier decades. Leaders kept borrowing and spending in an effort to keep growth alive, to no avail. Global growth fell back after 2010, from 4 percent toward its pre–World War II average of closer to 2 percent. In the remnants of the economic "miracle," by far the most prosperous age in human history, was a growing government debt bill.

A SELF-DESTRUCTIVE DOOM LOOP

Rather than recognize reality, many political leaders are still trying to push their economies to grow at the rates achieved during the postwar population and productivity booms. They are engaged in permanent stimulus campaigns that can't generate growth fast enough to hit their targets and are likely only to saddle their countries with deeper disappointment, as well as larger deficits and debt, which will further slow growth in the future.

President Donald Trump was the most hyperbolic example. He campaigned in 2016 on promises to make America great again, and to push growth back up to 4, 5, even 6 percent—a rate that has rarely been achieved in wealthy countries, and then only briefly, during recoveries from major crises. Once in office, Trump aides dialed that target back to 3 percent, still roughly double the actual potential of the U.S. economy, as estimated by the Federal Reserve, the Congressional Budget Office, and many other authorities. With this unrealistic target in mind, the Trump administration pushed through a large tax cut in 2017—providing aggressive fiscal stimulus and driving up the deficit late in an economic recovery, the first time this has happened outside of a major war.

The following year, analysts at Bernstein Research wrote that Trump's move capped a century-long decay in government "attitudes toward debt." While the authorities started out by running up debt only to fight the world wars, then only to fight recessions, they had in the past always intended to pay back the debts. By the 2010s, however, the attitude was "fight nothing, don't pay back." Borrowing "profligacy" had "unabashedly eclipsed" economic good sense.

The Bernstein researchers cast Trump as the latest in a line of postwar presidents who had set out to achieve an unreachable growth target of 4 percent or more. John F. Kennedy lamented the fact that the postwar recovery was slower in the United States than in Europe. During his presidential campaign, Kennedy quietly dispatched a delegation to Paris to study French state capitalism, and he arrived at the White House in 1961 with lofty ambitions. He told the country that the "primary object" of his economic plans was a growth rate of at least 4.5 percent, "which is well within our capability" and would ensure that "the Soviet Union will not outproduce the United States at any time in the twentieth century."

Even then, however, sustaining growth faster than 4 percent was beyond the potential of the U.S. economy. While Europe was rebuilding from the war, the United States had emerged largely unscathed, and there was no rebuilding boom to be had.

Heady ambitions spilled over into the Carter years. In 1978, Congress passed the Humphrey-Hawkins Act, which committed the government to achieving an unemployment rate even lower, and by implication a GDP growth target even higher than JFK's. After he left office in 2012, President George W. Bush set up a think tank that explicitly endorsed the "4 percent solution," and his brother Jeb later ran for the White House on the same goal. Their argument was that U.S. economic policy should be built on a "positive" vision of faster growth to lower its debt burden, rather than reducing its debts to promote growth.

As population growth slows, the other basic driver of economic growth swells in importance. Productivity matters now more than ever, as the only engine left that can keep economies expanding. In recent decades, as growth in output per worker slumped across capitalist societies, so did growth in wages and average incomes. By the 2010s, per capita GDP growth had dropped by more than half from its postwar peak to 1.5 percent a year in the United States, and to 1ß percent or less in the United Kingdom and the large economies of continental Europe, with Italy bringing up the rear. Japan's per capita GDP growth was just as weak as Europe's, and it was rising only because the population was shrinking. In 2023, on the occasion of Adam Smith's 300th birthday, University of Cambridge economist Diane Coyle asked whether the progress Smith described as a march toward "universal opulence," unleashed by the Industrial Revolution, had finally "ground to a halt" in developed economies.

Nostalgia for the postwar miracle is thus feeding the self-destructive cycle now eating away at capitalism, in which politicians feel compelled to stimulate economies all the time. These efforts are backfiring, not directly as a result of constant deficits, since more spending does mean more growth in the short term, but because of the resulting debts, which are corroding the capitalist system for the long term.

Productivity growth is as complex and hard to measure as population growth is simple and easy to measure, but by all indications it, too, has fallen sharply—nearly by half—since 2000 alone. And today, a growing body of evidence links the productivity slowdown to the expansion over the last four decades of government in all of the forms we have seen so far: as a spender and borrower, as a regulator, as a provider of easy money and bailouts.

While easy money encourages investors to take risks they would never take when money has a price, the promise of a bailout should those bets fail encourages investors to double down: the bigger the bet, the more likely the bailout. Inadvertently, government and central bank support for financial markets steered capital into increasingly large companies, or risky and inefficient ones, which together can explain a good part of the productivity slowdown, shedding new light on why capitalism is losing its spark.

PART II

THE PERILS OF CONSTANT RELIEF

TEN

IN SEARCH OF ZOMBIES

Around the year 2000, constant government support started to nurture the growth of corporate life forms that are destructive to the capitalist system. The most unusual and unwelcome are so-called zombie companies, which do not earn enough profit to cover even the interest payments on their debt and stay alive only by taking out cheap new loans. They barely existed anywhere twenty years ago but now count for around one of every ten publicly traded companies in the world's twenty largest economies, and possibly much more. Unlike the movie variety, corporate zombies can be tricky to identify.

When they first appeared, zombies were thought to be a uniquely Japanese phenomenon, the outgrowth of an insular society where clubby ties between politicians, bankers, and businessmen distort the way capital is allocated, often steering it to companies for social, not economic, reasons. The 1990 collapse of the Tokyo stock and housing market bubbles exposed a web of bad debts that had underpinned the much-hyped rise of Japan as a global economic superpower over the previous decade.

Outside of Toyota, Honda, and a handful of other export manufacturing powerhouses, it turned out that many domestic Japanese companies were surviving on generous loans from friendly banks, often pressured by politicians to keep these firms on their feet. In 2000, a paper by economist Takeo Hoshi revealed the existence of this broad class of unprofitable companies that would and probably should have failed, but for the banks keeping them alive. Hoshi named these companies "zombies."

Western media jumped on the story, often with thinly disguised relief. Japan was not destined to "rule the world" after all. Too soft, too full of bankers and policymakers unwilling to cut loose their indebted buddies. Far from a global industrial juggernaut, most of Japan was mired in bad loans and denial. The typical Japanese worker toiled away in this debt-soaked domestic economy, where productivity was far below the average in other developed countries.

The *New York Times* had some fun with Japan's zombie problem in a 2002 story titled "They're Alive! They're Alive! Not!" Reporter James Brooke wrote that if a corporate zombie like the chain store Daiei were American and not Japanese, it "would probably have gone the way of Woolworth's and Montgomery Ward by now." He quoted Tokyo-based economist Jesper Koll describing Japan as a "loser's paradise" where "feudal" corporate bosses "can get access to more revolving credit due to their political connections and their club memberships."

This club was at its backslapping worst inside the keiretsu, Japanese conglomerates that often own their own banks, and require those banks to extend cheap loans to their other subsidiaries. By 2005 the result was being derided in the *American Economic Review* as a process of "unnatural selection," in which weak banks had the "perverse incentive" to dole out new loans to the most "severely impaired borrowers."

In 2006 Hoshi teamed up with two MIT economists to produce another seminal paper documenting the extent of the zombies in Japan. They found that, by the early 2000s, zombies had spread far enough to account for 30 percent of the companies in six key domestic industries—including construction, real estate, and retail—up from just 5 percent a decade earlier. Hoshi and his coauthors compared Japan's zombies to firms that still existed in the post-Communist countries of Russia and Eastern Europe, where lingering state ownership and support were weakening the process of competition with "depressing effects on the private sector." Normally, they wrote, credit crunches lead to a rise in bankruptcies, but in places where the state supported more comprehensive bailouts, financial crises just gestate more zombies.

By this stage, zombies were also starting to spread outside of Japan, largely undetected. As the comparison to post–Soviet Russia implied, many economists may have assumed that zombies were not a problem of capitalism as practiced in Western countries, and so not worth looking for there. That changed as the aftershocks of the global crisis in 2008 led to a debt crisis in Europe, concentrated in countries on the edges of the continent, including Italy and Spain. The fear was that these weak links were pushing Europe into a "lost decade" like Japan in the 1990s, marked by weak growth and a crippled banking system.

By 2015, the search for zombies in Europe was spawning a rich literature, with major contributions from teams in international institutions including the Bank for International Settlements (BIS) and the OECD, academic institutions including New York University and Harvard, and investment houses like Deutsche Bank. Their stories cast a darker light on Western capitalism.

As the eurozone crisis gathered speed, the European Central Bank had stepped in to the rescue. The ECB vowed to buy the debt of member governments in virtually unlimited amounts, and in 2012 its president,

Mario Draghi, issued his now famous vow to "do whatever it takes" to stanch the crisis. "Believe me," he said, "it will be enough." Within two years, Draghi had admitted that while European banks looked much stronger, bolstered by capital infusions from their governments, the banks were not lending that capital to businesses. Not fast enough to inspire confidence in Europe's prospects, or encourage the investment required to revive economic growth. Somewhere between 30 and 50 percent of the bank debt in Italy, Spain, and Portugal was owed by companies that could not even cover the interest payments. The threat of "Japanification" loomed.

In 2016 came the first study uncovering what it called "unvital signs" that "Europe's weak economic recovery is a repeat of Japan's 'zombie lending' experience in the 1990s, when banks in distress failed to foreclose on unprofitable and highly indebted firms." Italy, where the economic contraction was especially sharp and banks were particularly laden with bad loans, was an especially good place to look for symptoms of Japanification. And indeed, in Italian provinces where lending was dominated by weaker banks, "zombie firms are more likely to survive, and healthy firms are more likely to fail."

What had once been considered a uniquely Japanese phenomenon was gradually being exposed as a wider problem of modern capitalism. In 2017, OECD researchers went looking for zombies in a sample of nine countries, including smaller ones on the periphery of the continent and larger ones, such as France and the United Kingdom. The findings made headlines around the world: in these countries, zombies accounted for as much as 20 percent of the capital stock (in Italy) and more than 10 percent of the jobs (Italy, Spain, and Belgium). As in Japan, there appeared to be a symbiotic link between zombie corporations and weak banks. Even more important, the researchers wrote, were "prolonged" easy monetary policy and the "persistence of crisis-induced" bailout programs.

That might have left America as the last redoubt of zombie-free capitalism, but no. The following year, the BIS executed the most comprehensive search to that point, screening more than thirty thousand companies going back to 1980 in fourteen countries, including the United States. It found a set of disturbing patterns, since widely confirmed. For one, the hope that zombies had appeared only in freak outbreaks, generated by the sweeping scale of bailouts in Japan during the 1990s and Europe in the 2010s, was put to rest.

Zombies barely existed in the 1980s; they started to appear in the 1990s, and to spread rapidly in the 2000s—long before the global financial crisis of 2008. Unfortunately, this was not a new, "episodic," or passing problem. Zombies had multiplied during recessions, and their number receded only partly during the subsequent recoveries. In other words, they appeared to be both created and indefinitely sustained by the widening habit of constant government rescues. The "cleansing effect" of recessions, which in the past had forced weak companies to fold or restructure in downturns, appeared to be fading, the BIS authors wrote. And America was not immune.

The true extent of the zombie population was hotly debated, and it depended on what one meant by "zombie firm." Over time, the definition had evolved, from an unprofitable company living on bank support to a company earning too little to cover its interest payments not just for one year but for three years running. Even this narrow definition produced very high estimates of the zombie population. One, from Deutsche Bank, put the zombie share of public companies at or near zero before 2000, rising to 20 percent in the United States and around 25 percent in the United Kingdom, France, and Germany by 2020.

Numbers that eye-popping started to draw media attention. A scan of English, German, French, Italian, and Japanese news outlets found that references to zombie companies rose from zero in 2005 to four thousand around 2016 and more than sixteen thousand by 2021. As the story gained traction, the wider news media began looking to name names, and by 2020 they had published some big ones indeed, from Delta to Boeing, Uber to Tesla, Bally's casinos to Carnival cruise lines and Mattel, the venerable toy company. The most notorious were the tottering firms that had become the darlings of pandemic day traders, like AMC Theatres and GameStop. Even ExxonMobil, the world's largest private oil company, showed up on a zombie list in 2020.

To many analysts, that was a step too far. ExxonMobil and Tesla are "zombies"? Companies in dying industries, like mall retailers, or movie theaters, or video game stores, might have dim prospects for covering their debts. Surely for a giant with vast oil reserves, or cutting-edge technology, any earnings shortfalls were a temporary condition. To identify companies that were entering a steady zombie state, not just visiting, one had to look at their prospects for paying off debt in the future.

So researchers began looking for zombies only among companies that had not only failed to cover their interest payments for the last three years but also had dim prospects of earning enough to make those payments in the future. Narrowing the definition in this way did not, however, make zombies disappear.

In 2022 the BIS found that since 1990, zombies, narrowly defined, had increased, from 4 percent to 15 percent of all companies in a sample of fourteen advanced countries, and to 20 percent in the United States. Depending on how they assessed future profitability, an inherently difficult exercise, researchers still turned up a range of estimates, but few disputed the upward trend. In a 2023 report on "Global Zombies," an NYU team led by Edward Altman found that the zombie share of public companies had quadrupled since the 1990s, to around 7 percent in twenty of the world's largest economies, including the United States.

By now, there were differing explanations for the rise of zombies, including their symbiotic relationship with "zombie banks," which also thrive on government support. With little or no profit and limited reserves, zombie banks are the least likely to write off bad loans to zombie customers, because that makes their own fragile books look even worse. Others cited a clumsy and slow system for declaring companies bankrupt and ushering them out of the market, particularly in Europe.

Still others cited the increasingly generous bailouts and other acts of "regulatory forbearance," including a willingness to go easy on banks and companies that were stretching lending requirements—the same habits that deepened the S&L crisis in the 1980s. It was a question of mounting excess, wrote a team led by economist Viral Acharya at New York University: smaller rescues delivered by "patient" government leaders could be beneficial, by keeping credit flowing through the system. Excessive bailouts delivered by "myopic" leaders, who do not see the long-term risk of soaking the system in too much debt, were raising "the spectre of worldwide 'zombification.'"

Zombies also thrived in a business environment flush with easy money. Like the OECD researchers, those at the BIS found a "highly significant" link between the proliferation of zombies and record low interest rates—in particular, persistently low rates over a period of five years. Though these firms would have shut down in "normal circumstances," they continued to operate—thanks to support from banks, shadow banks, and governments, and the abnormal conditions of the easy money era, the authors of the "Global Zombies" paper wrote: "Even before the pandemic began, the explosive growth of corporate debt in the United States and other countries, combined with historically low interest rates, has created a friendly environment for the growth of zombie firms globally."

Countries with lower interest rates tended to have the largest populations of zombies, a finding that on one level seemed odd. Mechanically, lower rates should have made it easier for zombies to start covering their interest payments and return to normal health. That did happen before 2000, when zombies tended to pay down debt faster than healthy firms, but not after.

As central banks "ratcheted down" interest rates with each new business cycle, zombies faced less pressure to pay down debt or close shop. They not only found it easier to take out new bank loans, they also found it easier to sell bonds in the public markets. This was a result of deliberate central bank policy, the whole point of which was to encourage investors to move out of safe government bonds and start funding riskier debt: none was riskier or paid a higher yield than junk bonds sold by zombies. No surprise, countries with the most developed junk bond markets also tended to have the largest populations of zombies. In short, falling interest rates were giving many players in the credit system—banks, shadow banks, and bond markets—an incentive to extend the life of zombies indefinitely.

When the pandemic hit, some zombies were forced to declare bankruptcy, which exposed more famous names. Among them were JCPenney and Sears. It turned out that zombie retail store chains had in fact been present in the United States, just as they were in Japan back in the 1990s. And declaring bankruptcy did not mean these zombies would "go the way of . . . Montgomery Ward," as the *Times* had once put it. JCPenney still survives in many locations, rescued this time by mall operators desperate not to let an anchor department store go under.

High-profile zombie failures were, however, the exception. Though headlines were warning that defaults and bankruptcies would rise sharply during the pandemic, few mentioned the opposite risk, that many companies which were failing before the pandemic would survive it, still losing money. In 2021 and 2022, business bankruptcies in the United States fell below fifteen thousand, shattering the record lows since the data begins in 1980. Leaders of the "Global Zombies" project wrote that they had expected zombies to die off in the pandemic; instead the zombie share of public companies barely budged, thanks in part to "unprecedented central bank intervention in financial markets and government support such as moratoriums on interest payments" for small corporate debtors.

By 2023, it was easy to find stories about zombies lurching from one survival stunt to the next. GameStop had attempted to find profitability by branching into cryptocurrencies and non-fungible tokens but soon had to shut down those projects as losses mounted. AMC Theatres had attempted to raise capital from the Reddit day traders who call themselves "apes" by offering them "APE shares," for "AMC Preferred Equity." When uncertainty about the legality of APE Shares forced the company to withdraw them, AMC stock collapsed 34 percent in a single day. Zombie firms had returned to "the forefront of the public debate" amid the unprecedented bailouts, wrote researchers at the International Monetary Fund that summer of 2023. "While this initial (mostly) untargeted support was essential to mitigating the negative shock on the economy, it may have helped zombie firms stay afloat, thus avoiding or delaying a necessary creative destruction process."

So how had zombies remained hidden in our midst for so long? Despite the media attention on a few famous corporate names, most zombies turned out to be relatively small. Even under a narrow definition, the BIS found, zombies had risen over three decades to account for nearly 15 percent of small and medium-sized firms in Germany, roughly 25 percent in the United Kingdom, France, and Australia, and more than 40 percent in Canada and the United States.

Gradually a more complete profile of the zombie life cycle had emerged. Zombies are more likely to arise in the certain industries, from energy and real estate to clothes and appliances. Zombifying firms tend to be old ones: firms in business for more than forty years are roughly two to three times more likely to become zombies than those in business for less than five years. They do not live forever, but only one of every four U.S. and European firms that have been zombified since 1980 has shut down.

They are notably lacking in ambition. Most zombies were by the last decade making no plan to improve profitability or reduce debt. The likelihood that a zombified firm would remain one through the coming year had risen from 40 percent in the late 1980s to 70 percent in the late 2010s. Though some of them would return to good health, covering their debts, at least for a time, the rest lurch along in a zombie state for increasingly long periods—now four years on average. "Zombiism" was turning into a chronic, recurring disease. Many recovered firms suffer a relapse. And recovered zombies are three times more likely to relapse than healthy firms were likely to succumb in the first place.

From its origins in Japan, the zombie virus had spread worldwide, steadily widening its reach since the turn of the millennium, lasting longer and resurfacing in its hosts more often. By 2023, in America and other capitalist countries, most researchers agreed, a surprising share of public companies, especially small ones, had been exposed as zombies. Whether the zombie share of the corporate population is approaching 10 percent or surpassing 20 percent was important but perhaps not critical, since most researchers would agree that, either way, this trend exposes a serious problem of debt decay. Though the condition is not necessarily deadly, there is a strong case to be made that capitalism would be healthier if fewer zombies were on government life support.

ELEVEN

RISE OF THE OLIGOPOLIES

Since Joseph Schumpeter coined the term in 1942, it's been understood that "creative destruction" would create large pools of wealth and power, which were a plus for capitalism so long as they did not become entrenched. Increasingly, however, they are entrenched. When competition is not free and open, as has been the case in recent decades, upstart firms can no longer "compete away" the profits at the top.

In recent decades, governments and central banks have been grinding away the gears of creative destruction. The textbooks say that when central banks lower the cost of borrowing money, easier access to financing should give businesses the wherewithal to invest more in new equipment, or new research, raising growth. For the last twenty years, however, central banks have lowered rates with exactly the opposite result: weak investment and disappointingly slow growth.

Princeton University economist Atif Mian was drawn into this mystery by a chance conversation. He was chatting with the son of small hotel proprietors in Spain, who complained that years of low rates set by the European Central Bank were helping the big hotel chains get bigger and run little guys out of business. Mian found the complaint unexpected, a direct challenge to longstanding assumptions that low rates are basically just a price, the same and equally accessible to all. He and his Princeton colleague Ernest Liu, along with Amir Sufi of the University of Chicago, went to work. They built a model of how easy money would affect not the economy as a whole and companies in general but competition between companies.

Their model predicted that, early on, lowering rates would in fact encourage investment by all companies, boosting economic growth. Owing simply to their size, the big companies would invest more than the small ones, leading to higher profits and a higher stock market valuation.

Before long, many smaller rivals would give up the chase, and stop investing, which means that the big companies could also lower their investments yet keep building on their very lucrative market lead. More and more industries would become oligopolies, dominated by just a few companies, and this tendency toward market concentration would grow as interest rates fell toward zero. "Industry leaders invest more aggressively to keep industry followers at bay, which in turn disincentivizes industry followers from investing," Mian, Liu, and Sufi wrote in 2019.

Next, they checked the predictions of their model against the actual events of recent decades. The match was nearly exact. After central banks started lowering rates in the early 1980s, easy money set off a period of heightened competition. Following the turn of the millennium, stagnation set in as dominant firms consolidated control over one industry after another, with fewer established companies dying off, and fewer new ones rising up.

In the view of Mian, Liu, and Sufi, easy money was the best explanation, even for the growing dominance of cash-rich giants like Amazon and Apple. They don't need to borrow in order to invest or to acquire smaller rivals. Yet they still benefit from easy money. Low yields on safe government bonds pushed investors toward stocks, and easy money gave dominant companies a strong incentive to do everything in their power to grow more dominant—to profit from the stock market boom.

WHEN PROFITS ARE NOT COMPETED AWAY

One might think that an expanding stock market would create more room for more competition, but that was not the case. Since Alan Greenspan promised Fed support after the 1987 crash, the stock market has grown from half the size of the U.S. economy to two times larger. And after 2000, the share of industry profits and the share of stock market returns that go to the largest companies rose sharply—as smaller firms died off.

This was a global story. As Jan Eeckhout, a professor at Pompeu Fabra University in Barcelona, puts it in his 2021 book on industrial concentration, *The Profit Paradox*, one surprise in his research was that profits are rising "from tech to textiles," and across countries, not just in the predictable American names like Google and Apple. Worldwide, the markup of the average firm has risen from less than 10 percent in 1980 to nearly 60 percent above their costs.

Three years later, a team at the Roosevelt Institute extended Eeckhout's work back to World War II, for the United States. The results were even more striking. Markups had remained flat for all U.S. firms through the 1970s, then started to rise, almost exclusively among the largest 10 percent of firms—from 50 percent to 250 percent above costs. During the surreal Covid market boom of 2021, the top firms saw their largest annual share gain since records begin in 1955.

A lion's share of earnings leads in a straightish line to a lion's share of the stock market. Recall that the corporate giants of the 1960s and early '70s had started to lose their grip on the markets following the purgatory recessions of 1973 and 1980, which were followed by an explosion in new firms. By the mid-1990s, the stock market share of the top ten firms— out of the five hundred in the S&P index—had dropped by nearly half in twenty years to around 17 percent. Then the easy money era kicked into high gear, giving large firms ample access to capital and slowing the process of competitive destruction.

In the late 1990s, the top ten share of the stock market started climbing again, and by 2023 it had redoubled to 34 percent—a record since the late '70s. And most of the gains were in the top five. In 2023 the market value of the top five firms was three times that of the next five, also a record since the late '70s. Their names at midyear: Apple, Microsoft, Alphabet, Meta, and Nvidia, the hot maker of chips used in AI programs.

The pandemic had tilted money flows to big firms and particularly to the biggest tech firms, which were seen as well positioned to prosper in a society shut in at home, forced to work and play online. In the 2010s there had been much debate about whether Apple would follow in the footsteps of U.S. Steel, the first billion-dollar stock when it was created by JPMorgan in 1901, to become the first trillion-dollar stock. Defying the skeptics, five companies would break the trillion-dollar barrier—all were tech firms. By late 2023, the biggest tech stocks accounted for half of U.S. stock market returns during the pandemic—and *all* of U.S. returns for the year. Apple had peaked above $3 trillion, the most highly valued company of all time by far.

Unrivaled size was translating into unprecedented staying power at the top. In the 1980s, only three American companies remained in the top ten from the start to the end of the decade. In the 2010s, six U.S. companies achieved that feat. More striking, the rate of churn remained much faster in Europe, China, and even Japan, where only two companies managed to hold on to a top ten position from 2010 to 2020.

The likelihood that a leading U.S. company in any industry would be bumped from its dominant position was falling sharply. After 1990, the share of U.S. companies that were less than five years old fell by about a third to just over 30 percent. In technology industries, too, the ones traditionally most alive with innovation and competition, the process of creative destruction was slowing.

In the past, each new wave of the computer age—the advent of the mainframe, the arrival of the PC—had brought new names to the top of the industry. "Silicon Valley" came to flow off the tongue as a prefix for "start-up." After the dot-com bust in 2000, the churn started to weaken. Survivors of the bust consolidated their grip on internet search, shopping, and more. Explaining how "big tech killed the internet," venture capitalist Chris Dixon wrote that the magical creativity of the early internet had given way to stagnation around 2010, as aging names like Facebook and YouTube became fixtures at the top of app store bestseller lists.

When the next wave of innovation hit a peak in 2023, as investors poured money into any firm that could claim a tie to artificial intelligence, there was little to no turnover at the top. Among the five biggest tech firms by stock market value, cited above, only Nvidia was a newcomer to this elite circle, and it was thirty years old. The median age of the leading tech firms had crept up by half to thirty-six years, compared to just twenty-four years at the dot-com peak. Brookings Institution researchers have called this corporate petrification process "the other aging of America."

If money corrupts, then what Wall Street now calls the "supernormal profits" of big tech will tend to corrupt absolutely. Sitting on cash piles in the tens of billions, the tech giants now have myriad options for stifling smaller rivals and undermining the process of creative destruction—which should be eroding their own dominant positions. One of those options has come to be known as "predatory infringement." Back in the late 1990s, Apple founder Steve Jobs said his company had "always been shameless about stealing great ideas," invoking a quote from Picasso as poetic justification: "Good artists copy, great artists steal." Over the years, this uncareful description of the creative process would become a strategy, writes George Mason University patent law expert Adam Mossoff, as "Big Tech companies like Google decided that they profit more by stealing smaller companies' intellectual property than buying or licensing it." If the victims dared object in court, they could be easily smothered in motions launched by a larger army of lawyers.

Occasionally the aggrieved did dare challenge intellectual property theft, and a few have won cases at the U.S. International Trade Commission. A wireless speaker company named Sonos accused Google of copying technology for use in its own Google line of speakers and won. Apple lost a case filed by two California firms who accused it of lifting patient-monitoring technology for the Apple Watch, but these setbacks are the exception. "In plain English, this is piracy," writes Mossoff, who calls it "a problem that threatens America's innovation economy and its international economic competitiveness."

WHAT'S TO BLAME

Easy money is, of course, only the newest explanation for the rise of oligopolies. Earlier work had cited at least four others: globalization, which gives big companies access to international markets by lowering barriers to trade. The internet, which gives superstar firms instant access to a global network of customers. Aging populations, which produce fewer young entrepreneurs to challenge incumbent firms. And, finally, an increasingly complex web of government regulation, which megafirms have the resources to shape and navigate in ways small companies do not.

When researchers began testing these explanations, the results shifted the finger of blame for multiplying oligopolies in the direction of government. Aging might explain why there were fewer entrepreneurs but could not explain why fewer start-ups were highly profitable and productive, or why fewer were trying to break into the most profitable industries.

Globalization might appear to favor economies of scale but it would force consolidating giants to compete and cut profit margins—yet profits were rising instead. Globalization also could not explain why most U.S. industries were consolidating, when only 13 percent of those industries have any significant dependence on foreign trade. Moreover, most of these export-oriented firms are manufacturers, and only a quarter of manufacturing profit could be attributed to costs saved in global supply chains; lower borrowing costs were much more important.

Scanning the competing explanations, economists Thomas Philippon and Germán Gutiérrez concluded in 2019 that there is "limited or no support" for economies of scale or aging populations or network effects as an explanation for growing industry concentration. If capitalism is operating normally, entrepreneurs will flock to the industries where profits are highest and opportunity is therefore greatest. If anything, this rush will grow as populations age, leaving fewer young entrepreneurs to challenge older incumbents; and that was in fact happening before the 1990s.

Something changed around 2000, they wrote. Regulatory shocks—a sudden increase in regulations targeting one industry—grew more common as lobbying by market leaders intensified. And big gains in profit for the large firms and declines for smaller ones started to follow "systematically" from these regulatory shocks. Turning capitalism upside down, entrepreneurs began to avoid the industries that strong profits should have made most promising. The most compelling explanation for this "failure of free entry" was neither aging populations nor changing technology and rising returns to scale. It was the increased spending on lobbying and campaign contributions by large companies, creating regulatory barriers to new business.

It's no secret that the lobbying industry has exploded, with annual spending more than doubling from around $1.4 billion in the late 1990s to north of $4 billion today, based on data reported to the U.S. Senate. And the unreported industry may be much larger. (Microsoft's annual lobbying budget alone, for example, has been put at $1 billion.) Among the top twenty American lobbyists, big tech firms are rising fast and now have four names on the list, led by Amazon and Alphabet, up from zero a decade ago. Big U.S. tech firms are also active in Europe, where they were a non-presence as recently as 2015. Now they account for five of the top ten corporate lobbyists, outspending the pharma, finance, and chemical industries combined; and they are increasingly controversial. European lawmakers have accused them of working through front organizations that appear to represent small business.

FALL OF THE SMALL

Even more than the rise of big, established companies, the fall of smaller, younger ones was visible across the capitalist world. By early 2020, startups represented a falling share of all companies in the United States,

Britain, Italy, Spain, Sweden, and many other industrial economies. Not only was capitalism generating fewer start-ups, it was also forcing fewer firms to shut down. The United States was generating start-ups at just half the rate and shutting down old companies at two-thirds the rate of the mid-1970s.

Though the U.S. economy had tripled in size since the 1970s, the number of public companies was falling at a stunning pace. The change came, once again, right around the turn of the millennium. During the period of heightened competition between the 1970s and the eve of the dot-com bust, the number of public companies rose from around 4,500 to a peak near 7,500. Then the era of easy money reached full stride, and as industries consolidated, the number of public companies fell back, to just over 4,000 in 2023.

This decline hit the small business community hard. Nine of every ten disappearing companies were small ones (with a market cap under $250 million). By the early 2010s, big U.S. companies outnumbered small ones for the first time, and soon by a significant margin, nearly two to one. Two-thirds of the major business sectors were consolidating in the hands of the three largest firms, in both the United States and Europe—a sharp increase from earlier decades.

This was not a matter of old analogue firms disappearing in the digital age, because the overwhelming majority of industries, not just smokestack industries, were hemorrhaging public companies. During the pandemic, Americans launching online enterprises from their living rooms pushed the number of small companies back upward—but it has yet to be seen whether that is just another passing and stimulus-inspired oddity of the Covid years.

As small and young companies were collapsing in number, they were collapsing even faster in value, accounting as a class for less than half of 1 percent of the total stock market in 2022, down from 13 percent four decades earlier. Worse, smaller companies were more and more likely to be falling into the ranks of the profitless.

Small companies that did not fail outright were dropping out of the public markets through two main channels, according to a 2019 paper by Rice University professor of finance Gustavo Grullon and his colleagues: they were getting acquired by larger companies, or they were going private. Both types of deals were enabled by easy money, and many of the companies going private were motivated by a desire to escape the growing burden of government scrutiny and regulation. This trend raised a hopeful possibility, that growing concentration across industries was just an illusion. Rather than concentrating in fewer companies, perhaps industries were just dividing into two groups—one publicly traded and shriveling in number, one privately held and thriving?

To address that question, Grullon and his coauthors dug into census data, which includes private companies. Their findings, including the private firms, mirror the story told by Mian, Liu, and Sufi: most U.S. industries were growing more competitive before the turn of the millennium, then "began undergoing a new fundamental change." Over the last two decades, three out of four U.S. industries have grown more concentrated, most dramatically so. Using a standard index that measures the dominance of leading firms by their share of industry sales, they found concentration intensifying at a "striking" pace, up 90 percent on average since 2000.

Worse, the biggest firms appeared to be extracting more monopolistic "rent" from the economy, wrote Jason Furman and Peter Orszag, former top economic advisers to President Obama. Facing less competition, the big firms would in theory tend to both invest less in training and equipment and take more profit for themselves. And they were. As returns fell for safe assets like government bonds, returns spiked for risky assets like stocks—driven mainly by the largest stocks. The gap between the returns of safe and risky assets quadrupled from 2 to 8 percentage points, with big firms extracting higher rents and enjoying higher returns as a result.

When the pandemic hit, some scholars argued, the rise of oligopolies had made the U.S. economy newly vulnerable. In normal times, concentrating power in three or four companies did not give any one of them a clear opening to hike prices, since competitors still exist. But as supply chains shut down, they had more room to jack up prices, confident that existing competitors could not raise their own production—for lack of materials. As both prices and profits shot up, it was difficult to discern which was cause and which was effect; either way, however, large companies were enjoying a windfall in earnings. Politicians and economists on the left were quick to blame the spike in consumer prices on "greedflation," symptomatic of an economy now dominated by giant companies.

Oligopolies in one industry tend to promote consolidation in others. One concern is the rise of the "big three" investment houses, BlackRock, Vanguard, and State Street. Together, these firms now manage around $22 trillion in assets, including much of America's retirement savings, and a big chunk of the stock market. Often, they own large stakes in all of the major players in an industry, "potentially leading them to favor uncompetitive behavior," wrote Furman and Orszag. For example, the top three investment houses are among the top five shareholders in both Coca-Cola and PepsiCo; the concern is that they don't have much interest in seeing the soda makers compete in earnest. Even John Bogle, founder of the original Vanguard index fund, warned before his death in 2019 that allowing further concentration of stock ownership in the hands of three companies would not "serve the national interest." If the trend continues, he wrote, "a handful of giant institutional investors will one day hold voting control of virtually every large U.S. corporation."

IT'S NOT A "WONDERFUL LIFE"

For all the concern lavished on whether American banks had grown too big to fail, most were in fact too small to survive. Since small banks are the financial lifeline for rural and small towns, their demise became a popular topic for reporters covering the American heartland. Few could resist evoking the beloved small-town banker played by Jimmy Stewart in *It's a Wonderful Life*, but that film came out in 1946.

Starting in the 1990s, the share of total bank assets held by larger ones, with more than $250 billion in deposits, rose from 5 percent to 55 percent, taking equal chunks away from both medium-sized and small banks. The number of community banks fell by more than 11,000 in those decades to 4,600, leaving one in three rural counties with no local bank at all. Many of the survivors were struggling to breathe under a mounting pile of paperwork.

Since the 1970s, the average number of new bank laws had tripled to ten a year, and the average length of each new law had risen tenfold to nearly two thousand pages. After the financial crisis of 2008, new regulations doubled the length of the typical bank filing to nearly ninety pages. Small banks fired loan officers and hired compliance officers to keep up with the task of writing these reports, many unsuccessfully. Though the number of local banks had been falling for years, the pace of decline surged after 2008.

The squeeze on small companies and banks spawned a chicken-and-egg question. Which came first, the increase in regulation or the increase in industry concentration? Were some industries simply investing more in research, growing more innovative and profitable, and attracting regulatory scrutiny? Or did the regulations come first, making it more difficult and costly for companies to grow, with the biggest ones coming out on top?

WHAT WENT WRONG WITH CAPITALISM

To address this question, economist and technologist James Bessen ran a series of tests to parse which factors were driving the rise in corporate valuations and profits, particularly after 2000. "Intangible" investments such as R&D could explain part of the rise, but an even larger share was driven by the same force cited by other researchers: increasing regulation and spending on political lobbying and campaign contributions. One test was chronological: across U.S. industries, profits and valuations showed a clear pattern of rising *after* the industry got slapped with significant new regulations.

The issue did not appear to be "regulatory capture," meaning that officials had been co-opted or just befriended by the businesses they were supposed to regulate. In the 1990s, for example, the Federal Communications Commission issued new regulations governing the hugely unpopular cable TV industry, and predicted that the rules would drive down cable prices and save consumers more than $1 billion a year.

The aim, in short, was to shift wealth from the cable monopolies back to consumers. Instead, the cable companies slipped through loopholes in the rules to cut service along with prices: for example, by charging a premium for popular channels. Many customers paid more for premium packages. Cable profits and stock valuations went up. The intent of the regulators was not so much captured as dodged.

One challenge for modern capitalism is that governments are increasingly ill-equipped to keep up with the accelerating pace of technological change. "Man's works have outgrown the capacity of the individual man," warned the future Supreme Court justice Louis Brandeis in 1908. Humans entered the twenty-first century with "Paleolithic emotions, medieval institutions, and godlike technology," said evolutionary biologist E. O. Wilson in 2009. And yet a regulator's job is to regulate, so they feel duty-bound to fight this losing battle with the gods. In *Recording America,* her new book on "why government is failing in the digital age,"

Jennifer Pahlka quotes a California state employee who considers himself the "new guy" after seventeen years on the job, because it would take a least twenty-five years to master layers of hacks, updates, and fine print that have been building up in the bureaucracy for nearly a century.

Trying to control big tech firms through regulation may only cement their positions. By late 2023 the European Union and the United Kingdom were moving to require internet companies to treat drivers for ride-hailing services and other "gig workers" as full-time employees, with benefits. Earlier, however, when California imposed a similar rule, it gave a big boost to the dominant ride-hailing service, Uber, which could more easily afford the benefits. Soon Uber was leaving smaller rivals like Lyft, less able to pay benefits, "in the dust." One tech analyst predicted a future in which Uber employed enough drivers to provide relatively expensive and subpar service, much like taxi services once did.

The rise of oligopolies is not always obvious to the average consumer. Most Americans will know that online search, shopping, and social media are dominated by one or two ubiquitous corporate names. They will be loosely aware that U.S. air routes are now dominated by just four companies (down from ten just twenty years ago), rental cars by three companies, beer sales by two companies. It's likely they know their favorite craft brewery is probably owned now by Anheuser-Busch, less likely they are aware that Tom's of Maine is owned by a conglomerate (Colgate) as is Burt's Bees (Clorox).

These brands nurture a small and local image but are owned by a giant parent. Go into a mall and shop at any of more than a dozen jewelry stores, from Zales to Jared and Kay, and all are owned by the same company, Signet. They pitch to slightly different mass markets, which is why they can all set up in the same malls. Two companies make more than 80 percent of the coffins and caskets sold in the United States—and similar trends are visible worldwide. Browse any one of forty-five global dating sites and you are on one owned by the Match Group. Former college backpackers who fondly remember Belgium in the 1980s as the land of a thousand distinct breweries may be a bit saddened to learn that most are owned by a global company called InBev, which also owns Anheuser-Busch.

Contrary to the rhetoric of so many American politicians, historically the main engines of job creation were not small businesses but new businesses, particularly the top 10 percent of new businesses, which are the ones that survive at least five years. Older small businesses had tended to be stable or stagnant mom-and-pop shops. After the turn of the millennium, something fundamental changed in this corner of American capitalism, too. The cream of the start-up class, that top 10 percent, was growing less impressively fast, compared to the old mom-and-pop shops.

Why is not exactly clear. Many start-ups were simply disappearing quickly into larger companies, as young tech entrepreneurs aspired only to launch a company they could sell quickly to Google or Facebook, not own and build themselves. In the pharmaceutical industry, some of the giants have been making "killer acquisitions," or buying smaller firms not to develop their drugs, but to block development of drugs that would compete with their own. The result by the late 2010s was that large and established firms appeared to have replaced small entrepreneurial ones as the main engines of U.S. job creation.

RETURN OF THE TRUSTBUSTERS

Before the New Deal, the U.S. government was a defender of small business and an enemy of private monopolies. After the landmark 1911 breakup of Standard Oil, then the nation's most powerful monopoly, majority-owned by its richest man, John D. Rockefeller, it looked like the end of an era. The battle over concentrated wealth and power was over, wrote the journalist Walter Lippmann: "It had become the settled policy of this country that no man would be permitted to make so much money," with the monopoly route to vast fortunes "outlawed by public opinion, forbidden by statute, and prevented by the tax laws."

We know now nothing was settled. FDR would shift from busting trusts in the 1930s to co-opting them for the war effort in the 1940s, leaving his legacy on this issue up for grabs. The conservative icon Friedrich Hayek opened *The Road to Serfdom*, his 1944 warning about the slippery slope from big government to socialist dictatorship, with a quote from an FDR speech on the evils of monopoly. The first two postwar presidents, Truman and Eisenhower, kept up the attack, launching a barrage of antitrust suits against the nation's biggest companies, including AT&T in communications and IBM in computers.

In a period when government was tough on trusts, it was easier to launch new companies. Leaders of the Progressive era had aimed to expand "industrial liberty" by creating space for craftsmen, farmers, and other small businesses. They largely succeeded. Half the veterans returning from World War II ended up starting their own businesses, which multiplied at a faster pace than the baby boom population. The number of corporations per every million Americans doubled from around four thousand in 1940 to eight thousand by 1968.

By the 1970s, however, antitrust was under attack, from the same unexpected alliance that was criticizing the regulatory state: pro-competition conservatives and pro-consumer liberals. The conservatives saw monopolies as the offspring of scientific progress and the natural winners of market competition. Liberal intellectuals largely agreed. They wanted big business not free of government but guided by government technocrats—their kind of people. With Galbraith, the leading postwar economist and a proponent of "command and control statism," they credited big business for creating "The Affluent Society," the title of

Galbraith's book on post–World War II America. Drawn to the sarcastic wit of the prominent sociologist C. Wright Mills, a soft Marxist, they dismissed small business as the "lumpen bourgeoisie," petty, provincial, ineffectual.

Throughout, theorists on both sides still agreed with Schumpeter that monopolies and oligopolies were dangerous when they become entrenched and gain the power to jack up prices. Galbraith downplayed this risk in his widely repeated theory of "countervailing power," that every giant creates an equal and opposite giant. A cereal monopoly that raised prices too high would be undercut by upstart cereal makers or chain stores, which would negotiate prices down on behalf of the consumer. Galbraith mocked a federal antitrust suit against A&P, the dominant grocery chain store of the time, for accusing the company of "too vigorous bargaining . . . on the consumer's behalf." These countervailing powers worked automatically, another law of economic science: "We can rely on countervailing power to appear as a curb on economic power."

This view ultimately came to shape the new consumer rights movement, led throughout the 1960s and '70s in the United States by Ralph Nader, a Harvard-trained lawyer. Though Nader would at various times bash big government, big unions, and big business, his concern was not protecting the small entrepreneur from "predatory pricing" by bigger rivals. It was lower prices for consumers. In 1975, heavily influenced by both Nader's Raiders and the Chicago School, a Democratic Congress lifted much of what remained of the rules controlling predatory and discriminatory pricing—a move historian Matt Stoller has called the "biggest step toward the destruction of the independent business enterprise and the small producer and small retailer in the history of America."

Just as liberals and conservatives had come to agree that industrial concentration is fine if it promotes "consumer welfare," consumer prices were about to start falling for reasons much larger than monopoly: the competitive pressures imposed by new technology, globalization, and particularly the opening of China. That opening effectively added hundreds of millions of Chinese workers to the global labor market, helping to contain price increases for the next four decades. And antitrust faded away in the United States.

By the mid-1980s, merger deals worth more than $1 billion, once confined to the oil industry, were sweeping across the U.S. corporate landscape, in industries ranging from tobacco and entertainment to aircraft and chemicals. "The experiment of enforcing the antitrust laws a little bit less each year has run for 40 years," wrote a team of Yale School of Management faculty in 2019.

From more than ten cases a year in the early 1970s, the number of prosecutions brought by the Justice Department under Section 2 of the 1890 Sherman Antitrust Act had dwindled to one to two a year by the 1980s. After bringing a major Sherman case against Microsoft in 1998, the United States did not bring another one until it went after Google in 2020. In a separate branch of trust-busting, the Federal Trade Commission challenged sixteen mergers a year in the two decades before 2000, and only three in subsequent decades. Before Biden started to revive antitrust and rethink its obsession with consumer prices, enforcement was moribund.

While efforts to cut back the regulatory state had failed, the campaign to restrain the trustbusters had largely succeeded. Why the different outcomes? Regulators are spread out across roughly seventy agencies, and many of the most important, including the Fed and the Securities and Exchange Commission, are independent from the White House. They are difficult for a president to track and control. Trustbusters work out of three agencies, making them easier to mobilize—or demobilize. Perhaps most important, while industries often work with regulators to craft rules in their favor, they see no possible gain in cooperating with trustbusters and fight them tooth and nail.

Thus government for the last four decades has been contributing to the rise of oligopolies three ways, by abandoning antitrust enforcement, by building up regulation in just about every other way, and by soaking the capitalist system in easy money.

Though the point is disputed, it is worth noting that by some measures, industry consolidation has been more pronounced in the United States than in Europe, which has no companies nearly as large or dominant as the American tech giants. Philippon and Gutiérrez have an interesting explanation for why that may be the case. Despite its reputation for coddling state champions, Europe is much tougher in busting up monopolies. When the EU member states began establishing regulatory agencies in the early 1990s, their main concern was to avoid falling under the thumb of other members. The French did not want German bureaucrats telling them what to do in the name of "Europe," and vice versa. The result, Philippon and Gutiérrez write, was a "fiercely independent" European administration, including "the world's most independent antitrust regulator."

While the United States had largely stopped enforcing antitrust laws, Brussels "slowly pushed Europe toward freer and more competitive markets." This is one of the instances in which a smarter government is more active, not less: when it is defending competition in general, not propping up or bailing out individual competitors.

When Biden came into office, he brought in trustbusters intent on promoting real competition, not only containing consumer prices, on the 1970s model. Their focus was on big tech, trying to prevent the giants from walling off access to their internet platforms, which have become global markets for commerce, communication, and much else. They went after Amazon for making it difficult for customers to cancel its shopping service, and punishing vendors for working with rival shopping services. And they challenged the tactics used by Google to cement its dominant position, including paying Apple to make Google the default search engine on iPhones.

The trick for the new trustbusters is to prevent tech giants from killing competition, without killing the giants. Smaller firms simply do not have the billions of dollars required to develop technologies like AI, which may be the key to productivity growth in the future. China was demonstrating how not to do it, its highly politicized and personal crackdown on big tech firms and their CEOs having contributed mightily to the country's economic slowdown. As destructive as oligopolies can be, even the most powerful need to be contained with a deft touch, not populist vengeance. Ideally, the aim would be to level the fields of easy money and overregulation in which trusts grow, so there is less urgent call to bust them up in the first place.

TWELVE

HOW MARKETS GREW TOO BIG TO FAIL

Today the economic leaders of the capitalist world are like the doctor who was trained to spot one affliction and ended up blind to all the others. Since the threat of consumer price inflation had nearly vanished in recent decades, many politicians and government officials came to think that central banks can continue pumping easy money into the economy without regrettable consequences. In the United States, one of the precious few things progressive Democrats and Trump Republicans shared was a fondness for easy money as a way to fund their spending agendas. Never mind that easy money feeds other, equally crippling infirmities.

Full of good intention, these doctors made the system much more fragile. As government money inflated financial markets, and the financial markets grew much larger than the economy, recessions increasingly followed from crises in the markets. Governments quickly learned to step in faster and faster, to make sure market shocks didn't spill over into the economy. By 2019, only 7 percent of the nearly two hundred economies tracked by the International Monetary Fund were in recession, and only 3 percent were expected to fall into recession during the following year—near a record low. The U.S. economy was in recession half the time in the late nineteenth century, one-fifth of the time between the end of World War II and 1980, and just one-tenth of the time after 1980.

If this looks like stability, it isn't. If constant support dampens the business cycle and makes recessions less frequent, it also builds up debt in the system, which makes downturns much more destructive when they do arrive. That is why the Great Recession of 2007–09 was reminiscent of the Great Depression: it was magnified by debts built up over the prior decade.

The long-term problem for capitalism is not fewer or lighter recessions. No one would complain, much less vote for angry populists, because recessions aren't more common. The problem is that the same government interventions that dampen recessions also undermine the subsequent recoveries. Each downturn leaves a bigger pile of debt, and more unproductive corporate creatures of debt, and this waste stunts the subsequent rebounds. In the United States, wild swings in growth—from below 5 percent to above 5 percent—were common before the 1950s but subside after 1980. Illustrated on a chart, this flattening trend looks like the EKG of a dying patient.

Across all advanced countries, creeping stagnation slowed the average pace of economic growth during recoveries from 4 percent before 1980 to 2.5 percent after 2009. In the United States, where the data goes back further, the pace of recoveries fell from more than 7 percent in the late nineteenth and early twentieth centuries to 4 percent after 1945, just over 3 percent after 1980, and less than 2 percent from 2009 until the pandemic hit in 2020—the longest and weakest expansion ever. Meanwhile, Wall Street had enjoyed four decades of increasingly prosperous bull markets, and the 2010s were the best yet.

THE COMMITTEE TO SAVE THE WORLD

In crises, media commentators had begun to celebrate governments and central banks as heroic firefighters, no matter the role they played in starting these fires. In 1999, *Time* ran a cover on "The Committee to Save the World," which captured the worshipful new mood. Published after U.S. authorities had quickly improvised bailouts to slow the spread of the Asian financial crisis, the cover image featured Alan Greenspan, grinning, front and center. Standing just behind Greenspan were Treasury secretary Robert Rubin and Rubin's imminent successor, Lawrence Summers. The story itself traced the personal ties between these financial leaders of the free world, who turn out also to have been tennis buddies.

During subsequent crises, this cooperation grew so tight, it no longer made sense to picture the Fed as a neutral technocracy. The Fed was working ever more closely with the Treasury to organize corporate bailouts, fund the government and its deficit spending, even fill Treasury coffers with proceeds from its exploding asset purchases. In 2008, Treasury secretary Henry Paulson and Fed chair Ben Bernanke worked together as a lobbying tag team, scaring Congress into passing a $700 billion bank relief program, warning that refusal to do so would lead to "financial Armageddon" and "rioting in the streets." When the heads of nine major banks balked, because accepting relief would raise doubts about their solvency, Paulson and Bernanke persuaded them to take it anyway, or expect a knock on the door from regulators. They wanted big banks to accept so that smaller, weaker ones would follow.

Bernanke and Paulson also found novel ways to funnel Treasury money through the central bank and into the economy. The critical departure came as the intensifying crisis started to spark sell-offs in what had been considered entirely safe investments like money markets and commercial paper—the 1970s innovation pioneered by Walter Wriston. Rumors swirled that trouble in the commercial paper market, used by corporations to fund daily operations, might prevent even household names like General Electric from meeting payroll.

To get around rules that limit its own authority to lend to corporations, the Fed teamed up with the Treasury to create "special purpose vehicles," in essence shell companies registered in Delaware, long a haven of light regulation. The Treasury placed funds in the shell company, which the Fed drew on to support the commercial paper market. The story had come full circle: commercial paper was originally invented to dodge Depression-era regulations, and now the Fed was working through lightly regulated Delaware to bail out commercial paper.

The United States was built on the idea that taxation without representation is tyranny, and Fed governors are not elected representatives. "With each new ad hoc emergency rescue program," run by the Fed and backstopped by the Treasury, the chance of blowback was rising. In the central bank's internal deliberations, Fed chairman Bernanke "was highly uneasy about this development for reasons of democratic legitimacy."

The crisis of 2008 also marked a turning point, in that the U.S. government became a major buyer in the financial markets as well as a seller. Before 2008, the government had been mainly a seller of Treasury bonds. This tends to raise interest rates and force corporations to offer even higher rates on their own bonds. During the crisis, the government through the Fed became a major buyer of Treasury bonds and a wide range of other debts, which tends to lower rates, stimulating corporate borrowing and risk-taking.

Long after the crisis of 2008 had passed, the Fed was still the largest buyer in the Treasury market, often buying more than half the U.S. government bonds on sale in a given month. By 2023 the Fed held 22 percent of the Treasuries in circulation, up from 8 percent in 2008. It was thus on a path similar to Japan, where the central bank now owns more than 50 percent of government bonds.

With government as the dominant buyer, seller, and owner of the most common bonds, it becomes an easy money machine, grossly distorting price signals. "The federal government is nationalizing large swaths of the financial markets," warned a *Bloomberg* columnist in early 2020, as the Fed escalated its bond buying in response to the pandemic. Three months later, financier Henry Kaufman warned that "with the central bank and Treasury firmly joined at the hip, the transformation of capitalism into statism is gaining momentum, perhaps irreversibly."

The merged Fed and Treasury have become a standing committee to save the world, a permanent new arm of the state. "The central bank had shown in 2020 that its emergency lending powers could be used to funnel money to just about anyone in times of crisis, given the Treasury's sign-off," writes Jeanna Smialek in *Limitless*, an account of the vast powers accumulated by the Fed during the pandemic. As the Fed reporter for the *New York Times*, Smialek makes the point gently, noting that one reason Fed officials were so slow to back off easy money policies—even with the economy in recovery—was a growing sense of their own importance. Particularly after playing the role of saviors in 2008, "they had become used to understanding themselves as the central players in the U.S. economy." This pivot to bigger government, run by officials who have lost sight of the cardinal rule—do no harm—threatens to further distort capitalism.

MORE FRAGILE

When the price of money is zero, the price of everything else goes bonkers. As interest rates fall toward zero, investors will borrow more money to make more of it. And when the yield on safe government bonds, adjusted for inflation, falls to less than zero, as it did last decade, then investors take the perversely logical next step. They look for higher yield anywhere they can find it, whether in fine art, fine wine, luxury homes, stocks, corporate debt, or better yet, corporate junk bonds, because they yield the most.

The link between stock market returns and interest rate shifts is extremely tight, which explains why Wall Street keeps a closer watch on central banks than on any other arm of government and has small armies of analysts devoted to monitoring and anticipating the next shifts in Fed policy. For the decade that ended in late 2022, by one estimate, half of the increase in U.S. corporate profit margins can be attributed to lower borrowing costs. So it is that four decades of easy money—injected into the world economy at an accelerating pace over the last decade, and at a historically astonishing pace in 2020 and 2021—have inflated financial markets to a scale that dwarfs the global economy.

In 1980, before central banks had contained inflation and started lowering rates, global financial markets including stocks, bonds, and other debt products, such as packages of mortgages, were worth a total of $12 trillion, which was about the same size as the global economy. By 2007, the markets had grown in value to $200 trillion, more than three times the size of the global economy. By late 2019, they had reached $350 trillion, nearly four times the size of the global economy. Then came the pandemic, and after a flash crash, the markets flowered anew in a shower of government money and hit a new record high, more than $390 trillion.

The larger markets get, the bigger the risk they pose. Market shocks make people feel less wealthy, so they spend less even on food and other daily staples, undermining the economy. This negative "wealth effect" grows as the scale of the markets grows, relative to the economy, placing even more pressure on governments to rescue the markets when they stumble. With each crisis, capitalism grows more vulnerable to the next market-driven crisis, yet governments feel increasingly compelled to fuel this self-destructive cycle.

Before World War II, about one in four recessions followed a collapse in stock or home prices (or both). Since the war, that number has jumped to roughly two out of three, and this link has grown tighter in the last three decades. Over that period, market shocks preceded all the big economic crises, including the meltdowns in Japan after 1990, in Asia around 1998, and across the world after 2008. Yet for the most part central bankers, trained to focus on consumer price inflation, were still saying that controlling asset price inflation is not their job.

The debt buildup generated by easy money added to this fragility. Downturns tend to be longer and deeper when the preceding boom is fueled by borrowing, because after the boom goes bust, flattened debtors struggle for years to dig out from under their loans. This is the main reason housing bubbles pose an even greater threat to the economy than stock market bubbles: relatively few investors borrow to buy stocks, while virtually every homeowner in developed countries takes out a mortgage to purchase a home. And lately, easy money has been enabling debt binges all over the world, from mortgage lending to a variety of niches in the corporate world. Fed chairman Powell warned publicly in 2019 that "a highly leveraged business sector could amplify any business downturn."

The constant flow of easy money had made it possible for a new population of debtors to live on the edge. Between 1980 and 2020, the U.S.

credit market, including government and corporate bonds, grew twenty-five-fold, accounting for 275 percent of GDP. Over this forty-year period, as free money poured into the system, the share of corporate bonds that get a junk rating rose from negligible, less than 1 percent, to 25 percent. By the end, another 40 percent was rated just one notch above junk. More than half of all corporate bonds were piled up on the lowest rungs of the debtors' food chain.

Then the pandemic hit, and the shock threatened to demote many companies down a rung, into junk status, or from junk into bankruptcy. Pension funds and other big investors, which are often required to avoid investing in junk companies, would dump their stock. Creditors would refuse further loans or charge much higher rates, driving up business costs and forcing layoffs. The fear gripping the authorities was that the disaster would spread rapidly, from Wall Street to Main Street.

Detailed new histories of the period since 2008, informed by recently released transcripts of Fed deliberations, suggest that the decision to respond with vast new experiments in government relief was not carefully planned. It would not amount to a revolution in thought about the government role in the economy, in the way Keynesianism can be traced to Keynes and his General Theory, published in the 1930s. It was more like an accidental journey, a series of hasty responses to what political science came to dub "states of exception," when normal rules were suspended in favor of "whatever it takes" to stem the crisis at hand. The result, argued political strategist Dan Alamariu, was an ad hoc accumulation of powers that "could trigger the very systemic risks they are trying to stem."

Studies that appeared on the eve of the pandemic showed that, in the era of easy money, markets came to assume that weak companies will not default—even as they borrowed more heavily. The expected default rate of the weakest and strongest borrowers had narrowed, and this was not a good sign. In fact, a growing expectation that even the weak would not default had become a highly reliable predictor of credit market trouble. This makes a kind of sense, in such an abnormal time. When crises are brewing, investors now expect bigger government bailouts, not more corporate bankruptcies.

After failing to anticipate the crisis of 2008, the authorities began combing the past for warning signs. Going back to the sixteenth century, they found, major financial crises have often been preceded by a sharp run-up in debt. So after the troubles of 2008 had passed, government and central banks around the world set up agencies and divisions to monitor "financial stability," through measures like rising debt or asset price inflation in the markets. But they are watching only for the next big meltdown, like 2008 or 1929. They are still largely oblivious to the grinding daily crisis caused by constant government support.

LESS EFFICIENT

When markets are free to allocate capital, they play several useful roles in the economy. They translate the information and insights gathered by millions of investors into prices, which essentially reflect the world's best-educated guess as to which companies and economies are positioned to grow (and to repay their debts) in the future. Those prices in turn steer capital to the companies and countries with the brightest prospects, which in turn fuels economic productivity and growth.

By the 2010s, however, government support or the mere hint of it was distorting prices in the markets. Instead of rising and falling in anticipation of accelerating or decelerating economic growth, markets started moving in one direction: up. Investors started reading signs of slumping economic growth as a good sign for financial markets, because it was sure to trigger new infusions of easy money from central banks.

As the government met each new crisis with more bailouts, more weak companies survived, pushing the rate of defaults far "below what one would expect in a free and competitive market," wrote Jim Reid of Deutsche Bank Research. When the pandemic hit early in 2020, forecasters expected 25 percent of U.S. corporations to go bankrupt in the economic lockdowns that year, breaking the record default rate set in the Great Depression. Within months, as the Fed and Treasury stepped in to rescue companies of all sizes, those forecasts were instead plummeting fast. As it turned out, the default rate peaked at just 6 percent, a rate far below not only the Great Depression but every recession since 1990. Since more troubled companies survived each crisis, each bailout needed to be bigger than the last.

In 2023 a former Fed board member described this snowballing bailout culture to me this way: when "everything the Fed does is exceptional," it creates an expectation in the markets that the response to the next crisis will be "exceptional squared."

Constant relief made markets deeply complacent, and the volatility of stock and bond prices fell to record lows. Between World War II and the global financial crisis, the global stock markets suffered on average a full 20 percent correction once every four years; between 2008 and the pandemic they didn't suffer a single drop of that magnitude (only two near misses). The same point holds if you look at drops of 5, 10, or 15 percent—like cycles of recession and recovery in the economy, the normal rise and fall of markets started to flatten out. Tremors in stock and bond prices were met with new offerings of easy money from central banks, so no global crisis drew much of a reaction from the heavily sedated markets.

For most of financial market history, prices had tended to swing gently around an upward-sloping trend line—and this natural oscillation had become one of the basic guides for investors. When prices rose unusually far above or fell far below the trend, they could be counted on more often than not to move back to trend—or "revert to the mean." The further from trend prices rose or fell, the more likely they were to revert to the mean. If one company or one industry had a great run, the best bet was that it would fall back to earth. Now, however, government had entered the system as a major buyer. And the basic laws of market movements collapsed utterly in the post-2008 world.

Podcaster and investor Joshua Brown pointed out that, as absurd as it might sound, the most successful investment strategy of the 2010s would have been to buy the most expensive tech stocks and then buy more as they rose in price and valuation.

When the cost of borrowing money is zero, it not only puts investors on low alert, it distorts their choices about which assets to buy. Physical assets are seen as relatively low-value in an era when cheap borrowing costs make tangible stuff—machines, factories—inexpensive to buy or replace. The result in the 2010s was that investors got more and more excited about intangible assets—hot brands and new ideas; software, not hardware. Stock prices for firms heavy in intangible assets rose astronomically relative to those of old brick-and-mortar companies. By late 2020, the market value of Uber was higher than that of any carmaker, though it owned no cars. Airbnb was worth more than any hotel chain, though it owned no property. The roughly $6 trillion in physical assets owned by S&P 500 companies amounted to less than 20 percent of their stock market value, a record low, and down from around 50 percent in the 1980s.

In early 2019, investor William Bernstein, asked to name the most important question no one was thinking about, said, "What if the cost of capital never rises again?" One clear implication was more of the same, with more money flowing to the techy and intangible, and a tougher job market for everyone who works in the world you can touch without a keyboard.

Another, as the well-known investor Jeremy Grantham warned in 2021, was that yet more government stimulus was likely to fuel inflation more than output. "If you think you live in a world where output doesn't matter and you can just create paper, sooner or later you're going to do the impossible, and that is bring back inflation," he said. "Interest rates are paper. Credit is paper. Real life is factories and workers and output, and we are not looking at increased output."

The disconnect between markets and the real economy reached a new extreme as the standing committee to save the world mobilized anew during the pandemic. More than doubling down on the steps they had taken in 2008, the U.S. Treasury and the Fed were promising trillions of dollars to prop up companies of all sizes and conditions. By the summer of 2020, the Fed owned debt issued by major companies in virtually every industry, from Apple to Microsoft, Walmart to Home Depot, AT&T, Toyota, Volkswagen America, even a utility held by Berkshire Hathaway. In effect, the government was offering unsolicited financial aid to Warren Buffett.

The message to the markets was that the government considered every company "systemically important," and none of them would be allowed to falter. Many Americans, confined to their homes but flush with new infusions of government cash, began day trading for the first time. Online traders like E-Trade and Charles Schwab saw monthly trading volumes explode by as much as 900 percent. By May, these small investors appeared to be driving an unexpected bull market for classic zombie companies like JCPenney. Its stock rose sixfold in the three weeks after it declared bankruptcy, driven in part by bettors figuring that the government would not allow even zombies to fail.

Commentators described this as a moment of "bizarre" and unprecedented market "insanity," pointing out that stock market investors are generally last in line when companies are dissolved in bankruptcy proceedings. Bondholders and other creditors come first. Often stockholders walk away with nothing. Looked at another way, a stock market boom for bankrupt companies was just the logical next step, after four decades of increasing government intervention on behalf of failing firms. "When you had 11 years of free money, people do stupid things," said investor Stanley Druckenmiller, citing as an example the $80 billion valuation of Dogecoin, "which was invented as a joke. I mean, that can only happen in the world of free money."

Junk bonds, the lifeblood of distressed firms, were having an unexpected heyday as well. Early in the pandemic, investors expected a huge wave of defaults, and nearly tripled the interest rate premium they demand to hold junk corporate debt. After the Fed and Treasury bailouts were announced, those expectations evaporated, and the price investors demand to prop up distressed corporate debtors began falling by May of 2020, even as the pandemic raged on.

Warren Buffett put it well in 2021 when he said that "interest rates are to asset prices as gravity is to matter." Yet the next summer, when I attended his investing festival in Omaha, Buffett had only praise for the Fed and criticism for Wall Street, which he blamed for the "gambling parlor" atmosphere then gripping the markets. His partner, Charlie Munger, who was ninety-six at the time, said that he had never seen "anything like we have now in terms of pure gambling activity going on daily." But by Buffett's definition, blaming Wall Street for the outbreak of speculation on rapidly inflating assets was like blaming Earth for its orbit around the sun. The Fed controls interest rates and the pull of easy money, which humans can resist no more than they can defy gravity.

It was not only the zombie population that was growing fast. So was a close cousin, the class of "profitless firms," which are defined only by their failure to make money (not cover their debts). These money losers were also spreading worldwide. Looking just at the persistently profitless, which have operated in the red for three years in a row, they now account for 25 percent of public firms in the United States, up from 3 percent in 1990.

Rushing to take advantage of the state-inspired market euphoria in 2020, many entrepreneurs moved forward their plans to sell stock to the public. Twenty-two start-up companies went public at an initial valuation of $1 billion or more that year, despite having little revenue to speak of, smashing the record set for profitless IPOs at the height of the dot-com mania. Capitalism had entered a dangerous phase, commentator Steven Pearlstein remarked, in which Wall Street can earn outsize rewards in good times while in bad times, "outsize risks are socialized through government rescues." Even the smart money was following the government money. By mid-2023, a leader of one of the world's largest investment houses admitted to me that his firm was moving into fields like batteries and other green tech—because that was where Biden administration subsidies were going. And most of the U.S. companies moving jobs and production home from China were targeting the same narrow set of industries that had been singled out by the administration for state support. This is not how money gets invested when the markets are working freely.

═══════════

THIRTEEN

WHEN BILLIONAIRES DO BEST

Many Democrats embraced America's growing experiments with easy money as a way to pay for social programs and narrow the wealth gap. But their least favorite president, Donald Trump, the self-proclaimed king of debt, is far from the only tycoon to thrive in a debt-soaked form of capitalism, though he is perhaps the only one to own it so candidly. Four decades of easy money accelerated the rise of a billionaire class that many progressives would like to abolish, and widened the income gaps they would like to close.

Instead of raising productivity and with it economic growth, government money has flooded into financial engineering projects—buyouts, share buybacks, and other strategies to boost stock prices, not build anything new. In the past, financial markets typically reflected and followed the economy, up and down. Now they float only upward, levitating on a magic carpet of stimulus. It is a fine time for the wealthiest investors, who are often of advanced age, but a frustrating time for the working middle class and the young.

Many voices objected—accurately—that Wall Street was gaining at the expense of Main Street. But only a minority recognized that easy money was an important driver of rising wealth inequality—perhaps the most important. Ironically, many of those critics work on Wall Street and spend their lives following the money: where it goes and who is gaining most. They understand, as President Obama once warned them, that unfairness this glaring can end in mobs and "pitchforks." In recent years, finance industry titans like Ray Dalio have warned repeatedly that central bank purchases in the financial markets were fueling wealth inequality and threatening to provoke "some form" of more or less violent "revolution," a view that now has broad support. In a mid-2022 survey, 50 percent of Americans agreed that "in the next several years, there will be civil war in the United States."

To be clear, the talk of abolishing billionaires is utopian, dangerous, and impractical. Nations that tried to eliminate an economic or financial elite ended up only concentrating power and wealth in a political elite, from the Jacobins through the Soviet Communists and the postcolonial autocrats in Africa and Latin America. No society that rewards merit will end up with equal incomes or wealth, but capitalist societies need to recognize when they are slipping too far out of balance, when wealth and income inequality is arising as much from dysfunctions in the system as from merit or hard work. Those imbalances inspire the kind of popular anger and frustration we are seeing now.

WEALTH INEQUALITY

Inequality poisons the politics of capitalist democracies as surely as it distorts their economies. But given how wildly conservatives and liberals disagree on even the basic facts of inequality, it's hard to decide which facts to use. The story of rising inequality below rests on the new World Inequality Database (WID), established by progressive economists who hope it will become the standard used by governments to track this flammable issue.

Talk of a second Gilded Age, evoking the era of the robber barons, has been bubbling for years. In many capitalist countries, the share of wealth held by the richest citizens has been rising for decades. In the United States, the wealth of the 1 percent peaked near 50 percent of the total in 1929. Then the 1 percent's share fell through the Depression and World War II to around 30 percent by 1950. During what many consider the thirty "glorious" years of postwar liberalism, when the welfare state was consolidating, the 1 percent saw their share fall to a record low, just above 20 percent, in 1980. It is at that point, with the shift toward mounting public debts and exploding financial markets, that the wealth of the super-rich started to expand again as a share of the total.

It's also important to narrow in on exactly who was gaining and who was losing share in this post-1980 period. The 1 percent saw their share of the wealth rise by more than half to 35 percent, and they were not the big share gainers; they were pretty much the only gainers. The next 9 percent were losing share, and so were the next 40 percent (those between 10 and 50 percent in the wealth distribution). In short the middle and upper middle classes were losing share to the rich.

The bottom 50 percent never held more than a negligible share of the national wealth, yet in the last decade, many managed to lose what little they had. The measures here are net wealth, which first adds up any assets a family can sell including stocks, bonds, and property, then subtracts its debts. For most of the period since the 1960s, the net wealth of the poorer half hovered between 1 to 2 percent of the total. Between 2007 and 2016, as easy money policies added to the fortunes of the top 1 percent, it pushed the net worth of the bottom half below zero. They owed more on college loans, mortgages, and other debt than they owned. And what little they did own outright was "often to be found parked on the street," writes Karen Petrou. It was the family car.

As interest rates dropped not only to new lows but also to newly stable lows in the early 2000s, the drama of rising inequality raced toward a climactic turn, when the wealth share of the 1 percent eclipsed that of the 90 percent for the first time in decades. This was the tinder for the political backlash against inequality that followed, uniting much of the middle class and the bottom 50 percent against the 1 percent.

Push the data back in time and worldwide, as Thomas Piketty has done, and you find a very similar story in Europe going back to 1900. The recent gains in wealth have been concentrated at the very top, and the bottom 50 percent never controlled more than 7 percent of the wealth in Europe. Again, the big declines are in the middle class.

These shifts in wealth are roughly the distribution in gains one would expect in a period when easy money is pumping up the value of financial assets, most of which are owned by the very rich. In the United States, the top 10 percent own 72 percent of all financial assets and 93 percent of all stocks. But most of that wealth is controlled by the top 1 percent: for example, they own 54 percent of all stocks by value, while the next 9 percent own 39 percent, and the bottom 90 percent own just 7 percent. That is a striking sign of how wealth is concentrated at the top, particularly the very top.

When analysts break down this trend year by year, it shows that the rich gain the most during boom periods, and also lose the most during bust periods. This means that the more governments intervene to prevent the busts and to keep asset prices rising all the time, the more they widen wealth inequality and generational inequality as well.

In 2021, Fed researchers ran their own analysis and found a very similar story to the one reflected in the WID, but based on how fast fortunes are growing at the top. Since the 1980s, wealth in the United States has quadrupled among the 1 percent, tripled among the next 9 percent, and doubled among the next 40 percent; it rose not at all for the bottom 50 percent.

Even Donald Trump, who often claimed that stock market gains are good for "your 401K," generally avoided the claim that they are equally good for everyone. Suggestions that the stock market is somehow broad-based because more than half of Americans own stocks are misleading, since the figure is not much more than half (58 percent), and most own very few shares.

Top Fed officials have often denied or downplayed the impact of easy money on inequality, arguing in part that low rates and heavy bond buying generate a "wealth effect" that encourages spending and lifts the whole economy. In 2013, Dallas Fed president Richard Fisher demurred. At a meeting of Fed governors, he warned that more bond buying would benefit mainly the bluest of blue-chip private investors: "It has, I believe, had a wealth effect, but principally for the rich and the quick—the Buffetts, the KKRs, the Carlyles, the Goldman Sachses . . . those who can borrow money for nothing and drive bonds and stocks and property higher in price, and profit goes to their pocket." Fisher may have sounded a bit like a frustrated socialist, but he is really a frustrated capitalist, a former investment banker and founder of his own money management firm.

Even most of the 1 percent cannot afford to invest with the private funds that Fisher is describing here. These are hedge funds, venture capital funds, or private equity funds that borrowed at near zero rates and used the proceeds to invest in assets that return more than zero, and not necessarily that much more. Even if they reinvest in safe government bonds that return 2 to 5 percent, big investors can multiply the scale of their returns by using leverage—heavy borrowing—to increase the size of their bets.

Funds that operate at this level cater mainly to institutions or "high net worth individuals," who own more than $50 million in assets. Over the last two decades, the global value of the debt-driven private markets rose elevenfold, or four times faster than the value of public stock markets. Often private funds require a minimum commitment of $5 million, so mere millionaires need not apply.

Ken Griffin, founder and CEO of Citadel, one of the world's largest hedge funds, responded to an interviewer's question in 2023 about the market frenzy around artificial intelligence by saying that AI was indeed a "big theme" for Citadel. The problem, as he saw it, was that it could not be a big theme for small investors, because the twenty-year boom in regulation had pushed so many promising AI companies out of public markets and into the land of the unicorns—the privately owned, billion-dollar companies. "This is a tragic mistake that we're making on behalf of American investors," he said. "Because for the average family, they don't have a chance to invest in the start-ups or the mid-size companies that become the Apples of today."

In money-magnet cities like New York, London, and Miami, the explosion in private wealth was feeding a parallel boom in private communities, exclusive getaway resorts, and eating clubs like Zero Bond, Enterprise, and Casa Cruz. These clubs call themselves restaurants, but with special privileges for "partners" who pay $250,000 a year to get in the door. New York University urbanologist Mitchell Moss sees these gilded salons as an unwelcome product of the era of easy money, telling the *Financial Times*: "Fundamentally, there is too much wealth in New

York City so joining a club is an easy, mindless way to park money in hopes of enhancing your nightlife."

Private funds are in many cases part of the shadow banking system, and the regulators who inadvertently encouraged the rise of shadow banks in the 2010s also accidentally nurtured these closed circles of vast wealth. In 2021, a National Bureau of Economic Research paper traced how shadow banks fuel inequality, and vice versa. Setting out to "unveil" who owns how much of U.S. household and government debt, their results also challenged a widespread belief that American borrowing has been funded for decades by a "global saving glut," meaning savings by foreigners, particularly savers in China.

To the contrary, the paper's authors found that half the surge in U.S. borrowing since the 1980s was "financed by the rest of the world, and half was financed by the top 1 percent" of American households. Not only have the rich been saving more as the rest of America saves less, but the rich "directly finance the borrowing of the non-rich and the government." In short, rising inequality "generates a saving glut of the rich, which can push an economy into a debt trap characterized by low interest rates, high debt levels, and output below potential."

At the same time, researchers were beginning to trace a link between periods of rising inequality and major financial crises. One reason may be related to the saving glut of the rich; as inequality rises, the rich save more and lend more to the less well-off, easing credit conditions and encouraging the kind of risky borrowing that melted down in 2008. In a 2020 paper, the San Francisco Fed looked at seventeen countries going back to the 1870s and found that a widening income share for the top 1 percent of households is a powerful predictor of financial crises. The upshot was that the growing inequality of the system is closely linked to its growing fragility.

Generational Inequality,
or Who Pays for Whom in Retirement?

By constantly propping up financial markets, the government is almost by definition providing welfare for the mainly older members of the 1 percent.

Between 1989 and 2016, families headed by a father or mother under thirty-five saw their net wealth stagnate at around $12,500. Families headed by a person over sixty-five saw their wealth nearly double over that period, to nearly $400,000.

And one big reason younger families were seeing no gain was the drag of mounting college or mortgage debts. Millennials now control only 3 percent of America's wealth—a record low for any postwar generation. Baby boomers controlled five times more when they were at the same stage of life, back in the '80s. Three out of four adults under forty are trying to build up savings, and dig their way out of debt, meaning they lost ground as the return on savings accounts hovered near zero through the 2010s, right up to 2022.

In that light, the unexpected surge in generational disaffection with capitalism, and support for socialists promising higher taxes on wealth, is not surprising. The potential for generational conflict in coming years is vast, given that nearly two out of three millennials say their retirement security depends on how much they inherit, while more than half of American parents count on help from their children in retirement. Today, half of American thirty-year-olds make more than their parents did, down from 90 percent in 1970, so fewer and fewer of them are in a position to help Mom and Dad in the golden years.

Government's contribution to inequality has also been dramatic in the market for housing: a generation ago, it took the typical young family three years to save up the down payment on a home; by 2019, thanks to no return on savings, it was taking nineteen years. Millennials were also nearly twice as likely to be stuck living at home as prior generations. Nearly half of the twentysomething generation live with their parents, up from a third in the 1980s, and most Americans now blame this new reality on a "broken economic situation" that makes it tough for the young to succeed financially. The pattern is similar in Europe, where, for example, the share of young Brits who own their own homes has fallen to 45 percent from 67 percent in the 1990s.

Though much was written about house prices skyrocketing during the pandemic, supposedly driven by an exodus from crowded cities, this exodus was a small part of the story. Prices began rising long before the pandemic hit in early 2020 and were rising in cities as well as in rural and suburban areas. The force driving the boom was not the pandemic; it was easy money. Throughout the 2010s, easy money was pushing up the price of stocks faster than houses, and expensive houses faster than cheap houses, with both forces contributing greatly to the rise in inequality.

By 2021, mortgage rates had reached a record low of less than 3 percent in the United States, and under 2 percent in Europe. That summer, though the economic recovery was well underway and housing prices were rising at a double-digit pace in many capitalist societies, the Fed was still intervening aggressively to prop up the market, buying up to $40 billion in mortgage-backed securities each month.

Those purchases drove mortgage rates down, pushing home prices up and out of reach for many young families. Typically, housing is said to become "unaffordable" when the average price exceeds three times the median family income. Numbeo, a research firm, tracks home prices in more than five hundred cities internationally, and the share that are affordable has fallen steadily for many years, dropping below one in ten by 2021. In the least affordable cities, including New York and Los Angeles, the median home price had reached more than ten times the average income.

Though the housing boom started before Covid hit, it continued through the recession that followed, which is highly unusual. Going back at least to the 1970s, housing had always slumped during recessions, both in the United States and worldwide. People lose jobs and stop dreaming of bigger homes. But in the second quarter of 2020, the low point of the worst recession since the 1940s, housing prices rose 4 percent worldwide, and 15 percent in the United States.

This was a property boom created by government at the expense of the middle- and low-income homebuyer, another sharp illustration of what's gone wrong with capitalism. When prices are shaped by easy money as much as or more than by genuine demand, the result is often a severely skewed allocation of resources. Many investors were buying homes during the pandemic not as a shelter but as an alternative to stocks and bonds, which were even pricier.

Younger generations are already more likely than earlier generations to be stuck in freelance jobs without benefits and to have no option other than to live with their parents. Now millennials were losing out of the real estate bidding wars in the pandemic. They would be ready to close on a house, only to have richer buyers or speculators outbid them at the last minute, in cash. No wonder they are disaffected, and eager to see someone step in and fix this twisted version of capitalism.

AN UNEXPECTED QUESTION FOR THE NEW GILDED AGE

The 2010s was the decade when inequality finally exploded as a political issue, and the main target was not the 1 percent, or even the 0.01 percent. It was billionaires, or the 0.00003 percent. Not since the first billionaire—John D. Rockefeller in 1916—had America ever questioned whether this class of wealth should be allowed "to exist." Now a call to "abolish" billionaires was bubbling up from the progressive left, and the issue took a front seat in the national conversation. "It is fascinating that for the first time in my life, people are saying, 'Okay, should you have billionaires?'" said Bill Gates in 2019.

Looking back, the timing makes perfect sense. The global population of billionaires had risen from three hundred at the turn of the millennium to two thousand by 2019. Then in the next twelve months, that number spiked by another seven hundred, to twenty-seven hundred, as government rescues and bailouts drove the stock market upward. The total wealth of billionaires worldwide rose from $8 trillion to $13 trillion in 2020 alone.

In the United States, the number of billionaires rose by one hundred—to a total of seven hundred. Driven by stock prices in sectors getting the biggest boost from easy money, namely big tech, the largest fortunes were growing from tens to hundreds of billions. Sums that once would have seemed impossible in a lifetime, larger than the annual income of most countries. Tesla founder Elon Musk saw his wealth increase in 2020 from $20 billion to $150 billion. Amazon founder Jeff Bezos saw his fortune expand from $114 billion to a peak of more than $200 billion: He gained more wealth in those twelve months than the bottom 25 percent of Americans have accumulated in a lifetime.

At the very top, however, Europe's leading tycoons are by some measures even more dominant than America's, if their wealth is measured as a share of their home economy. During the Gilded Age, oil baron John D. Rockefeller became the most dominant tycoon in modern history, with a fortune equal at its peak in the 1910s to 1.6 percent of U.S. GDP. By 2021 there were at least seventeen modern-day Rockefellers spread across nine countries—but not one in the United States. Though Jeff

Bezos was in that year the world's richest man, his net worth was still less than 1 percent of GDP in the United States.

Europe, where central banks had been rolling out easy money at least as fast as the Fed, was home to many Rockefellers. Sweden, despite its reputation as a socialist model, had the most: five billionaires with wealth in excess of 1.6 percent of their nation's GDP. Canada had one. The single most dominant tycoon was fashion king Amancio Ortega, whose fortune amounted to nearly 6 percent of Spain's GDP.

France had two latter-day Rockefellers, Françoise Bettencourt Meyers and Bernard Arnault, whose fortune rivaled that of Ortega's in scale, at more than 5 percent of French GDP. By 2022, demonstrators in Paris were marching against plans to raise the retirement age, suggesting funding pensions with higher taxes on billionaires instead: they carried an image of Arnault on Wanted posters. This second Gilded Age looks most like its nineteenth-century precursor in countries with a socialist reputation, like France and Sweden.

The political targeting of billionaires in Europe was more personal than in the United States. This may be due in part to where the European fortunes were coming from, not new technologies but from a luxury goods industry that dates to the seventeenth-century court of Louis XIV. By the summer of 2023, French luxury firms led by LVMH accounted for a record 30 percent share of European stock market gains over the prior twelve months. Arnault, the founder of LVMH, had for a time surpassed Elon Musk as the world's wealthiest person, with a net worth over $210 billion. If not outright decadent, as many critics had it, there was something at least outdated in Europe's luxury-driven version of capitalism.

In the United States, the anger was less likely to spill into the streets, but it was growing there as well. Before 2010, the fortunes of American billionaires amounted to about 10 percent of GDP—which was close to the average share in other developed countries. But that share had spiked to 15 percent of GDP by 2014, fueled by easy money pouring out of the Fed, and it was not long before the revolt began. Launching his bid for the White House in 2016, Sanders became the first presidential candidate to frame his campaign as an assault on "the billionaire class."

Even moderate Democrats were soon taking up the theme. During the 2020 presidential race, Joe Biden hammered the hundreds of billions added to billionaire fortunes during the Trump presidency. He promised not to abolish billionaires, as progressives would, but to rein them in by taxing their wealth heavily.

By that year, an overwhelming majority of Democrats, and a solid majority of Republicans, agreed that the United States was not as equal as it should be. The growing inequities were threatening to spark a revolt against the essence of capitalism: the process of wealth creation. Most Americans supported a wealth tax. Even in late 2022, as the return of tight money was cratering stock prices and the number of latter-day Rockefellers was falling from seventeen to twelve worldwide, the *New York Times* was still printing calls for "abolishing" billionaires through regulation and taxes.

EASY MONEY AND INCOME INEQUALITY

The Fed denies that it has become the "Engine of Inequality," the title of a 2021 book on the central bank by Karen Petrou. The Fed rejoinder is that if the impact of easy money is studied comprehensively, factoring in its effect on jobs and incomes, not just financial wealth, then on balance it does not fuel inequality. The last three Fed chairs—Powell, Yellen, and Bernanke—have all adopted this view, arguing throughout the 2010s that lower-income families were gaining as unemployment dropped to record lows. In 2015, after his tenure was over, Bernanke dismissed the impact of easy money on inequality as "almost certainly modest and transient."

Their peers abroad, including at the Bank of England, have been less adamant, deflecting rather than dismissing the charge. They say that their job as central bankers is to steady the growth in national income—how that income is distributed is a political question, best addressed by legislators.

And yet the rise in income inequality since 1980, like the rise in wealth inequality, coincides exactly with the era of easy money and easy-to-get government bailouts. The numbers below are also from the World Inequality Database. By late 2023, its story of rising income inequality was under challenge from scholars who argue that, corrected for taxes, benefits, and above all unreported earnings, income inequality has in fact barely risen in the United States since the 1960s. The result was bitter and highly politicized debate, resting in large part on conflicting guesstimates of who hides more business and investment income from the taxman—the rich or the rest. Until that debate is resolved, which may be never, popular perception will be shaped by evidence obvious to the naked eye. Cross from Gross Pointe into Detroit, the Upper East Side into East Harlem, or over any border between rich and struggling neighborhoods in America, and it is hard to dismiss widening inequality as a statistical illusion.

During the Roaring Twenties, the share of national income that went to the top 1 percent peaked above 20 percent, and stayed that high through much of the New Deal. In subsequent decades the share controlled by the 1 percent would fall by half to 10 percent, first as blue-collar wages rose during World War II, later as the Great Society programs of the 1960s and '70s shifted income shares to the middle class. Then came the era of constant government deficits, rising debts, and easy money, and the income share of the 1 percent started to rise steadily; by 2022 it had climbed back up to more than 20 percent. Talk of a second Gilded Age was no longer just talk.

Unlike wealth inequality, where the biggest gaps opened up between the super-rich and the middle classes, income gaps were opening up from the top to the bottom of the income scale. The top 1 percent gained more than the next 9 percent, who gained more than the next 40 percent, while the bottom 50 percent lost the most. More families saw their incomes fall to well below the median, which is to say they were falling below the lower middle class. That alone goes a long way toward explaining growing popular resentment.

This is a basic problem for the Fed's self-defense: incomes were growing for all classes, but were growing fastest for the richest Americans. The 0.01 percent were doing even better than the 1 percent. Since the early 1980s, the 0.01 percent have seen their share of national income more than double, outpacing all other classes, and the largest contributor to that gain was capital income—steady dividends and payouts from investments.

As more of the money printed by the Fed flowed into the financial markets, naturally "income growth thus shifted from labor to the owners of property," including stocks, bonds, and exotic derivatives, writes historian Jonathan Levy. The biggest income gains flowed to the finance industry, which now takes home nearly 10 percent of U.S. wages, double its share in 1980. One in seven members of the top 1 percent are finance professionals, and this share has also doubled since 1980. Incomes were also rising in services like restaurants or home health care, but not as fast, and demand for these services grew especially fast "where the best-off lived." Proximity increased the likelihood of friction between people who were enjoying rapid increases in income and those who were not.

The BIS—the global bank for central banks—put an interesting stamp on this story. In a broad survey of the literature, it found that when the Fed is buying assets in the financial markets, the boost to the economy fades in short order to zero but the boost to the markets lingers. Over time, the impact on stock prices is ten times larger than the impact on economic output. Other studies have confirmed the point: when the Fed steps in as a buyer in the markets, it has a passing effect on the real economy, and a lasting effect on asset prices, thus widening both income and wealth inequality.

This process reached absurd extremes during the pandemic, as open-ended promises of easy money continued to drive up the value of the markets, and particularly of the superstar tech giants. Concentrated control over markets for goods and services encourages its equally troubling twin, concentrated power in labor markets.

It's widely understood, and true, that a growing share of national income is going to corporate profit rather than wages—which include the income of very high-salaried executives. It's widely believed, but not really true, that this gap is opening rapidly inside companies. The top 1 percent in any given firm typically earns about twenty times more than the bottom 90 percent, and that gap is only slightly wider now than in 1980. CEO pay rose over that period from thirty times the median worker to about 375 times and then leveled off, even retreated a bit, after 2000. During the pandemic, CEOs saw their pay rise anew, lifted by their stock options, to 400 times that of the median worker.

The larger part of income inequality is explained by growing gaps between companies—or, as Peter Furman and Jason Orszag have put it, "all of the workers at successful companies like Google and Goldman Sachs are being paid more relative to all the workers at less successful companies." Not facing serious competition, and earning a dominant share of national profits, the giant companies can afford to pay higher wages and salaries than the rest. The growing gap between firms can explain two-thirds of the rise in wage inequality since 1980, and not only in the United States. This is "one of the most robust" findings of studies across capitalist economies, from the United States to France, Germany, and Sweden.

Some of the giants pay very well, which is why college grads scramble to land a job at Apple, Amazon, or Alphabet. But those big companies can employ only so many, and as they take a growing share of overall sales and revenue, the labor share of GDP is falling. The gap between the tech superstar firms, their well-compensated employees, and the rest has become a growing concern. "Corporate inequality" has joined wealth and income inequality on the list of threats to capitalism.

Dominant corporate influence over local labor markets in individual towns or counties is called monopsony, a close cousin of monopoly. A growing share of U.S. counties are dominated by a single employer, or just a handful of employers, which also helps to explain why America is not as mobile a society as it once was. Despite the flood of recent headlines about job hopping in the gig economy, the reality is that Americans are less likely to move to new places, industries, or occupations or to switch employers within the same occupation.

In the period before the early 1970s and the shift to constant deficits, big government, and solidifying corporate power, Americans were twice as likely to move to another state, 50 percent more likely to move within their state, and 25 percent more likely to switch employers within the same occupation. By the late 2010s, companies were not only creating jobs but also destroying jobs at the slowest rates recorded outside a recovery since the records begin in the 1970s. "Just about everywhere you look in the economy there is less dynamism, fluidity, and churn," wrote Furman and Orszag.

Internal migration, long fundamental to American dynamism, particularly relative to more sedentary societies of Europe and Japan, has slowed sharply—contrary to popular belief. In the early 1990s, about 3 percent of the U.S. population moved between states each month; now about 1.5 percent do—otherwise the ongoing exodus from California, New York, and the Midwest to Florida and Texas would be even more dramatic. There are many possible reasons for this creeping immobility, but the growing dominance of local labor markets by one employer helps explain it. Americans can't move to towns where there are limited job opportunities.

If the boss in a company town has a lot of control, the boss in a company county has more, leaving locals with fewer choices and less leverage in job negotiations. Most CEOs, and many highly skilled professionals, such as electrical engineers, are required to sign contracts that restrict their freedom to move to rival firms in the same industry. But recent research shows that these "non-compete" clauses "are surprisingly common throughout the labor market," extending even to fast-food restaurants. To the challenge of getting by on low pay as a checkout clerk is added this obstacle to leaving for a slightly higher-paying burger joint. One of every five American workers has signed one of these agreements; they are another way corporations are using growing market power to limit mobility and wages.

Americans don't like to see themselves as limited by their parents' accomplishments, but they are. Fifty to 60 percent of Americans' income can be explained by their parents' income, which makes the United States one of the least upwardly mobile societies in the developed world, ahead only of England.

One of the leading explanations for this stagnation is the "Great Gatsby Curve," which shows that countries with the widest income gaps—like the United States—tend to be the ones in which it is most difficult to climb the income ladder. Even conservatives who accept inequality as a natural outcome of competition should be concerned about a society that is solidifying into fixed income classes, because it undermines equality of opportunity—a cornerstone of democratic capitalism.

Further depressing the spending power of ordinary Americans, record low interest rates directly erode what they can earn by holding money in a savings account. Below the top 1 percent, Americans just stick most of their extra money in the bank. Since 2008, by one estimate, U.S. savers have lost $4 trillion owing to rock-bottom rates on savings accounts. One result was that many more Americans were living on the margins, and needed income support, when the pandemic hit.

Scholars of inequality have, of course, cited many other causes for the growing concentration of incomes and wealth at the top, and these often mirror the explanations for concentrating corporate power. Globalization has opened up worldwide opportunities for the largest companies, and their founders and investors. Technology has had a similar effect, concentrating the profits and income from global internet platforms in Silicon Valley. These forces have shifted the flow of income to capital and away from labor, accelerated by the decline of unions and the erosion of labor-bargaining power.

Some of these forces are now reversing. Globalization has given way to deglobalization, which may narrow one advantage of the largest firms and, as fewer jobs shift overseas, boost labor-bargaining power. Unions are staging a comeback—witness the big contract victories won by unions against the large U.S. automakers in 2023. As populations age and workforces shrink worldwide, negotiating leverage is likely to shift even further back toward labor, further boosting wages. A more limited government could promote these shifts by encouraging competition and reducing the flow of power and wealth to superstar firms.

It won't do, however, for politicians and central bankers to keep denying their role in fueling inequality. They need to recognize that an enabling state has created the business environment, cosseted in regula-

tions and rescues and overflowing in debt, in which the biggest corporations thrive at the expense of the rest. Yes, big firms are often global, and
the biggest are arising in tech, but as we've seen, these giants are arising
across industries, and raising the income and wealth of the 1 percent and
especially the 0.1 percent. The distortions of corporate inequality are
mirrored by widening personal equality.

Governments and central banks, by working together to sustain an
easy money culture they hoped would eliminate pain for everyone, are
making the inequality gap that much worse. Their blindness goes back
to the way their advisers, the elite economists, see the world, on high
from the ivory towers, focused on abstract models. The officials who
control the flow of easy money are unwilling to acknowledge its role in
driving wealth and income inequality, even when some of the biggest
beneficiaries of those flaws—financial tycoons—are warning loudly of
the dangers. But it is the tycoons who spend every waking moment
following the money—in the real world not in theory, writes Petrou.
"Money knows instinctively and mercilessly where inequality lies," she
writes. Government would be wise to listen to its warnings.

For now, political leaders appear intent on doing what they are
doing—playing a larger role in the economy as spender, buyer, and
regulator. To address inequality they propose to tinker with the rules.
Offering solutions based on their faith in big government and its tools,
liberals would, for example, raise wealth taxes, change labor laws, or
increase support for middle-class housing, education, or job training.
None of that, however, addresses the root causes of the gigantism infecting America's corporate and billionaire classes. If liberals are serious
about containing inequality, personal and corporate, they should learn
to hate the culture of easy money.

FOURTEEN

A NEW ANSWER TO THE PRODUCTIVITY PARADOX

I f you had to pick one explanation for why so many people are unhappy with capitalism, the rise in inequality would be a popular choice. Billionaires make for a fat target. But the fall in productivity is the more subtle and persuasive one. When each worker produces more, companies can raise wages without raising prices. The economy can grow without generating crippling inflation. The economic pie can grow steadily for everyone. If productivity growth is falling, as it has been for the last two decades, more and more people will be fighting over what is left.

Productivity growth is the number that reveals whether capitalism is working. Its broad decline over the last five decades—a period of rapid technological progress—has been called the Solow Paradox, after Nobel laureate Robert Solow. In 1987 Solow pointed out—in an offhand remark in a book review—that "you can see the computer age everywhere but in the productivity statistics." His evidence was from studies showing that over the previous fifteen years or so, service firms were investing more in computers than manufacturing firms but gaining less in productivity. Some economists were even arguing that the spread of computers was lowering productivity growth.

Ever since Solow, we have been looking for an answer to his paradox in the computer itself. Pessimists, led by the economist Robert Gordon, say that during the Industrial Revolution, innovations like steam power and electricity had sweeping applications, which lifted output per worker across many industries. By comparison, digital technology has a much less sweeping impact or, worse, is less a tool than a distraction. In this view, it is no surprise that output per worker would be falling, now that workers can watch cat videos and read *BuzzFeed* on the job.

Tech optimists offer two basic responses. One is that the productivity measurements do not capture the impact of digital technology: online search, for example, saves shoppers and researchers countless hours, but time not spent doesn't show up in output figures. Or, they say, digital technology will raise productivity eventually, just wait. Even during the Industrial Revolution, new technologies did not raise productivity until a critical mass of businesses had figured out how to apply the latest innovations, whether steam, electric, or combustion engines.

Once businesses learn how to apply the next big innovation, the next productivity boom will begin. By 2023, many commentators were saying that innovation is here, in the latest forms of artificial intelligence; a Brookings Institution team predicted that these "machines of the mind" could raise U.S. output by as much as 60 percent over the next twenty years.

Solow's offhand remark focused the search for answers on the computer and related digital technologies, but evidence for an alternative answer was accumulating elsewhere. Timing offers a clue as to what it might be. The productivity decline unfolded in two waves, the first from the early 1970s to the mid-1990s; the second, even more rapid decline started around 2005. Those periods of decline were interrupted by a brief revival, limited mainly to the United States.

What, other than the computer revolution, dates to the 1970s? The relentless rise in government intervention, and the dysfunctions that come with it, including the massive misallocation of capital into unproductive and profitless companies.

Constant deficit spending goes back to the 1970s; the culture of bank and corporate bailouts took root in the 1980s. The easy money era hit full stride around 2000, rewarding blind financial risk and undermining creative destruction. Bigger and more inefficient companies started to prosper at the expense of newer, more nimble ones. It is at that point, around the turn of the millennium, that the long era of expanding government shows up decisively in slumping productivity statistics.

THE IMPACT OF ZOMBIES ON PRODUCTIVITY

The same economists who in 2008 first described the spread of zombies in Japan found that these companies were damaging the economy two ways, through their own incompetence and in the corrosive effect their very presence had on other companies in the same industry. As it became clear that zombies were spreading worldwide, researchers began watching to see if they have a similarly enervating effect outside Japan. And they do.

Firms start to show signs of severe decay two years before they can no longer cover their interest payments, and fall into the zombie class. As they fall deeper into debt, they start investing less, and selling off assets. Compared to healthy firms, their investment growth is 2 to 3 percentage points lower for hard assets like factories and machines, and 3 to 4 percentage points lower for soft assets, like software or branding. Once they have transformed into zombies, their stock of assets of all kinds, machines or brand image, has fallen on average to less than half that of a normal company. Having so little to work with, zombies generate less profit and create fewer jobs. Their employment growth is nearly 10 percentage points lower on average than that of a normal firm.

It might seem that a class of companies this sluggish should pose little obstacle to reasonably healthy competitors. Though a zombie may be hard to kill, surely it is easy to outrun. Before 2000, that was still true. Healthy firms were able to borrow at significantly lower cost, and faced less pressure to sell off assets. Then, over the last two decades, increasingly friendly government "forbearance" narrowed what should be the natural advantages of healthy firms. With governments and central banks waging a campaign to keep weak companies alive, zombies became stubbornly difficult to dislodge.

The result is one industry after another clogged with zombies, generating "congestion effects" that undermine the health of all companies in that industry. Instead of killing off zombies, competitors start showing similar traits. Every dollar the zombies in an industry borrow, every worker they hire, and every machine they buy makes it more expensive for healthy rivals to borrow, invest, and hire. At the same time, zombies create an excess of supply that pushes prices down and makes it even more difficult for healthy companies to survive in the industry or for new competitors to enter it.

Zombie congestion tends to turn the normal dynamic of creative destruction on its head. The heavier the congestion, the more likely an industry is to see more healthy firms folding, and fewer new ones entering. The healthy firms that hang on in a zombie-infested industry show signs of stagnation, with investment growth around 30 percent lower and job growth around 15 percent lower than the average for healthy firms in industries less marred by zombification. The bottom line is that zombies are not only less productive than other firms, they lower the productivity growth of other firms in the same industry.

The destructive impact of zombies follows the now-familiar pattern, increasing after the year 2000, as the bailout culture extended its support to more and more companies. Junk debtors began falling into default at a slower rate than one would have expected based on growth in the economy. With fewer weak firms shutting down, productivity began its relentless decline. The Deutsche Bank researchers who reported this pattern were careful to point out that their work demonstrated correlation, which does not prove causation. But they suggested that it is likely not just coincidence that productivity has been falling during a period of ever more generous government support for dying companies.

In the summer of 2019, Larry Summers urged central bankers to at least consider the possibility that ultra-low rates were behind many of the ills of modern capitalism, including financial fragility, the rise of zombies, "and reduced economic dynamism."

Zombie banks, which also survive on government support, help magnify the productivity slump, too. In 2021, the team led by Viral Acharya at NYU argued that when governments are backstopping loans from all banks, the blanket subsidy encourages "diabolical sorting": in effect, zombie banks supporting weak companies. By building on the easy money culture that created this "zombie lending channel," governments risk transforming "transitory shocks into phases of delayed recovery and potentially permanent output losses." This sorting would only grow more diabolical, they wrote, if government guarantees continued to grow more extreme with each new crisis.

In its latest back-of-the-envelope calculation, the Bank for International Settlements suggests that the rise of zombies may explain half of the productivity slowdown in advanced economies since the late 1980s. And going forward, every 1 percentage point increase in the zombie population may shave another tenth of a point off productivity. If that doesn't sound like much, remember that since productivity is lately growing at an average rate barely over 1 percent in the United States, even less in Europe and Japan, each additional tenth represents a sharp deceleration. Should those estimates prove even roughly correct, that is a serious hit, since each step down in productivity growth is an equal step down in economic growth. Researchers at the OECD have warned, similarly, that zombies are a previously unrecognized cause of the global productivity slowdown, raising "questions about our societies' ability to make good on promises to current and future generations."

BIG, POWERFUL, AND A BURDEN ON PRODUCTIVITY

Though monopolies and oligopolies have an unfailingly bad reputation among the general public, economists have always taken a more ambiguous view. Even Joseph Schumpeter distinguished between good and bad monopolies. The bad ones rise and hold on to power by exploiting government contacts and regulations, invest little, and do nothing to raise productivity. Good ones rise on the strength of innovation, kill off rivals who do not innovate, and have a positive impact on productivity.

Back in the 1990s, Walmart gained a public image as an evil empire that was running Main Street shops out of business, but many experts saw it in a different light. If towns banned Walmart, the local market would lose fewer businesses and would appear less concentrated and more competitive. But Walmart was far more productive than the typical Main Street retailer because of the way it applies digital technology to managing its stores. If towns welcomed Walmart, weaker local retailers would go out of business, and the market might appear less competitive—but productivity would go up.

In fact, studies by the McKinsey Global Institute and other think tanks have shown that the late 1990s productivity revival in the United States was driven largely by the retail sector, which is to say largely by Walmart and its copycats finding a way to apply new data technology in useful ways. Walmart, Home Depot, Best Buy, and other big-box retail chains rolled out hugely practical innovations, from checkout scanners and credit card readers to digital tools for inventory control. Many independent retailers could not keep up and failed, but productivity rose fast enough in retail chains and a few other industries to push productivity up on average nationwide. At a moment like that, it is hard to make a free market argument against oligopolies, because rising productivity has such broad benefits for society.

That was the nineties, however. Not only have sales been concentrating in most U.S. industries since then, but they are more and more likely to be concentrating in the bad kind of oligopoly, rising more on the strength of easy money and lobbying than on investment in new plants, equipment, and R&D. In this new environment, it is easy to complain about oligopolies because they are sapping productivity, undermining public welfare, and fueling the growing popular disgust with capitalism itself.

Though in the 1990s concentrating industries tended to enjoy rising productivity, that link broke in the last two decades. Now, annual productivity growth is falling on average in the industries where the biggest companies are tightening their control most rapidly. Productivity is falling across the board in these industries, particularly in the laggard companies but even in the leaders, for two basic reasons. With no pressure from below the leaders don't need to invest as much, and if they do add more or better service, they only "cannibalize on their own market shares."

Mian, Liu, and Sufi, the economists who first cast oligopolies as creations of easy money, also argue that they became major contributors to falling productivity. Before 2000, falling interest rates were encouraging more competition, leading to the productivity boom of the dot-com era. Afterward, as rates fell closer and closer to zero, low rates encouraged industry consolidation by giving dominant players an even greater incentive to kill off competitors, slowing productivity growth. This, they wrote, offers a new "unified explanation" for the ills afflicting modern capitalism over the last two decades, with the rise of oligopolies, the fall of small businesses, and the resulting decline in productivity growth all driven by the same force: easy money.

This brings us back to the postwar decades that many now consider a "glorious" age, when government worked more closely with large corporations, generating higher productivity and economic growth. There were bigger forces in play, including the baby boom and the reconstruction of Europe and Japan, but the role of the largest corporations was also very different, because they were much more likely to represent the good kind of oligopoly.

Starting around 1970, the largest corporations in the United States, and the four largest in each industry, were growing more productive and efficient than their smaller peers, in terms of sales per employee. That period ended around 2000, as industries began to consolidate again; the productivity of the largest firms started to drop, and whatever gains they made were achieved by hiring away top talent—not raising the output of their own workers. The result was a sudden collapse in the contribution the largest firms made to productivity growth, which dropped by 40 percent after the turn of the millennium. In short, good oligopolies were giving way to the bad kind, "associated with lower investment, higher prices and lower productivity growth."

This cast doubt on the widespread view that the new Silicon Valley giants are historically unique "superstars," so valuable to the economy that trustbusters should be wary of touching them. "Contrary to common wisdom," wrote Philippon and Gutiérrez in 2020, the contribution that dominant firms make to productivity has fallen by a third in the last two decades and is no match for the contribution made by dominant firms of earlier decades. Stars of the digital economy like Amazon, Google, Facebook, Apple, and Microsoft are not as "special" as one might think, "if anything, they are smaller than market leaders of the past, and they matter less for overall GDP growth than General Motors, IBM, or AT&T did at their peak." This also suggests industries are consolidating in the bad way—the one that does little for society.

Thus the big picture: easy money is fueling the rise of two very different symptoms of dysfunction, powerful oligopolies and pathetic zombies, and both have a similar impact on the health of the system. They squeeze the life out of small- and medium-size companies, which were once the key drivers of productivity growth.

BUREAUCRACY AND PRODUCTIVITY

Author and columnist David Brooks recently described the growing bureaucratization of American life as "death by a thousand paper cuts." On one level, this is a tragicomedy of waiting in lines, sitting on hold, going through annual trainings to relearn basic lessons of appropriate office behavior. California requires some of these trainings to last two hours, challenging trainers to teach simple lessons at great length. The assumption behind all this is that "people are weak, fragile, vulnerable and kind of stupid," so they need to be schooled this way, writes Brooks. "Trumpian populism is about many things, but one of them is this: working-class people rebelling against administrators."

This is also a serious drag on productivity and growth. That case was made by Gary Hamel and Michele Zanini of the Harvard Business School, who pointed out in 2016 that since the early 1980s, a growing share of Americans have gone to work for big organizations, as managers or administrators. The United States now has one manager for nearly every five workers. The C-suite has expanded to include Chief Officers of everything from Analytics and Digital to Collaboration, Customers, Ethics, Sustainability, Learning, and Happiness. And every chief needs his or her administrative minions.

Though Hamel and Zanini did not blame government, per se, clearly the corporate bureaucracy springs to a large degree from the regulatory state, demanding ever more HR analysts and compliance officers to make sure staff are toeing the state line.

Workers in advanced capitalist countries now spend as much as 16 percent of their time dealing with reviews, trainings, attestations, and other forms of red tape. Academic surveys estimate that at least half that time has no productive value. The total losses for the U.S. economy amounted to $3 trillion in 2016, or about 17 percent of GDP that year. If this burden had been reduced by half over the next ten years, wrote Hamel and Zanini, productivity growth would have increased "by a compounded rate of 1.3 percent annually, essentially doubling the post-2007 productivity growth rate."

Extend this analysis to the rest of the developed world, and the gains would amount to another $5.4 trillion a year, a sum roughly equal to the economic output of Japan. With many of the leading capitalist societies in a prolonged productivity slump, fueling the rise of "us versus them" populism, leaders can't just sit around waiting for technology to save the day. Hamel and Zanini called instead for a "concerted effort to reverse the rising tide of bureaucracy."

BILLIONAIRES AND PRODUCTIVITY

The ways that a rising tycoon class can undermine a society are threads of an ancient tale, with roots in precapitalist and developing economies.

From Cuba to Peru, North Korea to Bangladesh, Zimbabwe to Zambia, the post–World War II period saw numerous popular revolts against a crony elite bring to power a charismatic populist who promised redistribution but delivered more corruption. The Castro regime, the Kim regime, the Mugabe regime, all emerged in part from what the International Monetary Fund has called "efforts to redistribute that themselves undercut growth"—in other words, revolts against the process of capitalist wealth creation itself. Thus the anti-billionaire revolts and calls for confiscatory wealth taxes in advanced capitalist nations like the United States and France are distant echoes of Zimbabwe before Robert Mugabe.

There are many ways that rising inequality erodes productivity short of a populist revolt. In an economy increasingly dominated by a narrow circle of larger, older companies, which invest less but pay their executives more generously, productivity falls as investment declines, while inequality rises as profits concentrate in megafirms. In this telling, the link between inequality and declining output per worker is part and parcel of the general decline in competition. Nobel laureate Joseph Stiglitz, a liberal icon, would likely reject any causal role for big government, but in his book on "The Price of Inequality," he defines the costs in similar terms; inequality starves millions of people of the resources to better themselves, making a mockery of the idea that capitalism rewards merit, thereby retarding productivity and slowing growth.

The simplest, most clearly documented connection is that, as income inequality rises, poorer families have less to invest in education. Their children begin to fall behind, completing fewer years of school, getting lower test scores, graduating with weaker skills. They enter the labor force as less productive workers than they could have been. Trapped in dead-end careers behind checkout counters, particularly in an increasingly immobile society like the United States, they will suffer from lack of access to on-the-job training as well.

The effects are long-lasting, passed down to younger generations, and impact not only the poorest segments of society but the bottom 40 percent of families by income, according to studies published in 2014 by the OECD. Over the previous two decades, the authors estimated, income inequality had widened rapidly enough in the major developed countries to knock a full third of a percentage point off economic growth each year for the next twenty-five years.

THE BIG-GOVERNMENT ANSWER

Hard to measure, the productivity slump is harder to explain definitively. Skepticism of grand, single-factor theories is well founded. But consider: the centerpiece of the mystery today, roughly speaking, is a 1 percentage point drop in productivity growth across the major capitalist countries since the mid-2000s. Leading international institutions have estimated that zombies may shave half a point off productivity growth. Rising income inequality may shave off another third of a point. Those two flaws alone could thus go a long way to explaining the productivity slump. Subtract more small shares for the impact of administrative costs, oligopolies, profitless companies, and other offspring of capital misdirected by bloated financial markets, and the paradox may be close to solved. With big government widening these flaws, as I have argued, then at a minimum there is strong reason for suspicion that government is more the problem than the potential cure.

The big-government explanation has advantages over those that dwell on the computer. It does not require that one dismiss twenty-first-century innovations as mere digital distractions, a view that clashes with daily experience. Anyone who can remember the inside of a library knows viscerally that an internet search is a quantum leap more productive than leafing through file cards. It does not lean on the fog of mis-measurement, which cannot explain why productivity gains from digital tech did show up in the measurements between 1995 and 2005 but were absent before and after.

It does, however, match up well with the timeline and global sweep of this tale. The one productivity-destroying force present across these capitalist nations throughout this two-decade decline was easy money and activist government.

As central banks and governments offered more relief to a wider array of weaker companies, eventually the numbing hand of the state overwhelmed the positive impact of technology. The cumulative effects of government intervention thus could explain why the U.S. productivity revival around the year 2000 suddenly faded, never to return. Easy money pouring out of central banks was swamping every corner of the globe. In a 2018 study of twenty developed countries over the last twenty-five years, researchers confirmed a very clear link between easy money and falling productivity: "the higher the growth rate of credit, the lower the growth rate of output per worker."

Though the 1990s and the 2010s were both marked by long recoveries in the United States, driven by a booming tech sector, the two decades didn't resemble each other in the end. The 1990s saw an increasingly competitive economy with a growth rate of 3.8 percent, and surging productivity toward the end. The 2010s saw a consolidation across U.S. industries, with falling productivity, slumping wages, and an average growth rate closer to 2 percent. Why this tale of two different tech booms? In a 2020 paper, former Fed regional president and internal dissenter Thomas Hoenig tied this bogging-down of American capitalism to the distorting effects of Fed experiments with free money.

Productivity has been falling across regions and industries, regardless of whether they are big users or producers of computers and digital technology. Over the last two decades, more than three in four U.S. industries have suffered a fall in the core measure, known as "total factor" productivity, which aims to capture, in essence, how well businesses deploy machines. "There was a widespread, generalized slide among the vast majority of industries," writes economist Shawn Sprague of the U.S. Bureau of Labor Statistics—the official tracker of productivity data. One of the worst slumps was in the computer industry itself, which presumably is good at applying digital technology.

Every region of the United States and forty-nine of the fifty states have seen productivity growth slump since 2005 to a level below, often far below, its postwar trend—even though they all apply digital technology at different levels of intensity. The exception, North Dakota, got a boost from oil shale technology.

The big picture is that the sweeping reach of the productivity slow-down seems to point to a force more omnipresent than the new computer technologies themselves. Note that the broad arc of the productivity slump extends back to the early 1970s, interrupted briefly in the United States between the late '90s and early 2000s. This broadly tracks the story of constant government deficits and rising public debt across capitalist countries since 1980, with one interruption in one country, the United States in the late '90s.

One basic characteristic of new digital technology is how quickly it gets adopted worldwide, and yet the productivity slowdown reaches virtually every major power. In the 2010s, the digital revolution unfolded much faster in China than in the United States, quickly replacing cash with smartphone payment systems in the major Chinese cities. This transformation magnified the fear in the West of falling behind. Yet core productivity growth fell even faster in China than in the United States, to a rate well under 1 percent.

In China more than in any other country, the roots of the productivity slowdown have been traced to the rise of state support for a zombie economy, particularly in the last decade under Xi Jinping. In a 2021 study, the International Monetary Fund attributed China's productivity slump to an interventionist Chinese state "prolonging the economic life" of nonviable companies. While the U.S. government does not meddle in the economy as deeply as Chinese authorities meddle in theirs, it is now moving in a similar direction. Clearly any country that wants to revive its economy should not be following China's backward march to statism.

It is also likely no accident that in Europe and Japan, productivity has declined more dramatically than in the United States. By the 2010s, the productivity growth rate was equally dismal in all these countries, hovering around 1 percent or less, but it had fallen further and from much greater heights in Europe and Japan. As they rebuilt after World War II, productivity growth peaked in the 1960s and 1970s above 9 percent in Japan and around 6 percent in large European economies. That was more than double the 2.5 percent peak in the United States. This story of uneven decline is well known to economists as the "transatlantic productivity gap," but one overlooked explanation for it is a greater willingness to mobilize government rescue and relief crews in Europe and Japan, at least until recently.

The wild card here is artificial intelligence. Despite the intriguing potential of AI, questions remain about its impact, and whether it can offset the drag of a heavy-handed government. The optimists are ahead of themselves. Based on current surveys, few companies have adopted AI and most won't until the 2030s, at the earliest. For now, AI is more likely to generate efficiency gains by taking over mundane tasks, freeing humans for more productive labor, than to emerge as a "superintelligence" capable of innovating on its own, faster than humans, wrote a Goldman Sachs team in late 2023. Moreover, they argued, whatever boost the world gets from AI will be offset by the broader productivity slowdown, leaving in their view a base case for only "moderate" growth gains, averaging 0.2 percent a year in the United States, and less in other developed countries, over the next decade.

The Paradox of the "Polycrisis"

In recent years, global commentators have resurrected the specter of "polycrisis," a word originally coined to describe the sense of cascading economic, environmental, and military threats that first emerged in the 1970s. The signal characteristic of a polycrisis is that together the threats seem more complex and daunting than each one would on its own. The answer for many is a bigger umbrella government.

Thus the Biden administration's New World Economic Order promises more concerted government action to boost economic growth and reduce inequality while investing in green tech to combat climate change, chip fabrication plants to compete with China, and arms to contain Russia. And that is a partial list. Each point on this agenda requires billions, perhaps trillions more in public spending. Implementing all of it will further soak the system in debt, and seriously risk deepening the productivity slowdown. If leaders chose instead to intervene less and spend more selectively, they could raise productivity growth, and generate more resources to fight each element of the polycrisis.

PART III

THE PATH TO BALANCE

FIFTEEN

WHERE CAPITALISM STILL WORKS

I n 2023, researchers at Harvard argued that as capitalist economies bogged down in recent decades, slowing income growth, the result was a rise in zero-sum thinking. In a sluggish economy, people lose faith in the capacity of the system to "grow the pie rather than just redistribute portions of it." They start to see getting ahead as improbable, hard work as pointless. Politics turn ugly as citizens jockey for toeholds in a darker future. Shrinking opportunities start to drain the life from what German sociologist Max Weber, in a work that first appeared in English in 1930, had called the optimistic "spirit of capitalism."

Back then, the Industrial Revolution had created an expectation of human progress for the first time in history, and with it a decline in zero-sum thinking. A growing sense of possibility manifested itself in the Victorian values of hard work, thrift, consumption, and entrepreneurship. Having been inspired in the first instance by economic progress, the capitalist spirit faded as progress slowed. Since the 1970s, as the average rate of per capita income growth fell worldwide from nearly 3 percent a year to under 1 percent, pessimism and "demotivating" zero-sum beliefs spread.

A Harvard University team tracked this trend using the World Values Survey, which also dates to the 1970s and now polls nearly two hundred thousand people in seventy-two countries. It shows a sharp rise in zero-sum pessimism. A growing share of respondents believe that "people can only get rich at the expense of others" or have abandoned hope that "wealth can grow so there's enough for everyone." What's more, people who grew up in the higher-growth decades of the 1950s and '60s were less prone to zero-sum pessimism than those born as growth slowed over the last four decades. The younger the respondent, the more dystopian the outlook.

Faith in capitalism was falling across the world, helping to explain the rise of popular anger and support for extreme populists. This trend was perhaps most surprising in the United States, where the economy had been growing faster than its developed peers, making the catalysts for this rage harder to discern. Yet America was leading the charge toward radical solutions, many reflecting the zero-sum impulse to close doors, shutter markets, and control the flow of capital in a pinched economy. The past decade in particular saw the surge in young Americans who disapprove of capitalism and see socialism or even communism as a viable alternative, and a new youthful majority who believe that government should "do more to solve problems."

Older conservatives reacted with alarm, arguing that people too young to remember the Soviet Union don't understand that socialism means state ownership of business, a proven recipe for economic collapse. Alexandria Ocasio-Cortez, America's most prominent millennial socialist, was born a few weeks before the Berlin Wall fell: What could she know about it? To lecture younger generations on the pitfalls of Soviet socialism was, however, to parody their views. When framed as a question about state ownership, millennial support for socialism plummets. The socialism millennials espouse is the democratic kind practiced in northern Europe, with respect for the role of markets.

Mixed capitalism, with a strong role for the state, is here to stay. Pure laissez-faire ideology died with the Depression, and the question now is how to get the balance right—between state regulation and individual freedom, growth and redistribution. America had stayed ahead of the competition for decades with a relatively limited government, leaving people more free to invent, to innovate, and to build in industries still comparatively unencumbered by the state. Then came a shift, and at an accelerating pace since the turn of the millennium, the model of limited government has been fading in America.

Still, there are countries where capitalism is not in decay. Different styles can be made to work, from the socialist democracies of Scandinavia to the ex-Soviet states of Eastern Europe, which learned the hard way to fear centralized economic management. The three cases below—Switzerland, Taiwan, and Vietnam—were selected as particularly well-balanced representatives of high-, medium-, and low-income nations where the state is not necessarily small but it is efficient. They are pragmatic not ideological, and have been moving in the right direction, in terms of the timing and scale of regulatory and tax shifts. Above all they spend the public's money wisely, which means targeting both growth and redistribution simultaneously, in order to boost the prospects of the poor without chasing millionaires off to Singapore or Dubai.

SWITZERLAND: THE LESS SOCIALIST UTOPIA

America's progressive leaders and their young followers often trace their vision of socialist paradise to Scandinavian countries like Sweden,

Denmark, and Norway. These are just as wealthy and democratic as the United States but have more equitable distributions of wealth, as well as affordable health care and free college for all.

There is, however, a European country far richer—and just as fair. This $700 billion economy is among the world's twenty largest and is significantly bigger than any in Scandinavia. It delivers welfare benefits as comprehensive as Scandinavia's with a more open and stable economy, lower taxes, and a more streamlined government. Its average income, nearly $95,000, is among the highest in the world and $23,000 more than the Scandinavian average. Money is not the ultimate measure of success, yet surveys also rank this nation as one of the world's five happiest.

This less socialist utopia is Switzerland.

While widening its income lead over Scandinavia in recent decades, Switzerland has been catching up on measures of equality. Wealth and income are distributed almost as equally as in Scandinavia, with the middle class holding about 70 percent of the nation's assets. The big difference: the typical Swiss family has a net worth around $685,000, highest in the world by far and twice its Scandinavian peers.

The Swiss model drew fifteen minutes of media attention around 2010, when Obamacare was still new—but only for its health care system, which requires all residents to buy insurance from private providers and subsidizes those who can least afford it. Admirers said that Swiss health care had something for everyone: universal coverage for liberals, private providers and consumer choice for conservatives.

For the most part, intellectuals ignore Switzerland as a model, perhaps put off by its exaggerated reputation as a shady little tax haven where Nazi gold and other illicit fortunes have been hidden behind strict bank secrecy laws. In 2015, Switzerland agreed under pressure to share bank records with foreign tax authorities, and the economy did not slow at all. Switzerland always was more than secretive banks.

Switzerland is capitalist to its core, its government spending well below the average for rich countries, as a share of GDP. The Scandinavian governments are unusually bloated in comparison. Government spending in Switzerland amounts to a third of gross domestic product, compared with half in Scandinavia.

Switzerland imposes lighter taxes on individuals, consumers, and corporations than most of the Scandinavian countries do. Though the top tax rate has been creeping up, it remained under 45 percent in 2023, compared to 50 percent on average in Scandinavia and as high as 55 percent in Denmark. And Switzerland is more open to trade, with a share of global exports around double that of any Scandinavian economy.

Streamlined government and open borders have helped make this landlocked, mountainous country an unlikely incubator of globally competitive companies. The Observatory of Economic Complexity, a spin-off from the Massachusetts Institute of Technology, ranks nations by the complexity of products they export, which reflects how deftly they can mobilize a broad array of skills. In the most recent ranking, Switzerland came second after Japan, and well ahead of the Scandinavian countries, whose average rank is twenty-four.

The Swiss excel in just about every major industry other than oil, often by targeting specialized niches, bringing their advanced skills into play. The country is home to fourteen of the top one hundred European companies, more than twice as many as in the three Scandinavian nations combined. And most top Swiss firms are far larger than Scandinavian peers. Nestlé, with a stock market value of $300 billion in 2023, was fifteen times larger than its closest direct rival in Scandinavia.

Though major multinationals are concentrated in big cities, the Swiss economy is as decentralized as its political system. Traveling southwest from Zurich to Geneva one day, I was struck by how many iconic Swiss exports also originate in its provinces—Swiss Army knives from Schwyz, watches from Bern, St. Bernard puppies from a mountain pass in Valais, cheese and chocolates from Fribourg. Small companies anchor the economy, accounting for two of every three jobs.

Only one in six Swiss work for the government, about half the Scandinavian average. And they prefer to work. In a 2016 referendum, Swiss voters rejected a guaranteed monthly income of $2,500 per adult and $625 per child by an overwhelming margin. Swiss critics called this proposal "money for nothing."

No other nation's currency has been strengthening faster against its trading partners'. Normally a rising franc should erode Swiss exports by making them more expensive. Instead, while most rich countries, including those in Scandinavia, saw their share of global export revenues fall over the past decade, Switzerland's continued to rise. Such is the reputation of its engineers and chocolatiers that customers readily pay more for their products.

The premium the world is willing to pay for Swiss goods and services helps deter capital flight and stabilize the economy. Switzerland has not been hit by a domestic financial crisis since the 1970s, and it weathered the global crisis of 2008 with less damage to its economy than most of the Scandinavian countries. The strong franc helped Switzerland stave off the 2022 energy price shocks from the Ukraine war with inflation of just 3.5 percent, much lower than the developed world average. Even in 2023, when stresses in global finance triggered the implosion of Switzerland's second-largest bank, Credit Suisse, the franc held its value better than advanced capitalist peers.

If there is any ominous flaw in the Swiss model, it is that in trying to slow the rise of the franc, Switzerland cut interest rates to record lows ahead of its European neighbors, triggering a lending boom that has driven private corporate and household debt up to 280 percent of GDP, a risky height. No paradise is perfect.

For all its local charms, Switzerland is worldly in the extreme. The Swiss are a polyglot mix of German, French, and Italian speakers, many intimidatingly fluent in multiple languages. American visitors have been known to feel their cab driver has a better handle on the King's English. The foreign-born population has been increasing for more than a century and accounts for a quarter of the whole, 40 percent of them from outside of the European Union.

The Swiss labor force gets an added boost from a meritocratic public school system that starts steering students as young as twelve toward their academic strengths. The world-class universities charge average annual tuition of only $1,000 and leave graduates thousands of dollars less in debt than most schools in Scandinavia, or for that matter the United States and the United Kingdom.

Liberals have begun to argue in recent decades that one cannot judge an economy just by the total output and income it generates; you have to look more holistically at outcomes for people's health, education, and well-being. Since 2015 the OECD has been doing just that in its "Better Life" rankings, which score nations on a range of factors from murder rates to reading scores and rooms per person. Sweden and Switzerland tend to run neck and neck, both top five in the world in the latest rankings.

Switzerland, however, achieved this ranking with public spending at 35 percent of GDP, compared to 55 percent in Sweden. Its government consistently ranks among the top three in the world for efficiency, Sweden's in the top fifteen. Switzerland, moreover, seemed to occupy a kind of sweet spot in terms of its government size compared not only to Sweden but to all industrial countries: those that spent more than the Swiss typically did not get better results in terms of what people care about, from health to education and happiness.

That is not to say that government spending between 30 to 35 percent of GDP is somehow magic: Turkey's spending was pretty much the same as Switzerland's, and its performance on broad social measures was the worst in the industrial world. The point is simply that good government is about spending the right amount sensibly, not spending more.

Die-hard admirers of Scandinavian socialism overlook the capitalist turn it took, starting in Sweden. After its strained finances collapsed in debt and banking crises during the 1990s, Sweden began downsizing its government under a conservative party, and the reforms proved so successful that they were continued under its liberal successors. Government spending came down in the last three decades from 70 percent to 50 percent of GDP. Public debt fell by half, even as the top tax rate came down from around 90 percent to 50 percent. Reforms tightened the rules on early retirement, linking pension payouts to accrued wages, and partially privatized even the state employment service. Sweden is now one of the few rich developed countries where welfare spending has drifted downward a bit over the last three decades.

Perhaps most strikingly, Sweden set a budget target, directing the government to run a surplus averaging at least 1 percent of GDP in recoveries, and hit it. By the eve of the global crisis in 2008, the country had a surplus of 3.6 percent of GDP, giving it deeper resources to spend on stimulus than other capitalist countries. It emerged as "the rock star of the recovery," and others followed.

One was Denmark, which was hit hard by the crisis of 2008 and its fallout across Europe. By the early 2010s, Denmark, too, was cutting back its welfare state, as critics questioned how nearly one in ten Danes had qualified for lifetime disability, and suggested prodding "dawdling university students" and premature retirees off the welfare rolls. Gently scolding Americans who "associate the Nordic model with some kind of socialism," Danish prime minister Lars Løkke Rasmussen said on a 2015 visit to the United States that "I would like to make one thing clear. Denmark is far from a planned socialist economy. Denmark is a market economy."

By 2023, Sweden and Denmark were at the forefront of a movement to repeal wealth taxes, which had been withdrawn in nine of the thirteen developed countries that had imposed them since the 1960s. The tax had proved unworkable and unpopular, hitting the middle and upper classes hard, while the super-rich fled the country. Tennis star Bjorn Borg decamped for Monaco. Members of ABBA, the legendary pop rock band, threatened to move to Switzerland. Sweden's richest person, Ingvar Kamprad, founder of the IKEA furniture stores, wound up in a small alpine village outside Lausanne. Sweden's government estimated in 2007 that the tax had driven $70 billion in wealth out of the country, money that "could have been invested in jobs and welfare in Sweden." Upon repeal, the outmigration of rich Swedes slowed precipitously. Growth revived, as the largest Scandinavian economy started to look more like Switzerland, streamlining government and leaving business more room to grow.

The real lesson of Swiss success is that the stark choice offered by many politicians—between private enterprise and social welfare—is a false one. A pragmatic country can have a business-friendly environment alongside social equality if it gets the balance right. The Swiss have become the world's richest nation by getting it more right than most. Their model of capitalism works and is hiding in plain sight.

TAIWAN: THE INDISPENSABLE ECONOMY

The postwar Asian miracle economies lifted themselves into the ranks of rich nations by generating long runs of strong growth. Japan, South Korea, and Taiwan advanced up the industrial ladder by investing more heavily in research and development than their emerging world rivals did. Now they are research leaders among developed nations, and the most intriguing model among them is Taiwan.

In recent years, Taiwan has surpassed South Korea and the United States as the technology and market share leader in the global production of advanced computer chips, which puts this island of just 24 million people at the center of the battle for global technological supremacy. Arguably, computer chips from Taiwan are the most valuable prize in the new cold war between the United States and China. They are critical building blocks for artificial intelligence, cloud computing, the Internet of Things, and other digital industries of the future.

Competent governments played a major role in the Asian miracles. South Korea nurtured giant conglomerates like Samsung and Hyundai, which exported consumer products under their own brand names. Taiwan cultivated smaller companies focused on making parts or assembling finished products for foreign brands, and that nimbleness helps explain how it emerged in the lead.

Taiwan began, like many of its peers, by copying or borrowing technology from Western nations. As early as the 1970s, electronics had replaced textiles as the island's leading industry. Through every phase of the computer revolution, from PCs to the mobile internet, Taiwan's factories managed to retool fast enough to remain important global suppliers.

Inspired by the feats of Silicon Valley, Taiwan's government in 1980 set up the first of its science parks. Each would have its own tech university, and the system offered bonuses for Taiwan-born engineers to return home. Mixing overseas experience with local graduates, the science parks became hothouses for entrepreneurial start-ups. With one in the north, one in the south, and one in the center of the island, these parks have also ensured regionally balanced growth in the economy.

This was industrial policy of the kind now endorsed by many Western countries, except that it was managed by a government that has remained determinedly streamlined. Today Taiwan's government spending amounts to less than 20 percent of GDP, or less than half the average in developed nations. The government employs only one in thirty of its citizens, a fraction of the norm in the United States, Japan, Germany, or the United Kingdom.

At a time when capitalism is bogging down in debt, Taiwan is an exception. Its private debt is relatively low, and its government debts are just 34 percent of GDP, a quarter of the developed nation average.

Its leaders responded with restraint even to the pandemic. Taiwan's combined fiscal and monetary stimulus amounted in 2020 to less than 7 percent of GDP, compared to 34 percent on average in the G4 economies: the United States, Europe, the United Kingdom, and Japan. Though Taiwan's corporate and personal tax rates are typical for a developed economy, the way its government spends that revenue is highly unusual: very light on social programs and health care, compared to its peers, and very heavy on education and research.

The result is a record of extraordinarily dynamic and steady growth. Since Taiwan was formally recognized as a developed economy in the late 1990s, it has averaged close to 4 percent growth, more than twice as fast as the average for other developed economies. Taiwan maintained this edge, despite a rapidly aging population, by generating productivity growth far faster than that of any G4 economy every year for the last four decades.

From 2020 to 2023, Taiwan's labor productivity was growing at an annual pace of nearly 4 percent, compared to 0.5 percent in the G4. One reason: manufacturing, the industry most closely associated with productivity gains, accounts for more than 30 percent of Taiwan's GDP, a stunningly high share for any country, developed or not.

It's been said that to become rich a country needs to make rich things, and in this Taiwan particularly excels. The Observatory of Economic Complexity ranks Taiwan third in the world for the sophistication of its exports, testimony to the extraordinary range of skills required to manufacture fast computer chips. The big powers racing to match that capacity, the United States and China, rank tenth and twenty-fifth, respectively.

Taiwan's light-touch government has not prevented tech start-ups from growing to global scale. By the 2010s, for example, Foxconn Technology, founded in the 1970s, was assembling 40 percent of the world's consumer electronic products, using plants in Asia, Europe, and Latin America. Today Taiwan is a major supplier of smartphone lenses, e-paper displays, and many other computer parts, but it is the essential supplier of computer chips.

To build a semiconductor industry that could compete worldwide, Taiwan recruited Morris Chang, a graduate of MIT and a veteran of Texas Instruments. Chang reviewed Taiwan's strengths and weaknesses, and rejected the idea of trying to go head-to-head with global brands like Intel. Instead he built a "pure foundry," a contract manufacturer quietly cranking out chips for the global brands, much the way Taiwan had once made plastic toys for Western brands.

Though foundries are a small corner of the $573 billion world chip market, they make all of the fastest and smallest chips (of 10 nanometers or less). Two-thirds of foundry chips come out of Taiwan, the overwhelming majority from Chang's creation, the Taiwan Semiconductor Manufacturing Company (TSMC). He bet big on multibillion-dollar investments in the most advanced chip fabrication plants, giving TSMC a lead that will be hard for rivals to overcome.

Now a fixture among the world's largest tech companies by market value, TSMC has been criticized in Taiwan for buying up all the best talent, widening inequality in a country that long prided itself on sharing its fast-growing wealth. To date, however, social tensions remain muted, in part because the billionaire class—often the target of social protest in other countries—is relatively small and concentrated in the highly productive and popular tech sector.

An economy still dominated by small and medium-sized enterprises has generated relatively few billionaires of comparatively modest wealth. Chang's fortune is just over $2 billion, barely a rounding error in the fortunes of the leading American tech tycoons. Meanwhile the median wealth of an adult in Taiwan is $95,000, significantly higher than his or her American counterpart at $80,000.

As a wide-open economy heavily dependent on exports, Taiwan tried to position itself as a neutral supplier, the "Switzerland" of chips, but found itself caught in the middle of the U.S.–China rivalry. While Taiwanese companies have factories worldwide, the chip fabrication plants are concentrated on the home island, just one hundred miles off the coast of mainland China. In the event of military conflict, American analysts have warned, U.S. access to those chip supplies could be vulnerable to missile threat or naval blockade.

This is a tense spot for a small island to find itself in, as well as a tribute to the unusual success of Taiwan's economic model. Taiwan has become a critical link in the global tech supply chain, thanks in good part to a government that has gotten the balance right, creating a business environment that generates start-ups alongside giants and great wealth, relatively well distributed. If it were not living in the shadow of China, which works hard to block international recognition of Taiwan, its thriving model of capitalist democracy would likely be more widely studied and copied.

VIETNAM: FUNCTIONAL COMMUNISM

One of capitalism's biggest problems is the widespread misunderstanding of how China emerged as Asia's latest "economic miracle." Many experts have pointed to China's five-decade run of strong growth as proof of how well a state-managed economy can work, and this in turn has created a vogue for "state capitalism."

China's economic miracle did not prove the value of state control, quite the opposite. At its peak under the Qing dynasty in 1820 China was the most dominant economy in the historical records, accounting for 33 percent of global GDP. That position would erode as the Qing declined and fell, dropping to just 5 percent by the time of the Maoist rebellion in 1949—and there it stagnated under Communist control. Driven by misery and memories of past glory, China changed fast after the last Maoist regime fell in the late seventies, and quickly widened economic freedoms. By the 2010s, China's share of global GDP was back over 15 percent, a hundred-year high.

It was expanding, however, because the state was easing control over the economy. Growth took off after Beijing started to free private farmers and entrepreneurs to run their own shows. Even as growth picked up in private sector industries vacated by the state, it remained weak in rust belt industries heavily supported by the state. By 2021, the once nonexistent private sector had risen in four decades to account for 50 percent of tax revenue, 60 percent of GDP, 70 percent of tech innovation, and 80 percent of urban jobs. Yet Xi Jinping was bringing back Maoism, reasserting state control—and growth was slowing sharply. Squeezing the space allowed to private entrepreneurs and businesspeople was a historic mistake, a threat to the Chinese economic miracle.

There is a communist state where capitalism is still on the march, but it is not China. Run by an economically competent government, focused on building an export manufacturing powerhouse, Vietnam looks much like China did twenty years ago, if at a smaller scale. Its population of 100 million is a fraction as large, so Vietnam will never have an equally transformative impact on the global economy, yet the lessons it reveals are similar. Stay open for business, manage the economy with a light touch, and capitalism can yield amazing results—even under autocratic rule.

Like China, Vietnam began reforming in response to a period of total economic collapse. By the late 1980s, more than a decade after the end of its calamitous war of reunification, Vietnam was living on handouts from the Soviet Union, growth was stagnant, and inflation was running at 700 percent.

Hanoi's answer was *doi moi*, a series of reforms designed to open the state-run economy to the outside world and to private business. At the time, 70 percent of the population worked on farms and—as had been the case in China—the reforms began with agriculture. Collective farms were abolished, and the land was leased instead to individuals, who were allowed for the first time to sell their produce at a profit, at home or abroad. Output rose fast. Soon Vietnam made the transition from chronic rice importer, battling hunger at home, to rice exporter.

The centerpiece of *doi moi* was dismantling the state-planned economy, streamlining the central bureaucracy, and scaling down or selling off state-owned monopolies. Round after round of sales reduced the number of state companies, from twelve thousand in 1989 to six hundred by 2016. The pace and reach of privatization ran much deeper in Vietnam than in any advanced capitalist country. That set the stage for a surge in economic growth, led by the private sector.

To be the next China, Vietnam had to become a manufacturing power, and it steered all its resources toward this goal. To make its currency more stable and competitive, Hanoi worked to bring budget deficits and inflation under control. To support the development of export factories, it invested heavily in transport networks to bring goods to market, and schools to educate workers. Vietnam now gets higher marks from the World Bank for the quality of its infrastructure than any nation at a similar income level.

Vietnam became a leading champion of free trade, joining the World Trade Organization in 2007 and cutting deals with its Southeast Asian neighbors as well as the United States and Japan. Even in the 2010s, as many nations turned inward and protectionist, throwing up "stealth barriers" like domestic regulation designed to disadvantage foreigners, Vietnam stayed the course. It completed a landmark agreement with the European Union in the summer of 2020. Global Trade Alert, which tracks stealth trade barriers, ranked Vietnam among the few large exporters not playing this protectionist game.

By the time the pandemic hit, turning many nations even further inward, Vietnam was well on its way to becoming the next Asian miracle. Following the path blazed by China, and before it by Japan, Korea, and Taiwan, Vietnam was rising as an export manufacturing powerhouse.

During their boom years, the economies of the original Asian miracles were driven by annual export growth close to 20 percent—nearly double the average for emerging nations at the time. Vietnam has sustained a similar pace for the last three decades. Even as global trade slumped in the 2010s, Vietnam's exports grew 16 percent a year, by far the fastest rate in the world, and three times the emerging world average.

It is hard to overstate how unusual the Asian miracles are, as success stories. Japan, Korea, and Taiwan had risen into the World Bank's "high-income" class by sustaining annual growth of 5 percent or more for five decades—a rare achievement. Vietnam has been growing faster than 5 percent for three straight decades now. Once one of the world's poorest countries, flattened by a long civil war, it now stands in the lower-middle-income class. Since the late 1980s its average income has increased fivefold to nearly $3,000.

Much like the original Asian miracles, Vietnam has managed to balance explosive growth with income equality and rapid poverty reduction. In 2013, it produced its first billionaire, Pham Nhat Vuong, founder of

Vingroup, now a sprawling conglomerate. After graduating from college in Russia, Vuong had opened a small restaurant in Ukraine, where he saw his first big opportunity in instant noodles—unknown to Ukrainians at the time. Now he has interests from real estate to smartphones. The blockbuster 2023 IPO of his electric vehicle company, VinFast, made Vuong one of the richest people in Asia.

As a self-made entrepreneur, he is the kind of billionaire more likely to become a hero than a villain, particularly in a nation where most people have seen steady progress. Since Vietnam's boom began, inequality (as measured by the Gini coefficient) has not widened. The share of the population living on less than $2 a day has fallen from 60 percent to less than 5 percent, which makes Vietnam a world leader in the war on poverty. In other countries at Vietnam's income level, based on World Bank data, the poverty rate is on average six times higher.

Vietnam, so far, is getting the balance right, building basic infrastructure while taking early but not unaffordable steps toward improving welfare services. The government invests more than 6 percent of GDP each year on new infrastructure, better than double the average in Southeast Asia. At the same time, it has managed to extend health care coverage to nearly 90 percent of the population and to largely eliminate illiteracy.

The state spending on transport, communication, and power networks benefits workers, as well as factories. Even in rural areas, where most people lived in the dark at the start of Vietnam's boom, less than 1 percent of the population now lives without power. From the start, as the International Monetary Fund has put it, Vietnam's focus was on "leaving no one behind."

Generous spending on high schools has produced international test scores in the global top ten. At times Vietnam's scores have come in so high—well ahead of more developed nations such as the United States and Britain—that some experts doubt their validity. None, however, doubt that Vietnam is, at a minimum, a high-performing outlier among lower-middle-income countries.

Skilled labor is helping Vietnam move up the ladder, perhaps faster than any rival, to manufacture more sophisticated goods. Tech surpassed clothing and textiles as the country's leading export in 2015 and accounted for most of its record trade surplus by 2020. Samsung, the Korean giant, was moving smartphone production to Vietnam from competing sites all over Asia. So were Google and Apple, which was moving MacBook production to Vietnam.

The paradoxes of China's digital economy, which in the 2010s grew rapidly under a mix of heavy censorship and light regulation, are shared by Vietnam. It gets terrible grades for internet freedom, but digital commerce has been growing at an annual rate of 30 percent, among the fastest in the world. The World Economic Forum's most recent ranking of nations by digital progress placed Vietnam first in Asia for "ecosystem" and "mindset," which cover factors from the cost and ease of launching a start-up to the level of digital skills and popular attitudes toward entrepreneurial risk-takers.

In general, however, authoritarian capitalism rarely works for long, and only in the early stages of a nation's economic development. China is a major exception, or at least was, before the recent reassertion of central authority began to undermine its growth. All the other Asian miracles eased political controls during their long march to prosperity, and eventually became democracies—albeit at a much higher income level (around $10,000) than where Vietnam is today.

The question facing Vietnam, still in the early stages of development, is how long its growth can survive autocratic rule.

History shows that autocracies at every income level produce much less steady growth than democracies do. Facing no internal checks, they can change policy on a whim, or push policies to irrational extremes.

Time and again, these shifts trigger collapses that drop the economy back to square one on the development path. That helps explain why today every large developed country is a full-fledged democracy, and the only partial exception is Singapore.

Vietnam's Communist Party has been in power for nearly fifty years, and its internal workings are as opaque as the economy is open to outsiders. It has had its wobbles, but not one big enough to knock it off the miracle path, and no spikes in government deficits or debt large enough to signal an imminent crisis. Perhaps the most visible risk is a problem traceable to the pre-reform Communist years and shared by China. Though Hanoi has sold off most of its state-owned companies to private owners, the survivors are huge, and still account for nearly a third of economic output—the same share as a decade ago. They also hold many of the bad loans in the banking system. If trouble comes, these bloated state companies are one place it could start.

It's worth noting that rising debts, which eventually triggered the financial crises that ended rapid growth in Japan, South Korea, and other Asian miracles, are now acting as a drag on China as well. No good run lasts forever. For now, Vietnam is exporting its way to prosperity, and proving communists can successfully manage capitalism, so long as they are easing state control.

FOLLOW THE PEOPLE

Neoliberalism's critics will concede that opening borders and markets promoted prosperity and lowered poverty worldwide over the last four decades; their concern is for the many communities left behind by the "race to the bottom," as companies rushed to set up shop in nations with the lowest wages. As factories and blue-collar jobs left the American

Midwest in the 2000s, often for China, the emptying out of industrial Michigan and Ohio became count one in the indictment of neoliberalism, cited as evidence that markets were not self-correcting, and that the answer was corrective government.

The recent return to statism in China has, however, repelled new investors as fast as the opening had attracted them. One no longer hears odes to Chinese bureaucrats, and how they could by deft reshuffling make the nation's growing debt pile, including an estimated $10 trillion in "hidden debts" held by local government, disappear as if by magic. The conversation has shifted to the risks of staying in China under an unpredictable regime. And in some cases American manufacturers have begun to bring production back home despite wages that are still nearly eight times the Chinese average.

One way to tell where capitalism is working is to watch where the money and people go. When they were finally freed to leave the Soviet Union after its fall, Russian scientists moved mainly to countries with the lowest top income tax rates, especially to the United States. Within the fifty states, the population has been shifting for decades to those that promise lower taxes, lighter regulation, and the resulting overall reduction in labor costs (not just cheap wages). It's difficult to directly compare internal and international migration, but since 1980 the United States has lost an estimated 3.5 million manufacturing jobs to China, while the Northeast and Midwest alone have lost more than 13 million people, including some 9 million working adults to the South and Southwest.

As the Biden administration rolled out new incentives to boost investment in computer chips and green tech, the South was attracting twice as much of that investment as the Midwest and becoming "America's industrial heartland." For the first time in at least four decades, the South had as many industrial jobs as the Midwest. All of the fifteen fastest-growing U.S. cities by both percentage gain and total number were outside the old industrial belt of Middle America, mainly in the South. Miami is becoming Manhattan South. Americans tend to see this as a zero-sum game, one state cannibalizing from another, without recognizing the inherent advantage of a decentralized system that creates room for competition among states. The most competitive states are attracting investment from all over the world, acting as models in their own way.

Capitalism works, drawing in new people and business where it is permitted and welcome. By the 2010s, as the state reasserted control in China, many Chinese were hedging their bets by buying homes or second homes in Singapore. And capitalists were keeping their options open by adopting a "China plus one" strategy: opening factories in more welcoming countries, including Vietnam. Of course, cheaper labor was part of the appeal, but more broadly this was a race to freedom—to places where it makes sense to do business because government allows capitalism to work.

=================

SIXTEEN

THE ONLY WAY OUT IS THROUGH

Despite all its flaws, the United States is still the closest thing the world has to that shining city on a hill, the destination country of choice for immigrants from all over. Even many foreign critics find it hard to summon a pure distaste for America; during the second Iraq War, at a Warsaw protest against the U.S. troop presence in Poland, I saw a placard that reflects a common sentiment: "Yankee go home, but take me with you."

That line goes back to the 1960s and has been used in nations from Mexico to India. I was among the many who came searching for the American dream, and found it. To this day the country's enduring energy, the dynamic cabal of academics, entrepreneurs, financiers, and engineers who combine to make it the global tech leader, leave me in awe. One in ten Fortune 500 CEOs and three in ten Silicon Valley engineers are of Indian origin, a breakthrough that could not have happened in a less open society.

Nonetheless, I am deeply concerned about where America is leading the world now. The daily crisis of capitalism is manifest in public disappointment. In 2023, the number of people who expect to be "better off in five years" hit a record low in all fourteen of the advanced countries surveyed by the Edelman Trust Barometer. The optimists were a minority in every country. In nations with larger governments and slower growth, like Italy and France, fewer than one in five said they expect to be better-off in five years. In the United States, trust in government was at a historic low in Pew polls that go back to the 1950s. Nearly four of five respondents in a separate poll doubted that "life will be better for our children's generation than it has been for us," a record since that question was first asked in 1990.

Capitalism is not working for any generation, however, because it has been twisted into a distorted form. An unlimited state is restricting economic freedom and individual opportunity worldwide, but the decline is most jarring in America, still a beacon for those with the will and heart to get here. Leading businessmen in India, in private conversations, express dismay at the turn to a nationalistic industrial policy in America; they see in it echoes of India's awkward tryst with socialism in the 1960s and 1970s.

The United States has dropped in the Heritage Foundation rankings for economic freedom to twenty-fifth in the world, down from fourth in the 2000s. The reasons include multiplying regulations and exploding debt, which will limit the freedom of younger Americans to spend as they choose in the future.

The capitalist spirit is beleaguered. In 2022, when I broke away from a giant New York company to start my own, industry veterans warned me that the regulatory costs of launching a new financial firm had increased perhaps tenfold over the last two decades. Having been in the industry for twenty-five years, I managed to muster the necessary resources, but several colleagues who attempted similar launches ended up as case studies of what academics call the "failure of free entry." They would not expect sympathy and certainly won't get it in New York. I am still a resident of the great city, paying more than half my income in taxes. Yet I, too, migrate in the winter to Miami, drawn to its effervescent spirit—a fact a university professor could not have known when she told me at a gathering of authors that New York will be better off without "all the rich douchebags moving to Miami."

Anti-capitalism grows glibly on the pervasive narrative about how a withered government allowed rich financiers to flourish. The Democratic mayor of New York, Eric Adams, has tried to impress upon the progressive wing of his party, to little effect, that the 2 percent pay 50 percent of the city's taxes. Budget math is not likely to contain cultural disdain for rich elitists holed up in their new private clubs, subdividing a cosmopolitan and democratic metropolis. But the market soil from which such excesses spring was sown by an expanding government.

HISTORY IS BENDING TOWARD BIG GOVERNMENT

Today there is a widespread sense that the era of easy money is over, and that this will force a change. The return of inflation compelled the Federal Reserve to raise interest rates sharply, and to signal that they will remain "higher for longer." Coming after nearly fifteen years in which the Fed kept rates near zero and signaled they would remain "lower for longer," this about-face does have the potential to stop some of what needs stopping. When money is not free, people treat it with more respect, make more careful investment decisions, and do fewer "stupid things."

When money has a price, the perverse incentives that fueled the rise of zombies, oligopolies, oligopolist billionaires, and the broad distortion of financial markets are no doubt much reduced. Even members of the political elite, who helped create and shape the easy money era, have started warning loudly that rising deficits put America in a "terrible place." That's a turn for the better, but it is just a start.

This age has not been characterized only by low interest rates, or constant deficits, and it did not begin only in the wake of the 2008 crisis. It encompasses the suite of government habits—spend, borrow, bail out, regulate, and micromanage the business cycle—that have been steadily accumulating over the past century. Animated by "the mentality that champions building," Bidenomics crystallizes what came before, and suggests an enduring commitment to unlimited government.

The United States sets the tone and reflects the global story. Vastly and secretly expanded after World War II, the agencies of the national security state grew steadily over time, explosively so after the terror attacks of 2001. The regulatory state expanded sharply in the 1930s, when it started to compile and track its rules, and grew metronomically in recent decades at a pace of around three thousand new rules a year. The welfare state, founded in the New Deal and expanded in the 1960s to include health and pension entitlements for the middle class, is now on track to go bankrupt on its unfunded promises. The habit of running constant deficits took hold in the 1970s, the habit of covering them by borrowing took hold in the 1980s; since then the federal government debt has steadily quadrupled to more than 120 percent of GDP today.

The borrowing culture rose in tandem with the bailout culture, which was new in the 1970s—helping a railroad here, a mid-size bank there—and controversial. Since then it has become standard and universal, culminating in the one-thousand-plus bailouts of 2008, then the multitrillion-dollar rescues of 2020, when even bankrupt sinking demons got help.

Bailouts are no longer reserved for individual companies or banks, they extend to industries and a commitment to perpetual growth in the economy as a whole. It was Lyndon Johnson who in 1964 implemented the first government stimulus to speed up a recovery, and two years later the first and last spending cut to slow an overheated recovery. With that, the original Keynes was dead, and the basic imbalance was established—spending would know mainly excess rarely restraint. Austerity would not mean spending cuts, it would mean deficits too small to satisfy demands for more growth.

The omnipresent state was a bipartisan project. It was a Reagan appointee, Alan Greenspan, who in 1987 delivered the Fed's first promise of support to a cratering market, a safety net that has never been withdrawn. Later Greenspan delivered the first rate cuts explicitly designed to speed up a recovery, and then to prolong a recovery even as financial imbalances built up. By the time all this easy money blew up with the collapse of the housing bubble in 2008, rates could hardly go lower, so the Fed borrowed a trick from Japan to push rates down by buying bonds in multibillion-dollar bulk. Then it pushed that buying spree to a shocking scale in the pandemic, breaking the price signals that make capitalism work.

What began in the New Deal as a safety net for the poor has become a system of socialized risk for the super-rich, with government guaranteeing markets that would move only one way, up. If the bias of policy makers before the start of the Depression was to "liquidate, liquidate, and liquidate," it has given way to the opposite bias, "liquify, liquify, liquify." Though often depicted as a bold departure, Bidenomics does not set a new direction, it wants more of everything that was already there: spending, regulation, bailouts for U.S. companies and the world, even an industrial policy to outdo China's.

This escalation is not unexpected. Friedrich Hayek warned that the road to serfdom would be paved by government planners, too sure of their economic science, but with full support from citizen consumers "willing to forfeit the burden of making choices in favor of the comforts of certainty." Some see these cultural shifts and sound the alarm but for the most part, the mainstream is committed to more spending in the cause of certainty. Liberal economist and columnist Noah Smith warned in early 2023 against the descent into intellectual "stasis" and "checkism," which he defines as "the progressive belief that all we need is the political will to write bigger checks."

On the right, a growing movement would push government in the same direction, based on the same misreading of history. Republicans, writes Princeton University historian Jeremy Adelman, "are burning the flag they once waved." Oren Cass, a forty-year-old former adviser to Republican presidential candidate Mitt Romney, and the go-to expert for the right on jobs and poverty, argues that four decades of blind "market fundamentalism" have corrupted "conservative economics," which should be confidently "shaping markets" to serve the "national interest." That, for example, would mean government shaping global supply chains to make sure they don't become "Chinese supply chains." Christian political philosopher Patrick Deneen, author of *Why Liberalism Failed*, says capitalism fell in thrall to the God of market price signals, and needs to return power to a Church-going community with higher values. He endorses government-run industrial policy, and banning work on the Sabbath. Florida Republican leader Marco Rubio, though he professes to be a fan of Reagan, titled his book on the post-Reagan era *The Decades of Decadence*. Like many of his enemies on the left, Rubio, too, blames the woes of American labor on excessively free global markets.

The myth of how shrinking government unleashed unbridled market power was easy to believe, because it appeared to fit the facts of globalization and financialization. Barriers to the free movement of goods and capital were falling, while financial markets were growing rapidly, and these developments did look like a triumph for free market thinking. That narrative is at best incomplete, misleading. Global financial markets were expanding but alongside, and encouraged by, government and central bank support. The authorities were less committed to free market ideology than to the quietly invasive culture of easy money and bailouts.

Whether liberal or conservative, most politicians and thinkers still nod to the notion that prices should be set by individuals working in markets, not individual bureaucrats. They do not, however, seem to recognize that big government is already acting as sand in the gears of the market price–setting mechanism.

HOW A COUNTERREVOLUTION MIGHT BEGIN

It is hard to envision how or why governments would suddenly rethink the course they have been on for nearly a century. Unfortunately, reversals of this kind come only when a government runs out of money— when it can borrow no more because the borrowing costs are prohibitive. Though these crises have become rarer over time, they do happen.

Greece, the birthplace of democracy, was seen almost as a parody of financial irresponsibility until the last decade, when the humiliations of catastrophic debt forced a remarkable turnaround. As the U.S. deficit was headed to historic heights in 2023, Greece's was still coming down, to less than a quarter of the U.S. level. The experience of Sweden, after its crises of the early 1990s, shows that even a committed socialist state can start downsizing. Running surpluses made Sweden "the rock star of the recovery" after 2008. It's a role model but not for the reasons American progressives imagine. It showed how less government can produce better economic results.

The United States is, of course, not just another economy. It is the dominant financial superpower and can play by looser rules than other nations, which leaves its leaders unconcerned about mounting public debt—a complacency that has undone empires before.

Starting with Portugal in the fifteenth century, every global empire has, by virtue of its place at the center of commerce, issued the currency other nations most want to hold in reserve. Because of this built-in demand, the "reserve currency" gives its holder the privilege to borrow cheaply abroad and pay its debts by creating money.

Portugal and its successors into the early twentieth century—the Netherlands, Spain, France, and Britain—managed to hold on to reserve currency status and the borrowing privileges that come with it only until foreigners began to suspect that, having lived beyond its means for so long, the empire of the moment would no longer be able to pay its debts in the future. The world's trust began to shift to the next empire in line, and a new currency.

After World War I, British sterling was displaced by the American dollar, and today the main argument for why the dollar won't go the way of its predecessors is not built on U.S. strengths. It rests on the weakness of rivals. There are only two which have the necessary economic scale, and neither has credibility. The first, the euro, is barely two decades old. European institutions are young and slow, burdened by the challenge of rule by deliberation among nearly thirty member states, and lack a centralized administration to control public spending. The second, the Chinese renminbi, is even less credible, managed by a one-party state that employs capital controls as and when it suits.

And so, America remains confident the dollar will face no challenge. Where else will the money go?

The decline could already be underway. The dollar share of global central bank reserves has been eroding steadily. The share of countries that use the dollar as their "anchor"—the standard against which they measure the value of their own currency—has fallen to 45 percent from 62 percent in the late 2010s.

Perhaps the most important sign of vulnerability is a country's net international investment position: in effect, what it owes minus what is owed. Since the early 2000s, the U.S. position has been plunging deeper into the red, its deficit more than tripling from 20 percent to 66 percent of U.S. GDP. Over the same period, other developed economies started out in the same position—with an average deficit equal to 20 percent of their GDP—then shifted into the black. Most made the leap from debtor to creditor. The only developed country more deeply indebted to foreigners than the United States is Portugal, an indication of how far old empires can fall.

While other countries are not flocking to a single alternative to the dollar, they are looking at many alternatives. As central banks began holding reserves in currencies other than the dollar, no single rival gained much, but the euro, the renminbi, the Canadian dollar, and the Australian dollar, all gained a little in terms of share. This movement picked up speed in the late 2010s, when the United States used its currency as a diplomatic weapon, sanctioning Iran, Russia, and other rivals by cutting off their access to a global financial system that takes payments only in dollars.

To many countries this smacks of imperialism. China, Brazil, and South Africa have joined in talks with Russia to create a new currency to challenge the dollar, and its controlling role in global finance. They hope gradually to chip away at the dollar share of central bank reserves, and more immediately just to trade among themselves in their own coin, without first converting to dollars. "Every night I ask myself why all countries have to base their trade on the dollar," Brazilian president Luiz Inácio Lula da Silva said on a trip to China in April 2023, arguing that an alternative would help "balance world geopolitics."

The same motives are inspiring similar uprisings worldwide. There are talks on creating a common South American currency, on nation-to-nation deals to trade in their own currencies, and on buying and selling oil, the most important global commodity, in currencies other than the dollar.

A parallel movement began looking for ways to save and trade that do not involve any of the traditional currencies. In the past, gold and the dollar had both been seen as safe havens, and tended to rise in value together during crises. Amid the banking troubles of early 2023 and the Israel-Gaza war later that year, gold surged but the dollar didn't. This time, the main buyers for gold were not investors looking for a haven from inflation, they were central banks, looking for an alternative to the dollar.

Central banks in 2023 accounted for a third of the global demand for gold, three times the norm of recent decades, and a high since the records begin in 1950. Nine of the ten biggest central bank gold buyers were in emerging countries, including Russia, China, and India—all deeply involved in the revolt against dollar dominance.

Gold is an ancient store of value, but central banks were looking to new technology as an option, too. Between 2021 and 2023, the number of central banks studying ways to launch their own digital currency had more than tripled to 130, representing virtually the entire global economy. Most of those efforts were in an advanced stage of development—including testing digital currencies for use in foreign trade.

Some economists dismiss the importance of the dollar's global status. They point out that non-imperial currencies like the Swiss franc and Japanese yen are held by harmonious, reasonably happy societies, carrying extremely heavy debt without serious signs of strain. Only those societies owe their debts to domestic not foreign lenders, and do not depend on the forbearance of the rest of the world. The United States does depend on the trust of foreigners, and the borrowing privileges afforded by the strong dollar are real. Depending on the estimate, the dollar's reserve currency status lowers the rate the United States needs to pay on its government bonds by 0.2 to 1.8 percentage points—and remember this is on bonds that until recently had been yielding around 2 percent.

Empires can see the end coming in their currencies. Once the currency no longer looks safe, investors lose faith, and the empire effectively runs out of money. It holds auctions to sell its Treasury debt, and buyers don't show up, or they show up only to demand cripplingly high yields in return for holding what they newly regard as shaky debts. It may not happen in a day but it can happen quickly. Suddenly the empire has no option other than to cut back and stop spending money it doesn't have.

Admittedly, the developed countries that have been forced to downsize their governments in recent decades were smaller ones, like Sweden and Greece, not empires. Still, the process of financial decline and revelation was much the same. Recognizing they were in crisis, they might have attempted a different fix, digging themselves into deeper economic trouble by creating more money to cover their debts and setting off hyperinflation—à la Argentina. Instead their governments chose to wake up and reverse course. The lesson of history is that if something can't go on forever it won't. No country, even a financial hegemon, should take its status for granted.

In *The Sun Also Rises*, Ernest Hemingway's novel of America's "lost generation" of the 1920s, one of the more decadent characters explains how he went bankrupt: "Two ways. Gradually and then suddenly." This slice of Hemingway dialogue was later translated into an enduring pearl of financial wisdom by the economist Rudiger Dornbusch, as he watched debt-fueled meltdowns starting with Mexico in the early 1990s. "The crisis takes a much longer time coming than you think," said Dornbusch, "and then it happens much faster than you would have thought." This is how crises have unfolded for centuries, and likely will again.

CAPITALISM FOR THE TWENTY-FIRST CENTURY

Some day that shock will come, big and sudden enough to force reform, possibly reform sweeping enough to slow or reverse the daily crisis of capitalism. Today, discussions of how to fix the system focus on new or revised rules, regulations, and codes. Many are sensible, but together they paste layer upon layer of paragraphs, sections, and pages onto the core of the problem, which is overprotective government and the bailout culture it has created. Nonetheless, if only to reject fashionable or fatalistic pessimism, it is worth pondering what a reinvigorated capitalist model for the twenty-first century could look like.

For starters, it is important to recognize that American faith in the capacity of its citizens to endure any pain has given way to an impulse to grab for the public purse at the first sign of difficulty. The American "revolution in pain management" recommended treating even moderate injuries with powerful opiates, which became the leading cause of accidental deaths in the United States. Despite kind intentions, these cultural reflexes are also enabling capitalism's debt addiction. The health authorities have begun searching for a way out of the trap, in which every dose of painkillers leads to a bigger dose. Economic authorities need to follow that lead, and could start with a line of advice adapted from poet Robert Frost; some degree of suffering is a given in life, and "the only way out is through."

There is a long literature on the economic impact of an ever-larger government. Much, not all, of it confirms a corrosive impact over time. In his book *Measuring Government in the Twenty-First Century*, economist Livio Di Matteo promises "a few" samples, and ends up citing twenty studies. They show, for example, that the impact follows a curve: in the early stages an expanding state tends to spend on roads and other basics, promoting growth; after a certain point, added spending has diminishing returns, as more goes to less productive targets. Economic freedom, on the other hand, delivers increasing returns. Nations in the top quartile of the economic freedom rankings have an average income of $45,000, nearly eight times those in the bottom quartile.

Though there is no clear number—a threshold beyond which government spending has grown self-defeatingly high—common sense offers some guides. Leaders need to know where their nation stands and which way it is going. If it is an outlier, building up a bigger deficit and burden of debt than its peers, it risks undermining its own competitive position and needs to consider dialing back. That was the United States in 2023, when it had the widest budget deficit in the developed world and the third highest public debt after Japan and Italy.

It makes intuitive and even moral sense that when a nation's government accounts for more than half of all spending in the economy or takes more than half of an individual's income in taxes, that nation is getting less free. Citizens are effectively working for the state, probably more as a result of inertia than choice, and a kind of silent tax revolt begins. History shows that precious few Americans paid any tax at top rates over 50 percent in the 1960s and 1970s—not that the rich won't pay taxes. As the top rate came down to well below 50 percent after 1980, the share paid by the top 1 percent of U.S. income earners roughly doubled; today they contribute more than 40 percent of U.S. federal income tax revenue.

Again it's a question of balance. The democratic revolutions of the eighteenth century began as tax revolts, and even in communal France, liberty got equal billing alongside equality and fraternity. Today governments need to be cognizant of whether they are shrinking the sphere of private freedom a degree too far. The policymakers who see themselves as innovative thinkers for mobilizing government are in fact classic status quoists; they are hoping that more ambitious interventions to ease every new crisis—the same approach their predecessors have pursued for decades—will somehow produce better results.

Leaders would also need to recognize that economies simply cannot grow as fast as they once did, now that the post–World War II baby boom has given way to bust. The number of countries in which the working-age population is shrinking has risen from two in 1980 to fifty today. It is on track to reach seventy-seven by 2040, with the United States falling into this group after 2050. Fewer workers means slower growth, period. And if political leaders try to push economies to run faster than they can by priming the engines with debt, they will only create deeper dysfunction.

The slowdown is already underway. After 2008, global growth slowed to less than 3 percent from its postwar average near 4 percent; over the next decade, no major advanced economy grew as fast as it had in any of the previous five decades. Government can take steps to limit the impact of demographic decline by opening doors for adults—underemployed men, women, retirees, economic immigrants—to enter or reenter the labor force. But the baby bust is global, so no country can escape it.

For advanced capitalist economies, the fastest possible growth rate is no more than 1 to 2 percent a year, half the rate of the post–World War II miracle years. Even to reach the higher end of that range, as labor force growth ebbs toward zero, will require a revolution in productivity. Leaders in the United States and other capitalist countries should be aiming to double productivity growth to around 2 percent—an ambitious but plausible target. Indeed, the economically literate among them are well aware that productivity growth is the only way to cope with population decline.

In her pitch for Bidenomics, Treasury secretary Janet Yellen presented the administration's plan as "modern supply-side economics," aimed at increasing investment "to raise the ceiling for what our economy can produce." This was a backhanded homage to Ronald Reagan, who popularized the original supply-side economics. Yellen argued that the Reagan approach—focused on unleashing the productive power of the private sector—failed. The proper role of government, for the Biden administration, is to put itself in charge of steering capital—into research and development to raise productivity, into poor communities to end inequality, into community college to end underemployment, and into batteries and green tech to slow global warming.

The Biden administration plans reflect an attempt to engineer outcomes—economic, social, environmental, geographic—without regard to the total cost. The administration has abandoned the traditional balance of cost-benefit analysis, directing its regulators to seek positive "opportunities" to write rules that advance this goal or benefit that community. Bureaucrats are to be in effect state-sponsored entrepreneurs, unleashed to disrupt the system with maximum social impact.

Central bankers are closer to the economic story and are well aware that growth over 2 percent is no longer possible in wealthy countries. Yet they, too, demonstrate what former Fed governor Kevin Warsh has called "a belief in the perfected science of monetary policy," capable of micromanaging the economy's ups and downs. Many seem almost in denial, unwilling to consider the evidence that easy money fuels inequality or undermines productivity, and afraid to step off their current course. Haunted by the specters of the 1930s, they want to intervene at the first sign of any economic trouble.

There can be no return to nineteenth-century laissez-faire capitalism. During recessions, authorities need to extend relief to the needy and unemployed and to take steps to keep capital and credit moving through the financial markets, when they are frozen by fear. But the experimental quest of recent decades for painless and endless growth is utopian, counterproductive. Capitalism's premise, that limited government is the necessary condition for individual liberty and opportunity, has yet to be tested in a modern setting.

A true capitalism of the twenty-first century would require leaders who acknowledge at least the main excesses of recent decades and aim to restore some sense of balance. They would rediscover humility and disavow the now oft-repeated claim that "we," the economic authorities, have learned how to control the ebb and flow of the business cycle. Presidents Trump and Biden pushed the campaign to generate endless growth to new extremes by unleashing massive new stimulus measures in a peacetime recovery, setting a risky precedent.

Deficits do matter, less for the red ink in any given year than for the way they drive up public debt over time, worsening society's addiction and undermining productivity. Running serious deficits only in hard times, and surpluses in a recovery in order to be ready for the next crisis, is in fact possible in a "modern" economy, as Sweden showed after its crisis in the 1990s. The mantra of government officials in recent crises—better to spend too much than too little—would be scrapped in favor of balance. Rescue spending would be crafted as a last resort, not to satisfy every bank, company, industry, city, state, and foreign ally that comes to the government's door, saying, "I'm here for help."

Central banks already recognize that inflation matters beyond just consumer prices and threatens the economy when it is driving up asset prices. But they would start acting on that knowledge. They would act to contain frothy markets before prices reach dangerous bubble proportions, not just clean up after. The current excuse—that bubbles are too hard to identify in advance, much less to contain without serious collateral damage to the economy—would be dropped as out of date.

Since the crisis of 2008, many researchers have gone looking for warning signs that would help anticipate the next one, and found them in rapid price increases, frantic trading, amateur investors rushing into the market. In "Predictable Financial Crises," a team of Harvard Business School researchers challenged the idea that crises are "bolts from the sky." They found a set of factors that could increase one's chances of accurately identifying a bubble to more than 80 percent.

The most consistent precursor of major financial crises is not the scale of debt but the pace of increase in debt. Debt manias are visible. Looking back to 1960 in 150 countries, my own research shows that when private sector debt is growing rapidly for five years or more, the economy typically slows over the next five years. The larger the debt buildup, the larger the slowdown. If, for example, debt was growing as a share of GDP by 5 percentage points a year, growth fell by a third in subsequent years. That finding aptly describes the United States before and after 2008. After a private debt boom goes bust, the state typically steps in to help clean up the mess by easing its own lending terms, leading to a spike in public debt.

Once a bubble is spotted, there are many templates for how to respond, grouped under the general heading of "lean against the wind" policies. These would generally have led to higher interest rates than what we have seen for the last two decades. A modern central bank would be working to put these ideas into practice as soon as possible, in order to address the biggest risks of today's world and move beyond those of the 1930s. Financial markets were a small fraction of annual economic output then and are much larger than the economy now.

The most radical step taken after 2008 was the decision to follow the path of Japan. Central banks across the capitalist world became a major—often the major—buyer of bonds and other assets in the debt markets. In the United States, the first round of purchases came in the Great Recession of 2007–09, but the rest came in the subsequent recovery. By the end of the 2010s, central bank purchases had exceeded in one decade the sum total of all purchases they had made back to the seventeenth century. Buying on that scale was bound to drive up inflation in the financial markets, making price signals go haywire, and it did. A capitalism for the twenty-first century would restrain these wildly experimental buying sprees, particularly in recoveries.

Policymakers need to avoid getting lost too deep in the conventional wisdom—that the solution to every problem of capitalism will be found in rewriting the rules. Of course, tax laws, lending rules, central bank mandates, the conditions imposed on recipients of social benefits, and the entire 240-volume code of regulations matter, in every detail. There are thousands of practical proposals floating around, about how to rationalize this rule or that. They do not add up to a fix. Tweaking any set or subset of the rules won't slow the spreading symptoms of decay—not when the government is pumping more money into the economy than its citizens can put to work rationally.

For half a century, governments have been building on their overbuilt foundations because they aim to please everyone, yet poll after poll shows they are increasingly unpopular and distrusted. They are digging this hole deeper, magnifying the global economic slowdown by contributing mightily—through their constant interventions—to the collapse in productivity. The most confidently interventionist states have seen the worst productivity growth slump, since the postwar peaks, from 9 percent to near 0 percent in Japan, 6 percent to half a percent in the large economies of Europe. Though the original home of limited government, the United States, has seen a relatively small slump, from 2.5 percent to around 1 percent, it is now leading the capitalist world toward a bigger, less efficient government. That is not likely to reverse what needs reversing.

Old mental models of the economy need to change. Capitalist leaders have come to think and speak of the market economy as a machine, controlled by human engineers who have the power to "fine tune" this "engine" of growth. But the economy is less a machine than a natural ecosystem, less an engine than a complex organism, like a forest or ocean.

The health and prosperity of any individual depends on the free interaction of billions, and humans intervene in these environments at great risk to the systems, and themselves.

The supreme irony: modern voters, particularly the young, now demand that leaders show respect for the fragility of natural ecosystems. They will not sit still if politicians propose to clear cut forests, or dam rivers, or raze mountaintops, in the name of prosperity. Faith in science, as a tool that allows humans to reshape nature without ill consequences, is all but gone.

At the same time, leaders are riding a popular wave when they propose to intervene in the market economy—the global ecosystem in which 8 billion people do business. Political leaders conduct increasingly radical experiments to revive and reshape the business environment, to this end or that, and the elite for the most part applaud. The hubris of economics, not nearly so hard a "science" as it would like to think, only grows. Governments and central banks face few objections, indeed they are encouraged by opinionmakers, to meddle: to force faster growth by injecting rivers of dollars into the economy, to divert capital flows through a concrete latticework of regulation, to nurture even zombies and other invasive species through bailouts.

The physical sciences teach that life is a cycle of constant transformation, ashes to ashes; political leaders ignore that lesson when they listen to economic advisers claiming to know the secrets of constant growth, with no death, no ash. That's not possible. They are claiming mastery over the cycle of life, and their arrogance needs to be recognized and contained, before it does more damage. Capitalism is still humanity's best hope for economic and social progress, but only if it is free to work.

ACKNOWLEDGMENTS

This book is a pandemic baby. It was conceived at the height of the global lockdown in the summer of 2020, when we were all sheltering in. That dark and lonely period was a catalyst for many life-changing decisions, which included leaving a firm I had been with for twenty-five years and launching my most ambitious book project yet.

What remained unchanged were several key people in my life, who for long had indulged my passion for writing. No person has been more important in this regard than Tony Emerson. We came to know each other two decades ago, when I began to write for *Newsweek*, where he would edit my columns. After we started to collaborate on book projects in 2011, hardly a day has gone by when Tony and I have not interacted, with him constantly shaping my line of thinking, filtering my opinions, and putting pen to many of my ideas. This book is primarily a fruit of his labor.

Simran Bhargava has been one of my closest friends and life coach for nearly twenty-five years. She is the best writer I know, and I am constantly tapping her incredible talent for sharpening thoughts, and the most telling suggestions. Simran claims to have little knowledge of economics but was a constant sounding board for much of the material in this book.

My younger sister, Shumita Deveshwar, has read more of my writings than anyone else. For many years, she would edit my columns before submission. Shumita has an amazing attention for detail and has thoroughly vetted all my books. Even though she is swamped with responsibilities, as a working economist and a very involved mother, she insisted on editing this book as well. Tony attested to the fact that Shumita's edits were once again masterful.

In twenty-five years at a single firm, Morgan Stanley, I developed very strong bonds, none stronger than my ties to Cyril Moullé-Berteaux. Cyril has the best analytical mind I know, and every time I get a new idea, I am always eager to test it on Cyril first. I was fortunate that he took time to go through the book in detail and offer suggestions so incisive, we rebuilt many key passages around them.

I also developed great relationships at Morgan Stanley with Vikram Pandit and Greg Fleming, two legendary figures in our business, who have also been my mentors. Vikram read an early version of the manuscript, and apart from offering valuable comments prodded me to publish the book as soon as possible. Greg has long valued macroeconomic thinking, and at Morgan he stood behind me when no other leader would, defending me as a writer when others inside the company found my published opinions too provocative. I am grateful for his unstinting support.

My discussions with Greg shaped my approach to building a team for my new venture, which combines a stable and familiar core with new blood. I couldn't be more delighted with the result. Our new macroeconomic research team, headed by Rohit Goel, along with Apoorv Bhargava and Zachary Apoian, formed the brain trust for this project. In a long career, in an industry known for long hours, I have never seen a more disciplined work ethic, and this project never could have been done on time were it not for the midnight oil burned by Rohit, Apoorv, and Zack.

Viral Acharya is another new connection who played a pivotal role in strengthening the arguments in the book. I was fortunate to have Viral, one of the brightest stars and practitioners in financial academia, spend so many hours on the manuscript, making detailed notes and bringing insights on the dynamics and dysfunctions of financial capitalism that only someone of his caliber and with his special expertise could offer.

Another life-changing decision I made during the pandemic was to move to a new publisher, and the reason I did so was the tremendous enthusiasm shown for the book proposal by Robert Messenger at Simon & Schuster. At a time when so many of my fellow authors lament the lack of high-quality editing at their publishing homes, Robert is an author's dream—a gifted and meticulous editor, with the energy to take full ownership of this project, from start to finish.

None of this would have been possible without my longtime literary agent, Andrew Wylie, an industry legend for his breadth of knowledge and quality, for always putting his authors' interests first, and for a lightning-fast response time. He instantly saw the merit in moving to a new U.S. publisher and was there to guide me through the entire process.

I have been lucky to publish in international markets through Penguin Random House, and the main reason for that is its well-known editor Stuart Proffitt. I was thrilled when Stuart chose to acquire this project as well, given our great experiences working with him in the past. Stuart is the kind of editor who sees the small and the large picture, remembers at page 200 what was said on page 2, and calls you on it. The kind you want. Fortunately with the Penguin Random House team in London comes its crack team in my home country, India, including senior members such as Gaurav Shriganesh, whose advice I value immensely.

Trying to write this book for as wide an audience as possible, I solicited the advice of people whose intellect I respect and opinion I trust. One was Frank Wisner, who I met when he was ambassador to India nearly three decades ago. Frank is one of the most well-traveled and well-read people I know, and I hope the finished copy does justice to his discerning observations on the manuscript.

My lawyer, Prakash Mehta, is a keen student of global affairs; he went through the draft a couple of times and made key suggestions. I am also thankful to my friend Rohini Malkani for doing the same. It is very uplifting when someone like Rohini, a professional economist for nearly three decades, shows such enthusiasm for my writings.

I did not want to put this book to bed without getting inputs from Steven Quattry, a member of my team at Morgan Stanley. Steven is perhaps the best and most voracious reader I know, and he came in with very useful comments on this book, too, and how its various passages were likely to be received.

Alongside all the accomplished people who helped shape this manuscript I would be remiss not to thank those who helped me make my way as an author. Fareed Zakaria is more than just a close friend. He is the don of the current affairs world, who wears his success lightly, and takes genuine interest in other people's careers. One reason this project became a book is that when I first ran the basic idea by Fareed, he said it was book material, no less. I am also thankful to Nandan Nilekani and Suketu Mehta for always being there at the other end of the line to help.

Britt Harris is one of the most highly respected figures in the investing world and a big believer in nurturing long-term relationships. As a professor at Texas A&M University, he encourages his students to become devoted readers, and in the early stages of this project he volunteered his grad class to summarize books that could provide relevant background for this project. Their terrific work proved useful source material. I am grateful to Britt.

I am also filled with gratitude to my close friends Radhika and Prannoy Roy for their interest and counsel on so many issues related to content. And also to my travel group for the many stimulating conversations during our elections trips and holidays, often leading to new insights that are part of this book.

What they all know is that there is one person who keeps the wheels of my life in motion: Paul Weiner. Without him, it would grind to a halt. He makes it all happen effortlessly and is ably supported by Christine Dsouza. When I told them I was leaving the comfort and stability of Morgan Stanley their instant response was, we're going with you, wherever that is. I was very touched.

These extraordinary individuals are my solid rocks of support. My foundation is my parents, whose love is unconditional, and who will always be my biggest cheerleaders. Regardless of how this book fares, having so many great backers and such a strong extended family on my side makes the project of writing—and of life—very special. Thank you all.

SOURCES: SUMMARY DESCRIPTION AND METHODOLOGY

INDICATOR	PERIOD	SOURCE (COUNTRY/REGION)	METHOD/NOTES
Central government tax to GDP	1980–2021	Cabinet Office of Japan and World Bank (Japan), Instituto Nacional de Estadística and World Bank (Spain). World development indicators, World Bank for rest of leading capitalist economies.	
Central government debt to GDP	1954–2022	IMF (Germany, France, Italy, Spain, UK), Bank of Japan (Japan), Office of Management and Budget (US).	
Fiscal deficit to GDP	1954–2022	Ministère de l'Économie et des Finances et de l'Industrie (France), Deutsche Bundesbank (Germany), Banca d'Italia (Italy), Banco de España (Spain), Cabinet Office of Japan (Japan), Office for National Statistics (UK), Office of Management and Budget (US)	Except for Japan and Germany, all are central/federal government
Government expenditure to GDP	1954–2022	US Treasury, Bureau of Economic Analysis (US), World Bank (France), Deutsche Bundesbank, Statistisches Bundesamt (Germany), Banca d'Italia, Istituto Nazionale di Statistica (Italy), Intervención General de la Administración del Estado/BdE, Instituto Nacional de Estadística (Spain), Ministry of Finance, Cabinet Office of Japan (Japan), Office for National Statistics (UK)	Except for Japan, all are central/federal government
Total debt to GDP	1960–2022	IMF, BIS, Bank of Japan, OMB (US)	Sum of government, household and non-financial sector debt
Financial market to GDP	1975–2021	World Bank, IMF, BIS, Bank of Japan, OMB (US)	Market capitalization of listed domestic companies (% of GDP) + total as above
Recession stimulus*	1980, 1981, 1990, 2001, 2008, 2020	Monetary stimulus–national sources: FRB, BEA (US), BoE (UK), BoJ (Japan), ECB, Eurostat (EU). Fiscal stimulus–national sources: OMB (US), ONS (UK), CAO (Japan), IMF (EU). Off-balance-sheet stimulus: UBS. *Some data is handpicked visually, as the peak stimulus is in a different year than the recession year.*	Monetary stimulus: change in central bank assets (% of GDP). Fiscal stimulus: YoY change in general gov primary balance (where N/A, used federal gov PB). Off-balance-sheet reflects the utilized loan guarantees.
Long-term labor productivity growth	1870–1998	Angus Maddison's *The World Economy: A Millennial Perspective*, Table E-8	Growth of GDP per hour worked
Recent labor productivity growth	1950–2023	Output, labor, and labor productivity dataset of the Total Economy Database, the Conference Board (April 2023)	Growth in labor productivity per hour worked
Recent TFP productivity growth	1955–2019	Penn World Tables 10.01 (January 2023)	Variable: g_rtfpna (growth of TFP at constant national prices [2017=1])

ENDNOTES

Reference to "Breakout Capital calculations" are to my in-house research, and the relevant databases, which include many of the standard international sources, from Haver Analytics to the World Bank and the IMF. The references to "Master Data" are to the custom data set I created, in order to compare the United States to other leading capitalist economies consistently, as far back in time as the data allows. The Master Data covers government spending, deficits, tax revenues, debt, size of financial markets, scale of stimulus in downturns, and productivity growth, using the most authoritative available sources. The choice of the seven leading capitalist economies, which we call the LCEs—the United States, Japan, the United Kingdom, and the four large European powers, Germany, France, Italy, and Spain—was based on both size of the economy and availability of comparable historical data. The specific data sources are listed on the previous page, with notes on calculation methods.

Prologue: Why I Fell for Capitalism

XIII *"As I rise, I am overpowered"*: Manmohan Singh, "Budget 1991–92," transcript of speech delivered at New Delhi, July 24, 1991, https://www.indiabudget.gov.in/doc/bspeech/bs199192.pdf.

XIV *China's has risen fortyfold to $12,500*: Breakout Capital calculations based on IMF.

XV *Political and popular support for*: "The American Left and Right Loathe Each Other and Agree on a Lot," *The Economist*, July 13, 2023.

Introduction: What Went Wrong

1 *"I've spoken of the shining city all my political life"*: Ronald Reagan, "Farewell Address to the Nation," Washington, DC, January 11, 1989, https://www.reaganlibrary.gov/archives/speech/farewell-address-nation.

3 *China may never make it*: Lindsay Maizland and Eleanor Albert, "The Chinese Communist Party," Council on Foreign Relations Back-grounder, October 6, 2022.

4 *"The capital markets are not free"*: Ray Dalio, Bloomberg TV, July 2, 2020, https://www.bloomberg.com/news/videos/2020-07-02/dalio -says-capital-markets-are-no-longer-free-markets-video (at 3:47).

4 *Bernie Sanders has a point*: Orion Rummler, "Sanders Defends Socialism: 'We Are Living, in Many Ways, in a Socialist Society Right Now,'" *Axios*, February 19, 2020.

5 *In 2016, the youth vote*: Stef W. Kight, "70% of Millennials Say They'd Vote For a Socialist," *Axios*, October 28, 2019.

5 *For the first time since the Pew polling agency*: Stef W. Kight, "Exclusive Poll: Young Americans Are Embracing Socialism," *Axios*, March 10, 2019; "Americans' Views of Government: Low Trust, but Some Positive Performance Ratings," Pew Research Center, September 14, 2020, https://www.pewresearch.org/politics/2020/09/14/americans-views-of -government-low-trust-but-some-positive-performance-ratings/.

5 *"the era of small government"*: Jamelle Bouie, "The Era of Small Government Is Over," *New York Times*, March 18, 2020; Gary Gerstle, "The Age of Neoliberalism Is Ending in America," *The Guardian*, June 28, 2021; Justin Lahart, "The Era of Big Government Is Back," *Wall Street Journal*, June 25, 2021.

6 *In Gary Gerstle's taxonomy of capitalist orders*: Gary Gerstle, *The Rise and Fall of the Neoliberal Order: America and the World in the Free Market Era* (Oxford: Oxford University Press, 2022), 121.

6 *In Jonathan Levy's account of capitalist ages*: Jonathan Levy, *Ages of American Capitalism: A History of the United States* (New York: Random House, 2021), 590.

6 *"thirty glorious years"*: J. Bradford DeLong, *Slouching Towards Utopia: An Economic History of the Twentieth Century* (New York: Basic Books, 2022), 14.

7 *The neoliberals resurrected the ideas*: Louis Menand, "The Rise and Fall of Neoliberalism," *New Yorker*, July 24, 2023.

8 *Half the government departments*: Seven of fifteen had not yet been

created—see "The President's Cabinet," InfoUSA, U.S. Department of State, https://usinfo.org/enus/government/branches/ben_cabinet.html.

8 *Half of all federal government employees*: U.S. Census Bureau, "Historical Statistics of the United States: Colonial Times to 1970, Series Y 308-317, Paid Civilian Employment of the Federal Government: 1816 to 1970," https:// ia600407.us.archive.org/4/items/HistoricalStatis ticsOfTheUnitedStatesColonialTimesTo1970/us_ historical_statistics _colonial_times_to_1970.pdf; "Federal Government—Employment: 1901 to 2002," https://www2.census.gov/library/publications/2004 /compendia/statab/123ed/hist/hs-50.pdf.

8 *Compared to the capitals of Europe*: "Bicentennial Edition: Historical Statistics of the United States, Colonial Times to 1970," U.S. Census Bureau, September 1975; Michael Schuyler, "A Short History of Government Taxing and Spending in the United States," Tax Foundation, February 19, 2014, https://taxfoundation.org/research/all/federal /short-history-government-taxing-and-spending-united-states/.

9 *Since 1930, spending by government*: The historical spending and tax collection data for general government (which includes state and local) is drawn from Public Finances in Modern History, IMF, based on Paulo Mauro, Rafael Romeu, Ariel Binder, and Asad Zaman, "A Modern History of Fiscal Prudence and Profligacy," *Journal of Monetary Economics*, 2015, vol. 76, 5–70.

9 *If revenues are so steady*: Breakout Capital calculations, World Bank, Indicator Code: GC.TAX.TOTL.GD.ZS.

9 *The big change was that the large capitalist*: Breakout Capital calculations based on the Master Data.

10 *surging to almost 120 percent*: Breakout Capital calculations, using data from IMF, Bank of Japan, and U.S. Office of Management and Budget (OMB).

10 *Elected legislatures were fracturing . . . "doing too much"*: Jeanna Smialek, *Limitless: The Federal Reserve Takes on a New Age of Crisis* (New York: Alfred A. Knopf, 2023), 139, 201, 218–34, 277, 282.

10 *Yet for much of this century*: Ibid., 139, 202, 282.

11 *"revolution in pain management"*: Vanda Felbab-Brown et al., "The Opioid Crisis in America," Brookings Institution, June 22, 2020, https://www.brookings.edu/articles/overview-the-opioid-crisis-in -america/.

11 *about 1 percent of GDP*: Breakout Capital calculations based on the Master Data.

12 *From slightly larger on average*: Breakout Capital calculations based on: Institute of International Finance, World Bank, and IMF.

12 *Though stocks comprise roughly*: Breakout Capital calculations based on the Master Data.

12 *"sinking demons"*: Shuli Ren, "Who's to Blame for Fallen Angels and Sinking Demons?," *Bloomberg*, April 6, 2020, https://www.bloomberg .com/view/articles/2020-04-06/coronavirus-fed-rescue-could-exacer bate-unhealthy-credit-market#xj4y7vzkg.

13 *But like population growth*: Breakout Capital calculations based on data from the United Nations, Haver Analytics.

14 *It is likely no accident*: Anu Bradford, *The Brussels Effect: How the European Union Rules the World* (New York: Oxford University Press, 2020), 16.

14 *As what researchers have called*: Richard J. Caballero and Mohamad L. Hammour, "The Cleansing Effect of Recessions," *American Economic Review* (December 1994).

15 *Billionaires barely existed*: Stephanie Krikorian, "'Tax the Rich' Protesters Descend on the Hamptons," *Vanity Fair*, July 18, 2022; Leila Abboud, "Blame the Billionaires? French Left Protests Against Emmanuel Macron's Pension Reform," *Financial Times*, February 1, 2023.

15 *Like the media establishment*: Josh Bivens and Jori Kandra, "CEO Pay Has Skyrocketed 1,460% Since 1978," Economic Policy Institute, October 4, 2022, https://www.epi.org/publication/ceo-pay-in-2021/.

16 *Even writers who normally*: David Brooks, "The Power of American Capitalism," *New York Times*, October 4, 2022.

16 *What impressed establishment publications*: "The Lessons from America's Astonishing Economic Record," and "America's Economic Outperformance Is a Marvel to Behold," *The Economist*, April 13, 2023.

16 *"better" than fifty years ago*: Andrew Daniller, "Americans Take a Dim View of the Nation's Future, Look More Positively at the Past," Pew Research Center, April 24, 2023, https://www.pewresearch.org/short -reads/2023/04/24/americans-take-a-dim-view-of-the-nations-fu ture-look-more-positively-at-the-past/.

17 *Its premise*: Jake Sullivan, "Renewing American Economic Leader- ship," transcript of remarks delivered at the Brookings Institution, Washington, DC, April 27, 2023, https://www.whitehouse.gov/brief ing-room/speeches-remarks/2023/04/27/remarks-by-national-secu rity-advisor-jake-sullivan-on-renewing-american-economic-leader ship-at-the-brookings-institution/.

17 *The head of the European*: David Wallace-Wells, "America's 'Neoliberal' Consensus Might Finally Be Dead," *New York Times*, May 25, 2023.

17 *Japan launched*: "Green Protectionism Comes with Big Risks," *The Economist*, October 2, 2023.

17 *German officials warned*: Guy Chazan, Laura Pitel, and Patricia Nilsson, "Germany Warns Companies to Reduce Dependence on China," *Financial Times*, July 13, 2023.

17 *Biden had campaigned*: Editorial Board, "Biden's Cradle-to-Grave Government," *Wall Street Journal*, April 28, 2021; Brian Deese, "Modern American Industrial Strategy," transcript of remarks delivered at the Economic Club of New York, April 20, 2022, https://www.whitehouse.gov/briefing-room/speeches-remarks/2022/04/20/remarks-on-a-modern-american-industrial-strategy-by-nec-director-brian-deese/.

17 *Biden was said by aides*: David E. Sanger, "40 Years After Reagan, a Bet Big Government Can Get Something Done," *New York Times*, March 31, 2021.

17 *As paramount leader Xi Jinping*: Breakout Capital calculations based on Haver Analytics, National Sources.

19 *Former U.S. trade representative*: Robert B. Zoellick, "Welcome to Biden's Tale of WOE," *Wall Street Journal*, June 7, 2023.

19 *Of that sum*: Based on a study by Breakout Capital of the major spending bills during the Biden administration, sourced from press reports, the Congressional Budget Office, Congress.gov, and other U.S. government sources.

19 *As Biden rolled out new spending*: Ruchir Sharma, "The Trouble with American Exceptionalism, *Financial Times*, July 16, 2023.

19 *In early 2024*: Scott Remer, "Biden Is Turning Out to Be More Like Obama Than FDR," *In These Times*, June 7, 2023, https://inthesetimes.com/article/biden-obama-fdr-debt-ceiling-neoliberal-manchin-bernie-sanders.

19 *The deficit thereafter*: "The 2023 Long-Term Budget Outlook," Congressional Budget Office, July 27, 2023, https://www.cbo.gov/publication/59014.

19 *In the coming years*: Breakout Capital calculations based on Master Data, Haver Analytics, and IMF forecasts.

20 *And deficits mean*: Sharma, "The Trouble with American Exceptionalism."

20 *Already third highest in the developed world*: The public debt figures here and throughout are calculated on a gross (not net) basis,

following the approach used by multilateral organizations like the International Monetary Fund for cross-country comparisons.

Chapter One: There Was No Golden Age

25 *Hamilton would prevail*: "From Alexander Hamilton to Robert Morris, [30 April 1781]," *Founders Online*, National Archives, https://founders.archives.gov/documents/Hamilton/01-02-02-1167; *The Papers of Alexander Hamilton*, vol. 2, *1779–1781*, ed. Harold C. Syrett (New York: Columbia University Press, 1961), 604–35.

26 *In fact Hamilton did model*: Anthony Howe, "From 'Old Corruption' to 'New Probity'; The Bank of England and Its Directors in the Age of Reform," *Financial History Review* 1, no. 1 (April 1994): 23–41; Philip Harling, "Rethinking 'Old Corruption,' " *Past & Present* 147, no. 1 (May 1995): 127–58.

26 *Nonetheless, a loosely Hamiltonian*: Rose Eveleth, "Before the Civil War, There Were 8,000 Different Kinds of Money in the U.S.," *Smithsonian Magazine*, December 12, 2012.

26 *In this period, the American South*: Levy, *Ages of American Capitalism*, 159.

26 *Powered first by water*: Levy, *Ages of American Capitalism*, 180.

27 *The North was, in essence*: Eric Foner, "The Hidden Story of the North's Victory in the Civil War," *New York Times*, March 8, 2022.

27 *He also consolidated*: Levy, *Ages of American Capitalism*, 201.

28 *"protect their own gold reserves"*: Michael D. Bordo, "A Brief History of Central Banks," Federal Reserve Bank of Cleveland, Economic Commentary, December 1, 2007, https://www.clevelandfed.org/publications/economic-commentary/2007/ec-20071201-a-brief-history-of-central-banks; see also Edward Chancellor, *The Price of Time: The Real Story of Interest* (New York: Atlantic Monthly Press, 2022), 76, 82.

28 *As the robber barons built*: Levy, *Ages of American Capitalism*, 266; Patrick J. Kiger, "10 Major Labor Strikes Throughout US History," History.com, May 3, 2023, https://www.history.com/news/strikes-labor-movement.

29 *Still, lingering resistance*: "The Founding of the Fed," Federal Reserve Bank of New York, https://www.newyorkfed.org/aboutthefed/history_article.html.

29 *Worldwide, per capita income*: Tom Clark, "The UK Is Facing Two Lost Decades on Living Standards," *Financial Times*, February 5, 2022.

29 *Germans, for example*: Joerg Baten and Matthias Blum, "Why Are You Tall While Others Are Short? Agricultural Production and Other Proximate Determinants of Global Heights," *European Review of Economic History* 18, no. 2 (May 2014): 144–65; John Komlos, "Shrinking in a Growing Economy? The Mystery of Physical Stature During the Industrial Revolution," *Journal of Economic History* 58, no. 3 (September 1998): 779–85.

30 *Since 1880*: "Striding Tall: US v. USSR," The Globalist, October 7, 2017, https://www.theglobalist.com/striding-tall-us-vs-ussr/; "A Great Leap Upward?," The Globalist, October 7, 2017, https://www.theglobalist.com/a-great-leap-upward/; "Denmark: A Head and Shoulders Above," The Globalist, October 7, 2017, https://www.theglobalist.com/denmark-a-head-and-shoulders-above/.

30 *From 1875 to 1915*: Kevin H. O'Rourke, "Tarrifs and Growth in the Late 19th Century," *Economic Journal* 110, no. 463 (April 2000): 456–83.

30 *One reason was a statist*: Edward L. Glaeser and Andrei Shleifer, "Legal Origins," *Quarterly Journal of Economics* 117, no. 4 (November 2002), 1193–229, https://doi.org/10.1162/003355302320935016.

30 *They resisted the construction*: Oscar Jászi, *The Dissolution of the Habsburg Monarchy* (Burke, VA: Borodino Books, 2018), e-book, 80.

30 *More than half a century*: James Hamblin, "A Mapped History of Taking a Train Across the United States," *The Atlantic*, February 21, 2013.

31 *While other societies were booming*: O'Rourke, "Tariffs and Growth in the Late 19th Century," 460–64.

31 *per capita GDP shrank in the Austro-Hungarian empire*: Alexander Klein, Max-Stephan Schulze, and Tamás Vonyó, "How Peripheral Was the Periphery? Industrialization in East Central Europe Since 1870," in *The Spread of Modern Industry to the Periphery Since 1871*, Kevin H. O'Rourke and Jeffrey G. Williamson, eds. (Oxford: Oxford University Press/Oxford Academic, 2017), e-book, 64–65, https://doi.org/10.1093/acprof:oso/9780198753643.001.0001.

31 *The artists of this period*: Charles Sheeler, *River Rouge Plant*, 1932, Whitney Museum of American Art, New York, oil and pencil on canvas, https://whitney.org/collection/works/1480.

31 *The Fed responded*: Marvin Goodfriend, book review of Allan H. Meltzer, *A History of the Federal Reserve, Volume 1: 1913–1951* (Chicago: University of Chicago Press, 2003), posted December 1, 2003 at minneapolisfed.org.

31 *Industrial production fell*: Matt Stoller, *Goliath: The 100-Year War*

Between Monopoly Power and Democracy (New York: Simon & Schuster, 2020), 31; Michael Bordo and Andrew Filardo, "Deflation in Historical Perspective" (Bank for International Settlements Working Paper No. 186, 2005), https://www.bis.org/publ/work186.pdf.

32 *Later, President Herbert Hoover's*: Charles Rappleye, *Herbert Hoover in the White House: The Ordeal of the Presidency* (New York: Simon & Schuster, 2016), 28.

32 *The boom of the twenties*: Chancellor, *The Price of Time*, 89.

32 *U.S. life expectancy*: Robert Shackleton, "Total Factor Productivity Growth in Historical Perspective" (Congressional Budget Office Working Paper 2013–01, 2013), https://www.cbo.gov/sites/default /files/113th-congress-2013-2014/workingpaper/44002_TFP_Growth _03-18-2013_1.pdf.

33 *By 1926 most cars*: Martha Olney, "Credit as a Production-Smoothing Device: The Case of Automobiles, 1913–1938," *Journal of Economic History* 49, no. 2 (1989): 377–91, https://EconPapers.repec.org /RePEc:cup:jechis:v:49:y:1989:i:02:p:377-391_00.

33 *The number of Americans*: Levy, *Ages of American Capitalism*, 361.

Chapter Two: None of Us Are Keynesians Now

35 *During his first year in office*: Rexford G. Tugwell, *The Democratic Roosevelt: A Biography of Franklin D. Roosevelt* (Garden City, NY: Doubleday, 1957), 350.

36 *Roosevelt would turn government*: David C. Wheelock, "The Great Depression: An Overview," Federal Reserve Bank of St. Louis, xi–xiv, https://www.stlouisfed.org/-/media/project/frbstl/stlouisfed/files/pdfs /great-depression/the-great-depression-wheelock-overview.pdf.

36 *The Fed used*: Smialek, *Limitless*, 160–61.

36 *Then in 2008*: Ben S. Bernanke, *21st Century Monetary Policy* (New York: W. W. Norton 2022), 123, 263, 312.

36 *The industrial shakeouts*: Greg Zyla, "Cars We Remember: From 2,000 to 4; A Short History of American Car Companies," *Gainesville Sun*, November 28, 2016.

37 *The car companies added faster*: "Packard Automobile Plant," Detroiturbex.com, 2013, http://www.detroiturbex.com/content/industry/packard /index.html.

37 *Packard cut the factory space*: Chancellor, *The Price of Time*, 142.

37 *key to economic progress*: Peter Coy, "Here's the Secret Ingredient in Economic Growth," *New York Times*, April 17, 2022.

37 *Historian Alexander J. Field would*: Shackleton, "Total Factor Produc-
    tivity Growth in Historical Perspective."

37 *He titled his book*: Chancellor, *The Price of Time*, 142 (Chancellor
    slightly mistitles the Field book); Alexander J. Field, *A Great Leap
    Forward: 1930s Depression and U.S. Economic Growth* (New Haven,
    CT: Yale University Press, 2012).

38 *British economist John Maynard Keynes*: Liaquat Ahamed, *Lords
    of Finance: The Bankers Who Broke the World* (New York: Penguin
    Press, 2009), 339.

38 *On balance, taking action*: Chancellor, *The Price of Time*, 88.

38 *The view of many observers*: Chancellor, *The Price of Time*, 100.

39 *The standard narrative*: Ben S. Bernanke, "Asset-Price 'Bubbles' and
    Monetary Policy," transcript of remarks delivered at the National Associa-
    tion for Business Economists, New York, October 15, 2002, https://www
    .federalreserve.gov/boarddocs/speeches/2002/20021015/default.htm.

39 *At the time, however, there was*: Bernanke, *21st Century Monetary
    Policy*, 136; Christopher Klein, "1929 Stock Market Crash: Did
    Panicked Investors Really Jump from Windows?," History.com,
    March 7, 2019, https://www.history.com/news/stock-market-crash
    -suicides-wall-street-1929-great-depression.

39 *The role of the Fed as lender*: Jason Giordano, "Federal Reserve
    Becomes Buyer of Last Resort," S&P Dow Jones Indices, March 27,
    2020, https://www.spglobal.com/en/research-insights/articles/
    federal-reserve-becomes-buyer-of-last-resort.

39 *Ever since the 1930s*: Claudio Borio, Magdalena Erdem, Andrew
    Filardo, and Boris Hofmann, "The Cost of Deflations: A Historical
    Perspective," *BIS Quarterly Review*, March 2015, 31–54, https://www
    .bis.org/publ/qtrpdf/r_qt1503e.htm.

39 *The growing instability*: Gerstle, *The Rise and Fall of the Neoliberal
    Order*, 259; Breakout Capital calculations based on Harvard Business
    School, Behavioral Finance & Financial Stability.

40 *"never in the history of the Fed"*: Christopher Leonard, *The Lords of
    Easy Money* (New York: Simon & Schuster, 2022), 285–86.

40 *The rescues were largely unquestioned*: Leonard, *The Lords of Easy
    Money*, 277–96.

40 *The share of American households*: "Understanding Taxes—Theme
    2: Taxes in U.S. History—Lesson 5: The Wealth Tax of 1935 and
    the Victory Tax of 1942," Internal Revenue Service, https://apps.irs
    .gov/app/understandingTaxes/teacher/whys_thm02_les05.jsp#:~:

text=Additional%20taxes%20were%20put%20in,with%20new
%20income%20tax%20revenue.

40 *its debt nearly tripled to more than*: James A. Dorn, "Fiscal
Dominance and Fed Complacency," *Cato at Liberty* (blog), April 8,
2021, https://www.cato.org/blog/fiscal-dominance-fed-compla
cency.

40 *The Defense Plant Corporation*: Stoller, *Goliath*, 147; Gerald T. White,
"Financing Industrial Expansion for War: The Origin of the Defense
Plant Corporation Leases," *Journal of Economic History* 9, no. 2
(1949): 156–83, http://www.jstor.org/stable/2113638.

40 *By the end of the war*: White, "Financing Industrial Expansion for
War," 156–83; Stoller, *Goliath*, 147, 150.

41 *early for battle, like Germany and Japan*: R. J. Overy, *War and
Economy in the Third Reich* (Oxford: Oxford University Press, 1994),
36–37; Michiya Kato, "Hidden from View? The Measurement of
Japanese Interwar Unemployment," *Annual Research Bulletin of
Osaka Sangyo University*, (2009), 94–95.

41 *the "great arsenal"*: Franklin Delano Roosevelt, "Fireside Chat on the
'Great Arsenal of Democracy,'" December 29, 1940, https://web.mit
.edu/21h.102/www/Primary%20source%20collections/World%20
War%20II/FDR,%20Arsenal%20of%20Democracy.html.

41 *"freedom from want"*: Franklin D. Roosevelt, 1941 State of the Union
Address, "The Four Freedoms," January 6, 1941, Voices of Democracy/
The U.S. Oratory Project, https://voicesofdemocracy.umd.edu/fdr-the
-four-freedoms-speech-text/.

41 *In the GI Bill*: Jim Reid, Henry Allen, Luke Templeman, and Adrian
Cox, "Long-Term Asset Return Study 2022: How We Got Here and
Where We're Going," Deutsche Bank Research, September 28, 2022.

42 *From the wartime highs*: "Government Spending Multiyear Download
for United States 1900–2028," usgovernmentspending.com, https://
www.usgovernmentrevenue.com/download?show=n; Tejvan Pettinger,
"UK Public spending as % of GDP," *Economicshelp.org* (blog), June 11,
2023, https://www.economicshelp.org/blog/5326/economics/govern
ment-spending/.

42 *"essential components of the welfare state"*: Thomas Piketty, *A Brief
History of Equality*, trans. Steven Rendall (Cambridge, MA: Belknap
Press, 2022), 124.

42 *Government spending*: "United States: 2023 Article IV Consultation—
Press Release; Staff Report; and Statement by the Executive Director

for the United States," International Monetary Fund, June 15, 2023, https://www.imf.org/en/Publications/CR/Issues/2023/06/14/United -States-2023-Article-IV-Consultation-Press-Release-Staff-Report-and -Statement-by-the-534755.

42 *in the developed economies on average*: "Why Long-Term Rates Must Continue to Fall?" Macquarie Research, "What Caught My Eye?" v. 153, September 21, 2021.

42 *It's as if the two*: Breakout Capital calculations based on IMF Article IV reports.

43 *"the only thing"*: Franklin D. Roosevelt, "FDR's First Inaugural Address Declaring 'War' on the Great Depression," March 4, 1933, National Archives, https://www.archives.gov/education/lessons/ fdr-inaugural.

44 *Eisenhower defended the wartime*: Gerstle, *The Rise and Fall of the Neoliberal Order*, 41, 43.

44 *"should any"*: Levy, *Ages of American Capitalism*, 522.

44 *"everything the government"*: Dwight D. Eisenhower, "Radio and Tele-vision Broadcast: 'The Women Ask the President,'" October 24, 1956, https://www.presidency.ucsb.edu/documents/radio-and-television -broadcast-the-women-ask-the-president.

44 *"We are all Keynesians now"*: Gerstle, *The Rise and Fall of the Neolib-eral Order*, 46.

44 *Still, Eisenhower remained*: Farewell Address by President Dwight D. Eisenhower, January 17, 1961; Final TV Talk January 17, 1961 (1), Box 38, Speech Series, Papers of Dwight D. Eisenhower as President, 1953–61, Eisenhower Library; National Archives and Records Ad-ministration, https://www.archives.gov/milestone-documents/pres ident-dwight-d-eisenhowers-farewell-address.

44 *The action was seen*: Alan S. Blinder, *A Monetary and Fiscal History of the United States, 1961–2021* (Princeton, NJ: Princeton University Press, 2022), 13.

45 *This inflation-free boom*: Blinder, *A Monetary and Fiscal History*, 12, 17–18, 20, 28.

45 *In 1966 former Kennedy aide*: Blinder, *A Monetary and Fiscal History*, 11.

45 *"a leader of war"*: Blinder, *A Monetary and Fiscal History*, 21.

45 *it was the first*: Blinder, *A Monetary and Fiscal History*, 27.

45 *"in the future"*: Blinder, *A Monetary and Fiscal History*, 22.

45 *"symmetric" policies*: Blinder, *A Monetary and Fiscal History*, 22, 360, 372.

46 *When cutbacks were the order*: Blinder, *A Monetary and Fiscal History*, 21.

46 *"we have learned at last"*: Richard Nixon, "Inaugural Address,"
    transcript of speech delivered in Washington, DC, January 20, 1969,
    American Presidency Project, https://www.presidency.ucsb.edu/node
    /239549; Stoller, *Goliath*, 212.

46 *Having appointed a friend*: Wyatt C. Wells, *Economist in an
    Uncertain World: Arthur F. Burns and the Federal Reserve, 1970–1978*
    (New York: Columbia University Press, 1994), 61.

46 *This was the only time*: Burton A. Abrams and James L. Butkiewicz,
    "The Political Economy of Wage and Price Controls: Evidence from
    the Nixon Tapes," *Public Choice* 170 (October 13, 2016): 63–78,
    https://link.springer.com/article/10.1007/s11127-016-0381-0#citeas.

46 *The resulting recession*: Blinder, *A Monetary and Fiscal History*,
    65–66, 68, 70, 106.

47 *Even some advisers*: Blinder, *A Monetary and Fiscal History*, 112–13.

47 *The United States had emerged*: "Destruction and Reconstruction
    (1945–1958)," International Monetary Fund, https://www.imf.org
    /external/np/exr/center/mm/eng/mm_dr_01.htm; M. G. O'Cal-
    laghan, *The Structure and Operation of the World Gold Market*, IMF
    eLibrary, December 1, 1991, https://www.elibrary.imf.org/view/jour
    nals/001/1991/120/article-A001-en.xml.

47 *It was hard to imagine*: Levy, *Ages of American Capitalism*, 470.

48 *Over the next two years*: Levy, *Ages of American Capitalism*, 553.

48 *This freedom was empowering*: Blinder, *A Monetary and Fiscal History*, 69.

48 *The deficits of the early*: Reid et al., "Long-Term Asset Return Study
    2022," 20, 26, 27, 112.

50 *He waxed eloquent*: Gerstle, *The Rise and Fall of the Neoliberal Order*,
    64–69; Jimmy Carter, "The State of the Union Address Delivered
    Before a Joint Session of the Congress," January 19, 1978, https://
    www.presidency.ucsb.edu/documents/the-state-the-union-address
    -delivered-before-joint-session-the-congress-1.

50 *Carter was also, however*: Jimmy Carter, "Inaugural Address of Jimmy
    Carter," January 20, 1977, Yale Law Library, https://avalon.law.yale
    .edu/20th_century/carter.asp.

Chapter Three: The Reagan Evolution

52 *Asked later*: Blinder, *A Monetary and Fiscal History*, 106.

52 *"How far should a central bank"*: Smialek, *Limitless*, 245.

52 *consumer prices and asset prices as "cousins"*: Leonard, *The Lords of
    Easy Money*, 56, 81.

52 *The stock market dropped*: Leonard Silk, "Volcker on the Crash," *New York Times*, November 8, 1987.

52 *Critics sent Volcker*: Chancellor, *The Price of Time*, 109; Yuki Noguchi, "Former Fed Chair Paul Volcker Dies at 92," NPR, December 9, 2019.

52 *Defeating inflation*: Levy, *Ages of American Capitalism*, 587.

53 *Reagan nudged Volcker to resign*: Robert D. Hershey Jr., "Volcker Out After 8 Years as Federal Reserve Chief; Reagan Chooses Greenspan," *New York Times*, June 3, 1987.

53 *The growth of government*: Paul Krugman, "What Was Going on Between the White House and the Federal Reserve in the Early 1980s?: Daily Focus," Washington Center for Equitable Growth, January 12, 2015, https://equitablegrowth.org/going-white-house-federal-reserve-early-1980s-daily-focus/.

53 *The job of fully restoring*: David Wessel, *What We Learned from Reagan's Tax Cuts*, Brookings Institution, December 8, 2017, https://www.brookings.edu/articles/what-we-learned-from-reagans-tax-cuts/; Justin Fox, "The Mostly Forgotten Tax Increases of 1982–1993," *Bloomberg*, December 15, 2017.

53 *Yet government spending*: Piketty, *A Brief History of Equality*, 123.

54 *Having remained under*: "Federal Budget Deficit Totals $1.4 Trillion in Fiscal Year 2009," Congressional Budget Office, November 6, 2009.

54 *The Republicans became the party*: Blinder, *A Monetary and Fiscal History*, 138.

54 *That changed dramatically*: Philipp Carlsson-Szlezak, "U.S. Economics: Pushing on Growth—the Future and Limits of the 'Compulsive Stimulus Model,'" Bernstein Research, May 22, 2019, 3.

54 *U.S. government debt peaked*: "Historical Debt Outstanding," Fiscal Data, October 10, 2023, Treasury.gov, https://api.fiscaldata.treasury.gov/services/api/fiscal_service/v2/accounting/od/debt_outstanding.

55 *In the past, presidents*: Blinder, *A Monetary and Fiscal History*, 174–80, 304.

55 *The vigilantes loved*: Blinder, *A Monetary and Fiscal History*, 190–92.

56 *The Democrat, Al Gore, said he would*: Ceci Connolly, "Gore Outlines Several Uses for Surplus," *Washington Post*, June 14, 2000.

57 *The overwhelming majority:* Breakout Capital calculations based on data from the Office of Management and Budget, Haver Analytics, Bloomberg, and NBER recession dates.

57 *More than three-quarters*: Breakout Capital calculations based on National Sources, Haver Analytics.

57 *In 2008, at the height*: M. J. Stephey, "A Brief History of the Times Square Debt Clock," *Time*, October 14, 2008.

57 *"more expansionary"*: Brian I. Baker, "Fiscal Impetus and the Great Recession," *Beyond BLS*, January 2015, Bureau of Labor Statistics, https://www.bls.gov/opub/mlr/2015/beyond-bls/fiscal_impetus_and _the_great_recession.htm; Alan S. Blinder, *After the Music Stopped* (New York: Penguin Press, 2013), 393.

57 *History, which had made a hero*: J. Bradford DeLong, "Was the Great Recession More Damaging Than the Great Depression?," *Milken Institute Review*, October 29, 2018, https://www.milkenreview.org/articles/was -the-great-recession-more-damaging-than-the-great-depression.

58 *Liberal economists*: Ibid.

58 *"this sounded Orwellian"*: Blinder, *A Monetary and Fiscal History*, 303.

61 *In 1990, the trouble*: Bernanke, "Asset-Price 'Bubbles' and Monetary Policy," 49.

61 *"very unusual"*: Leonard, *The Lords of Easy Money*, 73–74.

61 *The long recoveries of the '90s*: Leonard, *The Lords of Easy Money*, 75.

61 *"nobody in Washington"*: Blinder, *A Monetary and Fiscal History*, 432.

Chapter Four: The Origins of Easy Money

63 *The morning after*: Mark Carlson, *A Brief History of the 1987 Stock Market Crash with a Discussion of the Federal Reserve Response*, Board of Governors of the Federal Reserve, November 2006, 10, https://www .federalreserve.gov/pubs/feds/2007/200713/200713pap.pdf.

64 *The new mood*: Connie Bruck, *The Predators' Ball: The Inside Story of Drexel Burnham and the Rise of the Junk Bond Traders* (New York: Penguin Books, 1989), 10.

64 *from Japan to Norway*: K. Osugi, "Japan's Experience of Financial Deregulation Since 1984 in an International Perspective" (Bank for International Settlements Paper No. 26, January 1990), 19, Table 5, https://www.bis.org/publ/econ26.pdf; Tord S. H. Krogh, "Credit Reg-ulations in Norway, 1970–2008" (Report 37-2010), Statistics Norway, August 2010, 3–39, https://www.uio.no/studier/emner/sv/oekonomi /ECON4335/h14/rapp_201037_en.pdf.

65 *While the recession of 1990*: Leonard, *The Lords of Easy Money*, 75.

65 *When the Fed did start hiking*: Breakout Capital calculations based on Federal Reserve Economic Data (FRED).

66 *below zero in 2014*: "Key ECB Interest Rates," European Central Bank, https://www.ecb.europa.eu/stats/policy_and_exchange_rates

/key_ecb_interest_rates/html/index.en.html; Reid et al., "Long-Term Asset Return Study 2022."

66 *for the next eight years*: Earlier, in 1999, the Bank of Japan had become the first central bank to push the basic rate it charges bank borrowers to zero.

67 *Still, these were super-cheap*: Patrick Collinson, "Danish Bank Launches World's First Negative Interest Rate Mortgage," *The Guardian*, August 13, 2019.

67 *"not too hot"*: David Shulman biography, UCLA Anderson School of Management, https://www.anderson.ucla.edu/about/centers/ucla -anderson-forecast/about-us/david-shulman.

68 *After 1992, the Fed kept*: Chancellor, *The Price of Time*, 111; Leonard, *The Lords of Easy Money*, 81.

68 *"irrational exuberance"*: Alan Greenspan, speech to the American Enterprise Institute, December 5, 1996, https://www.c-span.org/video /?c4673470/user-clip-alan-greenspan-irrational-exuberance.

68 *Doubters inside the Fed*: Leonard, *The Lords of Easy Money*, 85.

69 *The Fed responded*: Ann Saphir and Jason Lange, "With Fed's 'Insurance' Cut, Powell Takes Cue from Greenspan," Reuters, August 1, 2019; Leonard, *The Lords of Easy Money*, 85, 143.

69 *Thus in the aftermath*: Leonard, *The Lords of Easy Money*, 88.

69 *"When you keep rates"*: Bernanke, *21st Century Monetary Policy*, 75–79; Leonard, *The Lords of Easy Money*, 93.

69 *"Japan trap"*: Bernanke, *21st Century Monetary Policy*, 94.

71 *By mid-2003*: Bernanke, *21st Century Monetary Policy*, 95.

71 *If anything*: Borio, Erdem, Filardo, and Hofmann, "The Costs of Deflations."

72 *The Bank of Japan's*: "Establishment and Abolishment of Principal Terms and Conditions in Accordance with the Introduction of the 'Quantitative and Qualitative Monetary Easing,'" Bank of Japan, April 4, 2013, https://www.boj.or.jp/en/mopo/mpmdeci/mpr_2013 /rel130404a.pdf; Inigo Fraser-Jenkins, "Portfolio Strategy: Has the Fed Gone Too Far?," Bernstein Research, June 23, 2020; Inigo Fraser-Jenkins, "Global Quantitative Strategy: Why Is Volatility So Low and What It Means," Bernstein Research, June 23, 2020.

73 *In Washington*: Bernanke, *21st Century Monetary Policy*, 170.

73 *The money is not "printed"*: Leonard, *The Lords of Easy Money*, 26, 113.

74 *The scale of these new bond-buying campaigns*: Leonard, *The Lords of Easy Money*, 6.

74 *in recession*: Breakout Capital calculations based on the Master Data.

74 *The same basic pattern*: Ibid.

75 *Investors are so obsessed*: Carola Binder, "Federal Reserve Communication and the Media," *Journal of Media Economics* 30, no. 4 (2017): 191–214, https://www.tandfonline.com/doi/abs/10.1080/08997764.2 018.1515767.

75 *As Bernanke wrote*: Leonard, *The Lords of Easy Money*, 30; Ben S. Bernanke, "Aiding the Economy: What the Fed Did and Why," Fed eralReserve.gov, November 5, 2010, https://www.federalreserve.gov /newsevents/other/o_bernanke20101105a.htm.

75 *That minority included board members*: Leonard, *The Lords of Easy Money*, 121.

76 *the* "Groundhog Day *scenario*": Federal Open Market Committee meeting transcript, December 11–12, 2012, 105, https://www.federal reserve.gov/monetarypolicy/files/fomc20121212meeting.pdf.

76 *Lacker warned that the Fed*: Leonard, *The Lords of Easy Money*, 30, 31.

76 *people holding their money in bank savings accounts*: Ibid., 32.

76 *The holdings of the Bank of England*: "Quantitative Easing: A Dangerous Addiction?," House of Lords, Economic Affairs Committee 1st Report of Session 2021–22, HL Paper 42, July 16, 2021, https:// committees.parliament.uk/publications/6725/documents/71894 /default/; Reid et al., "Long-Term Asset Return Study 2022."

77 *In the view of central bankers*: Bernanke, *21st Century Monetary Policy*, 89–94.

77 *by the Fed's own estimates*: John M. Roberts, "An Estimate of the Long-Term Neutral Rate of Interest," FederalReserve.gov, September 5, 2018, https://www.federalreserve.gov/econres /notes/feds-notes/estimate-of-the-long-term-neutral-rate-of-inter est-20180905.html.

Chapter Five: Bailout Culture

80 *They used these loans*: Stoller, *Goliath*, 298–99, 304.

80 *He delighted in chiding*: John Kenneth Galbraith, "Richard Nixon and the Great Socialist Revival," *New York*, September 21, 1970.

81 *Penn Central was forced*: George Drury, "Penn Central History Remembered," *Classic Trains*, May 1, 2023. All the bailout figures in this chapter are translated to 2020 dollars for comparison.

81 *faking his own kidnapping*: Sam Frizell, "Could a 40-Year-Old Bank Collapse Have Saved the U.S. Economy?," *Time*, October 8, 2014.

81 *In 1975 New York City*: George C. Nurisso and Edward S. Prescott,

"The 1970s Origins of Too Big to Fail," Federal Reserve Bank of Cleveland, https://www.clevelandfed.org/publications/economic -commentary/2017/ec-201717-origins-of-too-big-to-fail#D2; William Safire, "Too Big to Fail or to Bail Out?," *New York Times*, April 6, 2008.

81 *"Ford to City: Drop Dead"*: *New York Daily News*, October 30, 1975, https://www.nydailynews.com/2015/10/29/ford-to-city-drop-dead-in -1975/.

81 *The nation's largest commercial*: Levy, *Ages of American Capitalism*, 606.

81 *"the sort of person who drank beer"*: Leonard, *The Lords of Easy Money*, 63.

81 *Amid the oil boom of the 1970s*: Ibid.

82 *When oil prices started*: Leonard, *The Lords of Easy Money*, 65.

82 *But soon it emerged*: Ibid.

82 *"no private actor"*: Levy, *Ages of American Capitalism*, 606.

82 *"extraordinary" departure*: Ibid.

82 *"one of the most important legacies"*: Leonard, *The Lords of Easy Money*, 66.

82 *Ultimately, the taxpayer bill*: Kenneth J. Robinson, "Savings and Loan Crisis 1980–1989," Federal Reserve History, https://www .federalreservehistory.org/essays/savings-and-loan-crisis#:~:text=The %20RTC%20closed%20747%20S%26Ls,as%20high%20as%20 %24124%20billion.

82 *And its creditors included*: John Cassidy, "Time Bomb," *New Yorker*, June 27, 1999; Michael Fleming and Weiling Liu, "Near Failure of Long-Term Capital Management," Federal Reserve Bank of Richmond, November 22, 2013.

83 *This was another first*: Levy, *Ages of American Capitalism*, 665–66; Bernanke, *21st Century Monetary Policy*, 75.

83 *Saving LTCM ushered*: Reid et al., "Long-Term Asset Return Study 2022."

83 *The next industry bailout*: David Koenig, "Hit by Virus, US Airlines Seek Aid Far Exceeding Post-9/11," Associated Press, March 16, 2020; Frank Swoboda and Martha McNeil Hamilton, "Congress Passes $15 Billion Airline Bailout," *Washington Post*, September 22, 2001; Jaime Holguin, "9/11 Airline Bailout: So, Who Got What?," CBS Evening News, December 9, 2002; Kate Snow, Dana Bash, and Ted Barrett, "Congress Approves $15 Billion Airline Bailout," CNN, September 22, 2001.

83 *On the eve of the crisis*: Levy, *Ages of American Capitalism*, 692.

84 *As the market for these*: Levy, *Ages of American Capitalism*, 695.

84 *The ratings agencies*: Levy, *Ages of American Capitalism*, 696.

84 *As the guesstimated value*: Ibid.

85 *The mortgage agencies*: Jo Becker, Sheryl Gay Stolberg, and Stephen

Labaton, "Bush Drive for Home Ownership Fueled Housing Bubble," *New York Times*, December 21, 2008.

85 *Bankers started calling*: Levy, *Ages of American Capitalism*, 709; Timothy F. Geithner, *Stress Test: Reflections on Financial Crises* (New York: Crown, 2014), 205.

85 *To stem the financial panic*: Levy, *Ages of American Capitalism*, 83.

85 *However, in the intervening centuries*: James Narron and David Skeie, "Crisis Chronicles: Central Bank Crisis Management During Wall Street's First Crash (1792)," Liberty Street Economics, Federal Reserve Bank of New York, May 9, 2014, https://libertystreeteconomics .newyorkfed.org/2014/05/crisis-chronicles-central-bank-crisis-man agement-during-wall-streets-first-crash-1792/; "The Slumps That Shaped Modern Finance," *The Economist*, April 12, 2014.

86 *"We cannot rely"*: Sheila Bair, foreword to Yalman Onaran, *Zombie Banks: How Broken Banks and Debtor Nations Are Crippling the Global Economy* (New York: Bloomberg Press, 2011), ix.

86 *Greenspan would remark*: Bernanke, *21st Century Monetary Policy*, 72; Alan Greenspan, transcript of "Remarks by Chairman Alan Greenspan at the Haas Annual Business Faculty Research Dialogue," delivered at UC Berkeley, September 4, 1998, https://www.federalre serve.gov/boarddocs/speeches/1998/19980904.htm.

88 *"lender of last resort to the world"*: Bernanke, *21st Century Monetary Policy*, 124.

88 *"taper tantrum"*: Karen Petrou, *Engine of Inequality: The Fed and the Future of Wealth in America* (Hoboken, NJ: Wiley, 2021), 62, 76.

88 *"invisible bailout"*: Leonard, *The Lords of Easy Money*, 241.

88 *To keep markets settled*: Petrou, *Engine of Inequality*, 198; Leonard, *The Lords of Easy Money*, 236, 238.

88 *And the powers used*: Bernanke, *21st Century Monetary Policy*, 58–59.

89 *But all that changed*: Cynthia Kroet, "A Timeline of the Eurozone's Growth," *Politico*, December 26, 2014, https://www.politico.eu/article /a-timeline-of-the-eurozones-growth/. Greece joined a bit later, in January 2001.

89 *Portugal and Greece were dubbed*: Reid et al., "Long-Term Asset Return Study 2022," 28.

89 *Contagion threatened the creditors*: Reid et al., "Long-Term Asset Return Study 2022," 26.

89 *The easy money culture was*: Onaran, *Zombie Banks*, 25.

90 *Even nations that had*: David Beers, Obiageri Ndukwe, Karim
McDaniels, and Alex Charron, "BoC-BoE Sovereign Default
Database: What's New in 2023?," Bank of Canada, July 2023,
updated August 2023, https://www.bankofcanada.ca/2023/07
/staff-analytical-note-2023-10/.

91 *the "main thing"*: Ruchir Sharma, "Why America's Big Companies
Keep Getting Bigger," *Financial Times*, April 10, 2023.

91 *Indeed, the bailout*: John Micklethwait and Adrian Wooldridge,
"A New Chapter of Capitalism Emerges from the Banking Crisis,"
Bloomberg, March 22, 2023.

92 *topped 50 percent*: Daniel Goldstein, "Why the Federal Government
Now Holds Nearly 50 Percent of All Residential Mortgages," *Market-
Watch*, October 16, 2015.

93 *"This is the new normal"*: Mark Dittli, "[Russell Napier:]'We Will See
the Return of Capital Investment on a Massive Scale,'" The Market
NZZ, October 14, 2022, https://themarket.ch/interview/russell-na
pier-the-world-will-experience-a-capex-boom-ld.7606.

93 *The economic war-fighting*: Ibid.

93 *Yet the mainstream*: "CBO Outlines Negative Implications of High and
Rising National Debt," *Committee for a Responsible Federal Budget*
(blog), August 17, 2023, https://www.crfb.org/blogs/cbo-outlines
-negative-implications-high-rising-national-debt.

Chapter Six: The Surreal Logic of 2020

95 *In doing so, he had driven*: Brian Riedl, "Trump's Fiscal Legacy: A
Comprehensive Overview of Spending, Taxes, and Deficits," Manhattan
Institute, May 12, 2022.

96 *"my gut tells me"*: Smialek, *Limitless*, 106.

96 *Most days Trump was thumbing his nose*: Christopher Condon,
"Key Trump Quotes on Powell as Fed Remains in the Firing Line,"
Bloomberg, August 22, 2019.

97 *Within months, total U.S. government*: Dorn, "Fiscal Dominance and
Fed Complacency."

97 *The recession of early 2020*: National Bureau of Economic Research,
https://www.nber.org/sites/default/files/2023-03/BCDC_printed
_spreadsheet.pdf.

97 *It ended in May*: Amanda Moreland et al., "Timing of State and Ter-
ritorial COVID-19 Stay-at-Home Orders and Changes in Population
Movement," Centers for Disease Control and Prevention, *Morbidity*

and Mortality Weekly Report 69, no. 35 (September 4, 2020): 1198–203, http://dx.doi.org/10.15585/mmwr.mm6935a2.

97 *Aiming to preempt critics*: Smialek, *Limitless*, 187.

97 *The unemployed got $600*: Tami Luhby, Vanessa Yurkevich, and Christopher Hickey, "In Some Reopening States, Unemployment Can Pay More Than Lost Jobs," CNN, April 30, 2020, https://www.cnn.com/2020/04/30/politics/unemployment-benefits-higher-than-work-wages/index.html.

98 *Midsize businesses*: Main Street Lending Program, Board of Governors of the Federal Reserve System, https://www.federalreserve.gov/monetarypolicy/mainstreetlending.htm.

98 *These supports extended*: Ren, "Who's to Blame for Fallen Angels and Sinking Demons?"

98 *bankruptcies fell*: Adam Slater, "Low Global Bankruptcies Mask Underlying Malaise," Oxford Economics Research Briefing, February 2, 2021.

99 *A Bloomberg TV announcer*: Jeanna Smialek, "The Federal Reserve's Economic Policy Powers Might Be Limitless, but Should They?," *Marketplace*, February 27, 2023, https://www.marketplace.org/2023/02/27/federal-reserves-economic-policy-powers-might-be-limitless-but-should-they/.

99 *Yes, poverty fell*: "Covid-19 Has Transformed the Welfare State. Which Changes Will Endure?," *The Economist*, March 6, 2021.

99 *"eviction 'tsunami'"*: Kristian Hernández, "Evictions Rise to Pre-Pandemic Levels," *Stateline*, https://stateline.org/2022/02/01/evictions-rise-to-pre-pandemic-levels/.

100 *Government dollars*: "Robust COVID Relief Achieved Historic Gains Against Poverty and Hardship, Bolstered Economy," Center on Budget and Policy Priorities, June 14, 2022, https://www.cbpp.org/research/poverty-and-inequality/robust-covid-relief-achieved-historic-gains-against-poverty-and-0.

100 *By one count*: Lorie Konish, "How Effective Were Those Stimulus Checks? Some Argue the Money May Have Fueled Inflation," CNBC, June 11, 1022, https://www.cnbc.com/2022/06/11/the-pandemic-stimulus-checks-were-a-big-experiment-did-it-work.html.

100 *Bank deposits swelled*: Andrew Castro, Michele Cavallo, and Rebecca Zarutskie, "Understanding Bank Deposit Growth During the COVID-19 Pandemic," FEDS Notes, June 3, 2022, https://www.federalreserve.gov/econres/notes/feds-notes/understanding-bank

-deposit-growth-during-the-covid-19-pandemic-20220603.html;
Center for Microeconomic Data, New York Fed, "Quarterly Report
on Household Debt and Credit," November 2022, https://www.new
yorkfed.org/medialibrary/interactives/householdcredit/data/pdf
/HHDC_2022Q3.

100 *Credit scores improved*: "Credit Card Holders and Their Credit
Scores; New Insights from the Research Division of the St. Louis
Fed," *The FRED Blog*, October 16, 2023, https://fredblog.stlouisfed
.org/2023/10/credit-card-holders-and-their-credit-scores/.

100 *Another big chunk*: Breakout Capital commissioned report by BCA
Research 2023.

100 *Americans making less*: Katherine Greifeld, Claire Ballentine,
and Vildana Hajric, "Stock Froth Boiled After $600 Checks. Now
$1,400 May Be Coming," *Bloomberg*, January 16, 2021, https://www
.bloomberg.com/news/articles/2021-01-16/stock-froth-boiled-after
-600-checks-now-1-400-may-be-coming#xj4y7vzkg.

100 *"Buy. Buy. Buy"*: Leonard, *The Lords of Easy Money*, 290.

100 *"Fundamentally we have now"*: Leonard, *The Lords of Easy Money*, 282.

101 *business and consumer confidence, far from plunging*: "Recent Developments," Board of Governors of the Federal Reserve System, https://
www.federalreserve.gov/releases/z1/20230608/html/recent_develop
ments.htm.

101 *"People were job-hopping"*: Te-Ping Chen, "These Tech Workers Say
They Were Hired to Do Nothing," *Wall Street Journal*, April 7, 2023.

101 *"Get in the boats"*: Brian Cheung, "Powell Compares Fed Actions to
Dunkirk: 'Just Get in the Boats and Go,'" Yahoo! Finance, March 25,
2021; Brian Chappatta, "Wall Street Economists Channel Powell's
Fiscal Vision," *Bloomberg*, September 14, 2020.

101 *The U.S. government issued*: Bill Fay, "Timeline of U.S. Federal Debt
Since Independence Day 1776," Debt.org, October 12, 2021, https://
www.debt.org/faqs/united-states-federal-debt-timeline/.

101 *The same basic escalation*: "Letter from Chair Powell to Secretary
Mnuchin Regarding Emergency Lending Facilities," Reports to
Congress Pursuant to Section 13(3) of the Federal Reserve Act in
Response to COVID-19, Funding, Credit, Liquidity and Loan Facil-
ities, November 20, 2020, https://www.federalreserve.gov/funding
-credit-liquidity-and-loan-facilities.htm.

102 *The United States would unleash*: Breakout Capital calculations based
on the Master Data.

102 *"too large, too broad"*: Martin Wolf, "Inflation's Return Changes the World," *Financial Times*, July 4, 2023.

102 *Though the Fed can create*: Smialek, *Limitless*, 132–33.

102 *Powell announced the conclusion*: Jerome H. Powell, "New Economic Challenges and the Fed's Monetary Policy Review," transcript of speech delivered via webcast at Jackson Hole, Wyoming, August 27, 2020, https://www.federalreserve.gov/newsevents/speech/powell20200827a .htm.

102 *Instead of trying to identify*: Smialek, *Limitless*, 242.

103 *Though conservatives worried*: Leonard, *The Lords of Easy Money*, 279.

103 *"mission creep"*: Merryn Somerset Webb, "Central Banks Need to Stop Mission Creep," *Financial Times*, August 27, 2021; Greg Ip, "Mission Creep at the Fed," *Wall Street Journal*, August 26, 2020.

104 *The farther it reached*: Gee Hee Hong and Todd Schneider, "Shrinko-nomics: Lessons from Japan; Japan Is the World's Laboratory for Drawing Policy Lessons on Aging, Dwindling Populations," International Monetary Fund, March 2020, https://www.imf.org/en/Publi cations/fandd/issues/2020/03/shrinkanomics-policy-lessons-from -japan-on-population-aging-schneider.

104 *That warning proved timely*: Michael D. Bordo and Mickey D. Levy, "Do Enlarged Fiscal Deficits Cause Inflation: The Historical Record" (National Bureau of Economic Research Working Paper 28195, 2020), DOI 10.3386/w28195.

105 *Never mind that even a back-of-the-envelope*: Chris Hughes, "Why Americans Need a Guaranteed Income," *New York Times*, May 1, 2020.

105 *One commentator hailed Biden*: Farhad Manjoo, "Biden Has Helped the Quiet Revolution of Giving People Money," *New York Times*, September 23, 2022.

105 *As the number of Americans*: Lauren Weber, "Burned Out, More Americans Are Turning to Part-Time Jobs," *Wall Street Journal*, February 25, 2023.

105 *"right to laziness"*: Robert Zaretsky, "Are French People Just Lazy?," *New York Times*, January 29, 2023.

105 *nation's "most toxic myth"*: Alissa Quart, "Can We Put an End to America's Most Dangerous Myth?," *New York Times*, March 9, 2023.

106 *"Let's Launch a Moonshot"*: Ezra Klein, "Let's Launch a Moonshot for Meatless Meat," *New York Times*, April 24, 2021.

106 *And not everyone*: Wolf, "Inflation's Return Changes the World."

106 *Former Treasury secretary*: Jordan Williams, "Larry Summers Blasts
$1.9T Stimulus as 'Least Responsible' Economic Policy in 40 Years,"
The Hill, March 20, 2021.

106 *Summers warned that stimulus*: Lawrence H. Summers, "On
Inflation, We Can Learn from the Mistakes of the Past—or Repeat
Them," *Washington Post*, February 3, 2022.

106 *"pining . . . for the swashbuckling days"*: Gerstle, *The Rise and Fall of
the Neoliberal Order*, 98–99.

Chapter Seven: Beyond Borrowing and Spending

109 *Dramatically and for the most part*: "The Evolution of the U.S. Intelligence Community—An Historical Overview," https://www.govinfo
.gov/content/pkg/GPO-INTELLIGENCE/html/int022.html.

110 *A major expansion*: "The U.S. Intelligence Community Is Composed
of the Following 18 Organizations," Office of the Director of National
Intelligence, https://www.dni.gov/index.php/what-we-do/members
-of-the-ic.

110 *The TSA alone*: "Leadership and Organization," Transportation
Security Administration, https://www.tsa.gov/.

110 *The Immigration and Naturalization Service*: U.S. Citizenship and
Immigration Services History Office and Library, "Overview of INS
History," 11, https://www.uscis.gov/sites/default/files/document/fact
-sheets/INSHistory.pdf.

110 *"National security"*: Lindsay M. Chervinsky, "FDR Is the Easy Comparison, but Biden Is Taking a Page from Eisenhower's Playbook," *The
Hill*, June 8, 2021.

111 *Reagan's quarrel with the growing*: Gerstle, *The Rise and Fall of the
Neoliberal Order*, 96.

111 *Government spending accounted*: Breakout Capital calculations based
on data from the Federal Reserve of St. Louis as of September 2023.

112 *By the eve of the pandemic*: Ibid.

112 *They calculated that government benefits*: Phil Gramm, Robert
Ekelund, and John Early, *The Myth of American Inequality: How
Government Biases Policy Debate* (Lanham, MD: Rowman & Little-
field, 2022), 2.

112 *He confesses that when*: Matthew Desmond, "America Is in a Disgraced
Class of Its Own," *New York Times*, March 16, 2023.

113 *"Neoliberalism' is now part of the left's lexicon"*: Matthew Desmond,
"Why Poverty Exists in America," *New York Times*, March 9, 2023.

113 *The story outlined*: Livio Di Matteo, *Measuring Government in the 21st Century* (Vancouver, Canada: Fraser Institute, 2013), 3, 8.

114 *"obligatory levies"*: Piketty, *A Brief History of Equality*, 122.

114 *When all states were weak*: Piketty, *A Brief History of Equality*, 54.

114 *Until the early twentieth century, however*: Piketty, *A Brief History of Equality*, 123.

114 *"more or less everywhere"*: Piketty, *A Brief History of Equality*, 131.

115 *The economic boom*: Piketty, *A Brief History of Equality*, 139.

115 *As top personal tax rates fell*: David Dollar and Aart Kraay, "Trade, Growth, and Poverty," *Finance and Development* 38, no. 3 (September 2001).

115 *The dodges are as intricate*: Gerald Auten and David Splinter, "Income Inequality in the United States: Using Tax Data to Measure Long-Term Trends," September 29, 2023, https://davidsplinter.com/AutenSplinter-Tax_Data_and_Inequality.pdf.

115 *Since confiscatory taxes*: Niels Johannesen et al., "Taxing Hidden Wealth: The Consequences of U.S. Enforcement Initiatives on Evasive Foreign Accounts," *American Economic Journal: Economic Policy* 12, no. 3 (August 2020): 312–46.

116 *In peacetime*: "The Public Finances: A Historical Overview," House of Commons Library Briefing Paper Number 8265, March 22, 2018, 4.

116 *digging itself deeper into debt*: Reid et al., "Long Term Asset Return Study 2022."

116 *"Capitalism as we know it"*: Nick Timothy, "Capitalism as We Know It Has Failed. Not Even the Tories Can Defend It," *The Telegraph*, July 2, 2023.

116 *For a variety of reasons*: James Capretta, "Federal Unfunded Liabilities Are Growing More Rapidly Than Public Debt," RealClearPolicy, November 17, 2022, https://www.realclearpolicy.com/articles/2022/11/17/federal_unfunded_liabilities_are_growing_more_rapidly_than_public_debt_865384.html.

117 *The White House encouraged*: Jake Sullivan, "Remarks by National Security Advisor Jake Sullivan on Renewing American Economic Leadership at the Brookings Institution," April 27, 2023.

117 *In 2021, Biden told Congress*: Joe Biden, "Remarks by President Biden in Address to a Joint Session of Congress," April 28, 2021, https://www.whitehouse.gov/briefing-room/speeches-remarks/2021/04/29/remarks-by-president-biden-in-address-to-a-joint-session-of-congress/.

118 *Fellow Democrat*: Steven Rattner, "Biden's Big Government Should Be Handled with Care," *New York Times*, April 9, 2021.

118 *It's true that*: "All Employees, Government (USGOVT)," U.S. Bureau of Labor Statistics, retrieved from FRED, Federal Reserve Bank of St. Louis, October 6, 2023, https://fred.stlouisfed.org/series/USGOVT.

119 *By the end of his term*: Paul C. Light, "The True Size of Government Is Nearing a Record High," Brookings Institution, October 7, 2020, https://www.brookings.edu/articles/the-true-size-of-government-is -nearing-a-record-high/.

119 *These sales gained steam*: Chris Edwards, "Margaret Thatcher's Privatization Legacy," *Cato Journal* 37, no.1 (Winter 2017): 91, https:// www.cato.org/sites/cato.org/files/serials/files/cato-journal/2017/2/cj -v37n1-7.pdf.

120 *Over the same period, Canada*: William L. Megginson, "Privatization and Finance," *Annual Review of Financial Economics* 2 (2010): 145–74, https://papers.ssrn.com/sol3/papers.cfm?abstract_id=1707918.

120 *If governments were still selling*: "Privatisation in the 21st Century: Summary of Recent Experiences," Organization for Economic Cooperation and Development, March 30, 2010, https://www.oecd.org/daf /ca/corporategovernanceofstate-ownedenterprises/43449100.pdf.

120 *Efforts to sell the state airlines*: Ruchir Sharma, "India Has a Policy of Privatisation by 'Malign Neglect,'" *Economic Times*, June 23, 2016.

120 *The unexpected twist*: Chris Edwards, "Options for Federal Privatization and Reform Lesson from Abroad," CATO Institute, June 28, 2016, Policy Analysis No. 794.

121 *Prisons sprang up*: Gerstle, *The Rise and Fall of the Neoliberal Order*, 185.

122 *Typically "much more complicated"*: Robert C. Clark, "Why So Many Lawyers? Are They Good or Bad?," *Fordham Law Review* 61, no. 275 (1992), https://ir.lawnet.fordham.edu/flr/vol61/iss2/1/.

122 *Under Nixon*: Ken Hughes, "Richard Nixon: Domestic Affairs," Miller Center, https://millercenter.org/president/nixon/domestic-affairs.

123 *Spurred by the activists*: Gerstle, *The Rise and Fall of the Neoliberal Order*, 66–67.

123 *During his campaign*: George Lardner Jr., "The Numbers Game: Wiped Out Agencies May Not Stay Dead," *Washington Post*, April 11, 1977.

123 *At the end of Carter's presidency*: "Demographics," Profile of the Legal Profession 2022, American Bar Association, https://www.abalegal profile.com/demographics.php.

123 *"perpetuate puffery"*: Susan E. Dudley, "Perpetuating Puffery: An Analysis of the Composition of OMB's Reported Benefits of Regulation," *Business Economics* 47, no. 3 (August 2012).

123 *"undo 50 years"*: Bill Prochnau and Valarie Thomas, "The Watt Controversy," *Washington Post*, June 30, 1981.

123 *"like asking Dracula"*: Walter Isaacson, "Thunderers on the Right," *Time*, March 16, 1981.

124 *Since 1996, the bureaucracy*: Clyde Wayne Crews Jr., "Ten Thousand Commandments 2023," Competitive Enterprise Institute, https://cei .org/wp-content/uploads/2023/11/10K_Commandments.pdf. For a summary of the project: https://cei.org/studies/ten-thousand-com mandments-2023/.

124 *"benefits from—indeed, requires"*: Adam J. White, "Regulatory Reforms and Counter-Reformations," *Regulatory Review*, March 12, 2019.

124 *The way the system works*: Clyde Wayne Crews Jr., "Ten Thousand Commandments, An Annual Snapshot of the Federal Regulatory State, 2022," 41, 47, Competitive Enterprise Institute, https://cei.org /wp-content/uploads/2022/10/10000_Commandments_2022.pdf.

124 *His signature Telecommunications Act*: "The Clinton Presidency: Eight Years of Peace, Progress and Prosperity," January 2001, https:// clintonwhitehouse5.archives.gov/WH/Accomplishments/eight years-index.html.

125 *They are simple and raise*: Daniel Bunn and Lisa Hogreve, *International Tax Competitiveness Index 2022*, Tax Foundation, October 17, 2022, https://taxfoundation.org/research/all/global/2022-interna tional-tax-competitiveness-index/.

125 *Scholars of the regulatory state*: "Title 33," Code of Federal Regulations, Appendix C to Part 325, National Archives, October 12, 2023, https://www.ecfr.gov/current/title-33/chapter-II/part-325/appendix -Appendix%20C%20to%20Part%20325.

125 *In the mid-1970s*: Thomas Philippon, "Causes, Consequences, and Policy Responses to Market Concentration," Economic Strategy Group, Aspen Institute, November 21, 2019, 23, https://www.eco nomicstrategygroup.org/publication/causes-consequences-and-policy -responses-to-market-concentration/.

126 *He came into office*: Breakout Capital calculations based on Clyde Wayne Crews Jr., "Ten Thousand Commandments 2022," Competitive Enterprise Institute, 93, "Part B: Number of Documents

in the Federal Register 1976–2021," https://cei.org/wp-content /uploads/2022/10/10000_Commandments_2022.pdf.

126   *And it was undone*: Crews, "Ten Thousand Commandments 2022," 45.

126   *Biden was setting the stage*: Clyde Wayne Crews Jr., "Ten Thousand Commandments 2021," Competitive Enterprise Institute, 56, https:// cei.org/wp-content/uploads/2021/06/Ten_Thousand_Command ments_2021.pdf.

127   *In short, Biden increased*: Breakout Capital calculations based on Reg Rodeo, a database compiled by the American Action Forum.

127   *In Margaret Thatcher's*: Steven K. Vogel, *Freer Markets, More Rules: Regulatory Reform in Advanced Industrial Countries* (Ithaca, NY: Cornell University Press, 1996), 3.

128   *Since then this new regional*: Bradford, *The Brussels Effect*, 32–40.

128   *Those critics could cast even*: Gerstle, *The Rise and Fall of the Neoliberal Order*, 177.

128   *the one-third minority*: Sneha Gubbala, "People Broadly View the EU Favorably, Both in Member States and Elsewhere," Pew Research Center, October 24, 2023.

129   *from transport to social policy*: Bradford, *The Brussels Effect*, 34.

129   *On one level, however, Brexit*: Dominic Green, "Amid Strikes and Scandal, Britain Is Grappling with 'Bregret,'" *Wall Street Journal*, February 1, 2023.

129   *By 2023, more than a quarter*: Wilfried Eckl-Dorna, "Quarter of Smaller German Companies Consider Giving Up, DPA Says," Bloomberg.com, July 16, 2023.

130   *Many of these*: Antonin Bergeaud, John Van Reenen, Philippe Aghion, "Regulation Chills Minor (But Not Radical) Innovations," VoxEU column, Centre for Economic Policy Research, February 1, 2021.

130   *Far from a race*: Bradford, *The Brussels Effect*, 32–40.

Chapter Eight: Whack-a-Mole

133   *Even the Vatican*: Chancellor, *The Price of Time*, 24.

134   *But the same histories*: Norman Strunk and Frederick E. Case, "Where Deregulation Went Wrong: A Look at the Causes Behind Savings and Loans Failures in the 1980s," US League of Savings Associations, 1988.

134   *"low paid, heavy drinking"*: "The Savings and Loan Crisis and Its Relationship to Banking," in *History of the Eighties—Lessons for the Future: An Examination of the Banking Crises of the 1980s and Early*

1990s, Federal Deposit Insurance Corporation Annual Report, vol. 1, 172, https://www.fdic.gov/bank/historical/history/167_188.pdf.

135 *By the early 1980s*: Stoller, *Goliath*, 268.

135 *While deregulation of the airlines*: "Origins and Causes of the S&L Debacle: A Blueprint for Reform," National Commission on Financial Institution Reform, Recovery and Enforcement, 1993, 2, 3, HathiTrust Digital Library, http://catalog.hathitrust.org/Rec ord/011334544.

136 *There were one hundred zombie thrifts*: Onaran, *Zombie Banks*, 2.

137 *To cope, banks shifted*: Apoorv Bhargava, Lucyna Gornicka, and Peichu Xie, "Leakages from Macroprudential Regulations: The Case of Household-Specific Tools and Corporate Credit" (International Monetary Fund Working Paper, April 29, 2021).

138 *In 1999, for example*: Norbert Michel, "The Myth of Financial Market Deregulation," Heritage Foundation, April 28, 2016.

138 *The permutations were virtually*: Bhargava, Gornicka, and Xie, "Leakages from Macroprudential Regulations," 5.

139 *By the time the crisis hit*: Bernanke, *21st Century Monetary Policy*, 113.

139 *But 90 percent of derivatives*: "The Global OTC Derivatives Market at End-December 1999," press release, Bank for International Settlements, May 18, 2000, https://www.bis.org/publ/otc_hy0005.pdf.

139 *the over-the-counter market*: Breakout Capital calculations based on IMF, Haver Analytics.

139 *"create a new market that's opaque"*: Onaran, *Zombie Banks*, 128.

140 *By comparison, Glass-Steagall*: Philip Coggan, *More: The 10,000-Year Rise of the World Economy* (London: Profile Books, 2020), chapter 18.

140 *Dodd-Frank was supposed*: "Shadow Banking in America: Back in the Spotlight," TD Economics, May 20, 2014, https://www.tdbank.com /investments/exc/pdfs/ShadowBankingInAmerica_U.pdf.

141 *"Thus the tendency"*: Franklin Allen, Itay Goldstein, and Julapa Jagtiani, "The Interplay Among Financial Regulation, Resilience, and Growth," *Journal of Financial Services Research* 53 (2018): 157.

142 *By the end of that period, the typical U.S. company*: "Private Markets Rally to New Heights," McKinsey Global Private Markets Review 2022, https://ccl.yale.edu/sites/default/files/files/McKinsey%20 -%20Private%20Markets%20Annual%20Review%202022%20 (Chapter%206).pdf. "Earnings" here are EBITDA—earnings before

interest expense, taxes paid, depreciation, and amortization—which, by accounting for costs that make it more difficult for a company to pay down debt, offers a clearer picture of its debt burden.

142 *With so many company owners*: Leonard, *The Lords of Easy Money*, 187.

142 *"The world has moved on"*: Michael Howell, "The Federal Reserve Is the Cause of the Bubble in Everything," *Financial Times*, January 15, 2020.

143 *"the less costly the rules"*: Petrou, *Engine of Inequality*, 69. See also Andrew Filardo and Pierre Siklos, "The Cross-Border Credit Channel and Lending Standards Surveys" (Bank for International Settlements Working Paper No. 723, May 2018), https://www.bis.org/publ /work723.pdf.

143 *By 2022, nearly 100 percent*: Leonard, *The Lords of Easy Money*, 216.

143 *Lenders no longer seemed to care*: Ruchir Sharma, "How Private Markets Became an Escape from Reality, *Financial Times*, December 19, 2022.

143 *The assets they managed*: Leonard, *The Lords of Easy Money*, 181.

144 *So it was that in 2008*: Bernanke, *21st Century Monetary Policy*, 115.

144 *Yet as late as the fall*: Petrou, *Engine of Inequality*, 70.

144 *China is a middle-income country*: Ruchir Sharma, "How Shadow Banks Threaten the Global Economy," *Financial Times*, May 22, 2022.

145 *The takeaway, he says*: Blinder, *A Monetary and Fiscal History*, 243.

146 *A 2018 Harvard Business School study*: Robin Greenwood, Andrei Shleifer, and Yang You, "Bubbles for Fama," *Journal of Financial Economics* (September 14, 2018).

147 *This is what the small-government*: Gerstle, *The Rise and Fall of the Neoliberal Order*, 88, 89.

Chapter Nine: Why States Rarely Shrink

150 *like the passage from summer to fall*: Tony Blair, full text of speech, Brighton, United Kingdom, 2005, http://news.bbc.co.uk/2/hi/uk _news/politics/4287370.stm.

150 *Clinton captured the mood*: Bill Clinton, full text of speech, March 9, 2000, Johns Hopkins University, Baltimore, MD, https://www.iatp .org/sites/default/files/Full_Text_of_Clintons_Speech_on_China _Trade_Bi.htm.

150 *When Xi Jinping came to power*: Richard D'Aveni, "The U.S. Must

Learn from China's State Capitalism to Beat It," *The Atlantic*, November 5, 2012.

150 *After all*: Nicholas Kristof, "Looking for a Jump-Start in China," *New York Times*, January 5, 2013.

151 *By early 2022, when Putin launched the invasion of Ukraine*: Andrei Kolesnikov, "How Russians Learned to Stop Worrying and Love the War," *Foreign Affairs*, February 1, 2023; David Remnick, "The Weakness of the Despot," *The New Yorker*, March 11, 2022.

152 *Bill Clinton again caught the mood*: Gerstle, *The Rise and Fall of the Neoliberal Order*, 170.

152 *The rise of advanced surveillance*: James Griffiths, *The Great Firewall of China: How to Build and Control an Alternative Version of the Internet* (London: Zed Books, 2019).

153 *Gary Gerstle says this order*: Gerstle, *The Rise and Fall of the Neoliberal Order*, 230.

153 *Before World War I*: Livio Di Matteo, "Measuring Government in the 21st Century; An International Overview of the Size and Efficiency of Government Spending," Fraser Institute, 2013, https://www.fraserinstitute.org/sites/default/files/measuring-government-in-the-21st-century.pdf.

153 *Most of the major combatants*: DeLong, "Was the Great Recession More Damaging Than the Great Depression?," 269.

153 *During the first leap*: Reid et al., "Long-Term Asset Return Study 2022."

154 *"over-stretched elastic"*: Andrew G. Haldane and Piergiorgio Alessandri, "Banking on the State," based on a presentation delivered at the Federal Reserve Bank of Chicago twelfth annual International Banking Conference on "The International Financial Crisis: Have the Rules of Finance Changed?," Chicago, September 25, 2009, 2.

155 *Nixon had a grand plan*: "Nixon's Revolutionary Vision for American Governance," Richard Nixon Foundation, January 24, 2017, https://www.nixonfoundation.org/2017/01/nixons-vision-for-american-governance/.

155 *risen from $20 to $70 billion in constant dollars*: Mark Febrizio and Melinda Warren, "Regulators' Budget: Overall Spending and Staffing Remain Stable: An Analysis of the U.S. Budget for Fiscal Years 1960 to 2021," Regulatory Studies Center/George Washington University and Weidenbaum Center on the Economy, Government, and Public Policy/Washington University in St. Louis, July 2020, https://regulatorystudies.columbian.gwu.edu/regulators-budget.

155 *This expansion unfolded*: Michael G. Krukones, "The Campaign Promises of Jimmy Carter: Accomplishments and Failures," *Presidential Studies Quarterly* 15, no. 1 (Winter 1985): 136–44, https://www.jstor.org/stable/27550171.

155 *Over time, the public comes*: Livia Gershon, "Why Ronald Reagan Became the Great Deregulator," *JSTOR Daily*, February 9, 2017, https://daily.jstor.org/why-reagan-became-the-great-deregulator/.

155 *Much remained, however*: Claire Cain Miller and Alicia Parlapiano, "The U.S. Built a European-Style Welfare State. It's Largely Over," *New York Times*, May 11, 2023.

155 *Into the fall of 2023*: "Monthly Budget Review: July 2023," Congressional Budget Office, August 8, 2023, https://www.cbo.gov/system/files/2023-08/59377-MBR.pdf.

156 *Whatever the fate of any one subsidy*: Don Schneider, "New Developments in Tax Refunds and Student Loans," Piper Sandler Macro Research, September 19, 2023, https://research.cornerstonemacro.com/ResearchPortal/LatestResearch#.

156 *Many governments have tried*: Jonathan V. Last, "Make Boomsa for the Motherland!," *Slate*, April 25, 2013; John O'Callaghan, "Tiny Singapore Risks Economic Gloom Without Big Baby Boom," Reuters, August 30, 2012; Vanessa Brown Calder and Chelsea Follett, "Freeing American Families: Reforms to Make Family Life Easier and More Affordable," Cato Institute, August 10, 2023.

157 *The added boost came from productivity*: Robert E. Lucas Jr., "The Industrial Revolution: Past and Future," Federal Reserve Bank of Minneapolis, May 1, 2004, https://www.minneapolisfed.org/article/2004/the-industrial-revolution-past-and-future.

157 *"The entire human race"*: Ibid.

157 *With a lag*: Breakout Capital calculations based on UN population statistics, Haver Analytics.

158 *In the United States*: Breakout Capital calculations based on Haver Analytics, Institute of International Finance, IMF, and National Sources.

159 *Flattened borrowers*: Breakout Capital calculations based on Institute of International Finance, IMF, and Haver Analytics.

161 *Borrowing "profligacy"*: Philipp Carlsson-Szlezak, "U.S. Economics Weekend Blast: Thrift and Profligacy in America," Bernstein Research, September 14, 2018.

161 *"primary object"*: John F. Kennedy, transcript of news conference, State

Department Auditorium, Washington, DC, June 28, 1961, https://www
.jfklibrary.org/archives/other-resources/john-f-kennedy-press-confer
ences/news-conference-13.

162 *After he left office in 2012*: Bernanke, *21st Century Monetary Policy*,
28; Timothy Noah, "Jeb's 4 Percent Solution," *Politico*, June 15, 2015.

162 *In recent decades*: Breakout Capital calculations for average growth in
per capita GDP 2013–2022 based on World Bank data.

162 *In 2023, on the occasion*: Diane Coyle, "Adam Smith at 300," Project
Syndicate, June 23, 2023, https://www.project-syndicate.org/com
mentary/revisiting-adam-smith-theory-of-economic-growth-by-diane
-coyle-2023-06.

Chapter Ten: In Search of Zombies

167 *Unlike the movie variety*: Edward I. Altman, Rui Dai, and Wei
Wang, "Global Zombies," Turnaround.org, November 23, 2021, rev.
January 6, 2023, https://ssrn.com/abstract=3970332.

168 *Hoshi named these companies*: Takeo Hoshi, "Naze Nihon wa Ryūdōsei
no Wana kara Nogarerareainoka? (Why is the Japanese Economy
Unable to Get Out of a Liquidity Trap?)," in Mitsuhiro Fukao and
Hiroshi Yoshikawa, eds., *Zero Kinri to Nihon Keizai* (Zero Interest
Rate and the Japanese Economy) (Tokyo: Nihon Keizai Shimbunsha,
2000), 233–66. See also Ricardo J. Caballero, Takeo Hoshi, and Anil
K. Kashyap, "Zombie Lending and Depressed Restructuring in Japan"
(National Bureau of Economic Research Working Paper 12129, April
2006), http://www.nber.org/papers/w12129.

168 *Reporter James Brooke*: James Brooke, "They're Alive! They're Alive!
Not!; Japan Hesitates to Put an End to Its 'Zombie' Businesses," *New
York Times*, October 29, 2002.

168 *By 2005 the result was being derided*: Joe Peek and Eric S. Rosengren,
"Unnatural Selection: Perverse Incentives and the Misallocation of Credit in Japan," *American Economic Review* 95, no. 4
(September 2005): 1444–66, https://www.aeaweb.org/articles
?id=10.1257/0002828054825691.

169 *They found that*: Caballero, Hoshi, and Kashyap, "Zombie Lending
and Depressed Restructuring in Japan."

169 *The fear was that*: Fabiano Schivardi, Enrico Sette, and Guido
Tabellini, "Credit Misallocation During the European Financial
Crisis" (Bank for International Settlements Working Paper No. 669,
November 2017), 2, https://www.bis.org/publ/work669.pdf.

170 *Not fast enough to inspire confidence*: Viral V. Acharya, Tim Eisert, Christian Eufinger, and Christian W. Hirsch, "Whatever It Takes: The Real Effects of Unconventional Monetary Policy" (SAFE Working Paper No. 152, April 11, 2017), https://papers.ssrn.com/sol3/papers .cfm?abstract_id=2858147.

170 *The threat of "Japanification"*: Ibid.

170 *And indeed, in Italian*: Schivardi et al., "Credit Misallocation."

170 *As in Japan, there appeared*: Müge Adalet McGowan, Dan Andrews, and Valentine Millot, "Insolvency Regimes, Zombie Firms, and Capital Reallocation" (Organization for Economic Cooperation and Development Working Paper No. 1399, June 28, 2017), 11, https://www.oecd-i library.org/economics/insolvency-regimes-zombie-firms-and-capital -reallocation_5a16beda-en.

170 *Even more important*: Sid Verma, "Zombie Companies Littering Europe May Tie the ECB's Hands for Years," *Bloomberg*, July 24, 2017.

171 *That might have left America*: Ryan Banerjee and Boris Hofmann, "The Rise of Zombie Firms: Causes and Consequences," *BIS Quarterly Review*, September 2018, https://www.bis.org/publ/qtrpdf/r _qt1809g.pdf.

171 *In other words, they appeared to be both*: Ryan Banerjee and Boris Hofmann, "Corporate Zombies: Anatomy and Life Cycle" (Band for International Settlements Working Paper No. 882, January 2022), https://www.bis.org/publ/work882.pdf.

171 *"cleansing effect"*: Ibid.

171 *One, from Deutsche Bank*: Jim Reid, John Tierney, Luke Templeman, and Sahil Mahtani, "The Persistence of Zombie Firms in a Low Yield World," Deutsche Bank, March 1, 2018.

171 *Numbers that eye-popping*: Banerjee and Hofmann, "Corporate Zombies: Anatomy and Life Cycle."

172 *zombie lists in 2020*: In Europe, where the hunt for names was less intense, the broad definition of a zombie—three years of earnings lower than interest payments—would have generated prominent ones as well, including Spotify, Delivery Hero, easyJet, TomTom, and Aston Martin.

172 *In 2022, the BIS found*: Banerjee and Hofmann, "Corporate Zombies: Anatomy and Life Cycle."

172 *Depending on how they assessed future profitability*: Most research-ers use a measure based on a firm's market value as an indicator of its future profitability; the BIS, for example, uses Tobin's Q, which

compares a firm's market value to the replacement cost of its assets. In 2022, Fed researchers using a different measure—slumping sales growth—came to a conclusion at odds with most of the new research. They concluded that while zombies represent just under 10 percent of the corporate population, they tend to be small, and had not expanded their presence in the economy over time. The "cleansing effect" of recessions was alive and well.

172 *In a 2023 report on "Global Zombies"*: Altman, Dai, and Wang, "Global Zombies."

173 *Others cited a clumsy*: Bruno Albuquerque and Roshan Iyer, "The Rise of the Walking Dead: Zombie Firms Around the World" (International Monetary Fund Working Paper, June 16, 2023).

173 *"the spectre of worldwide"*: Simone Lenzu, Olivier Wang, and Viral Acharya, "Zombie Lending and Policy Traps," VoxEU, October 29, 2021, https://cepr.org/voxeu/columns/zombie-lending-and-policy-traps.

173 *"highly significant"*: Banerjee and Hofmann, "The Rise of Zombie Firms: Causes and Consequences."

173 *"normal circumstances"*: Altman, Dai, and Wang, "Global Zombies."

174 *In short, falling interest rates*: Ibid.

175 *Leaders of the "Global Zombies" project*: Ibid., 2.

175 *"apes" by offering*: Scott Mendelson, "AMC Entertainment Stock Tumbles 34% as CEO Announces End of APE," *The Wrap*, August 14, 2023, https://www.yahoo.com/entertainment/amc-entertainment-stock-tumbles-34-175854284.html#:~:text=With%20a%20revised%20settlement%20approved,trading%20Monday%20following%20the%20announcement; Lawrence Scotti, "GameStop Rolling Back Crypto & NFTs After Losing Millions," Dexerto, December 8, 2022, https://www.dexerto.com/gaming/gamestop-rolling-back-crypto-nfts-after-losing-millions-2006389/.

175 *"the forefront of the public debate"*: Albuquerque and Iyer, "The Rise of the Walking Dead."

175 *relatively small*: As yet, searches for zombies in private markets have yielded inconclusive results, for a simple reason: privately held companies often don't have to report the debt and earnings detail that would allow researchers to identify them as zombies.

176 *They do not live forever*: Banerjee and Hofmann, "Corporate Zombies: Anatomy and Life Cycle."

176 *"Zombiism" was turning into a chronic*: Ibid.

176 *And recovered zombies*: Ibid.

176 *serious problem of debt decay*: Against all these alarming conclusions, there was an interesting dissent, from within the Federal Reserve itself. In 2021, a team of Fed researchers asked whether zombies are numerous and "consequential" in the United States, and found that they are neither. The authors concluded that zombies are relatively small, concentrated in just a few industries, and had not in fact expanded their presence in the economy over time. They estimated that the zombie share of U.S. companies had held steady at just under 10 percent going back to 2000, and importantly, had tended to fail in hard times; in other words, the "cleansing effect" of recessions was alive and well. Perhaps not unexpectedly, given how much blame for the rise of zombies had been heaped on the Fed, its researchers found that these distressed firms are "not a prominent feature" of the U.S. economy. See Giovanni Favara, Camelia Minoiu, and Ander Perez-Orive, "U.S. Zombie Firms: How Many and How Consequential?," FEDS Notes, July 30, 2021, https://www.federal reserve.gov/econres/notes/feds-notes/us-zombie-firms-how-many-and -how-consequential-20210730.html.

Chapter Eleven: Rise of the Oligopolies

177 *Princeton University economist Atif Mian was drawn*: Neil Irwin, "What if All the World's Economic Woes Are Part of the Same Problem?," *New York Times*, March 5, 2019.

178 *"Industry leaders invest more aggressively"*: Ernest Liu, Atif Mian, and Amir Sufi, "Low Interest Rates, Market Power, and Productivity Growth" (National Bureau of Economic Research Working Paper 25505, January 2019, rev. August 2019), 2, https://www .nber.org/system/files/working_papers/w25505/revisions/w25505 .rev2.pdf.

179 *And after 2000*: Sharma, "Why America's Big Companies Keep Getting Bigger."

179 *As Jan Eeckhout*: Jan Eeckhout, *The Profit Paradox: How Thriving Firms Threaten the Future of Work* (Princeton, NJ: Princeton University Press, 2021), 29–31.

180 *During the surreal*: Mike Konczal and Niko Lusiani, "Prices, Profits, and Power: An Analysis of 2021 Firm-Level Markups," Roosevelt Institute, June 2022, https://rooseveltinstitute.org/wp-content/up loads/2022/06/RI_PricesProfitsPower_202206.pdf.

180 *Defying the skeptics*: Eeckhout, *The Profit Paradox*, 275.

180 *Unrivaled size was translating*: Sharma, "Why America's Big Companies Keep Getting Bigger."

181 *After 1990, the share of U.S.*: Jason Furman and Peter Orszag, "Slower Productivity and Higher Inequality: Are They Related?" (Peterson Institute for International Economics Working Paper 18-4, June 2018), https://www.piie.com/publications/working-papers/slower-productivity-and-higher-inequality-are-they-related.

181 *Brookings Institution researchers*: The age of big tech firms is from Breakout Capital calculations based on U.S. Census data; Robert E. Litan and Ian Hathaway, "The Other Aging of America," Brookings Institution, July 31, 2014, https://www.brookings.edu/articles/the-other-aging-of-america-the-increasing-dominance-of-older-firms/.

182 *"always been shameless"*: Steve Jobs, interview, posted on YouTube by George McClellan, August 12, 2014, https://shorturl.at/vLY12.

182 *"Big Tech companies like Google"*: Adam Mossoff, "Google's Loss to Sonos Settles It: Big Tech Has an IT Privacy Problem," *TechCrunch*, January 13, 2022, https://techcrunch.com/2022/01/13/googles-loss-to-sonos-settles-it-big-tech-has-an-ip-piracy-problem/.

182 *two California firms*: Peter Coy, "The Patent Fight That Could Take Apple Watches Off the Market," *New York Times*, October 30, 2023.

183 *And, finally, an increasingly complex web*: David Autor et al., "The Fall of the Labor Share and the Rise of Superstar Firms," *Quarterly Journal of Economics* 135, no. 2 (October 2019): 645–709.

183 *Moreover, most of these export-oriented firms*: "Robots and Artificial Intelligence: Margin Amplifiers," Empirical Research Partners, December 2022, https://www.empirical-research.com/.

183 *If capitalism is operating normally*: Germán Gutiérrez and Thomas Philippon, "The Failure of Free Entry" (National Bureau of Economic Research Working Paper 26001, June 2019), https://www.nber.org/papers/w26001.

184 *The most compelling explanation*: Gutiérrez and Philippon, "The Failure of Free Entry," 16.

184 *Among the top twenty American lobbyists*: Richard Waters and Arjun Neil Alim, "How Brad Smith Used Microsoft's $1bn Law and Lobbying Machine to Win Activision Battle," *Financial Times*, October 14, 2023.

184 *Now they account for five*: Max Bank, Felix Duffy, Verena Leyendecker, and Margarida Silva, "The Lobby Network: Big Tech's Web of Influence in the EU," Corporate Europe Observatory and LobbyControl eV,

August 31, 2021, https://corporateeurope.org/en/2021/08/lobby-ne
twork-big-techs-web-influence-eu; Clothilde Goujard, "Big Tech Accused
of Shady Lobbying in EU Parliament," *Politico*, October 14, 2022.

185 *The United States was generating start-ups*: Ruchir Sharma, "When
Dead Companies Don't Die," *New York Times*, June 15, 2019.

185 *Then the era of easy money*: Breakout Capital calculations based
on data from the Office of the Advocate for Small Business Capital
Formation (OASB).

185 *Nine of every ten disappearing*: Breakout Capital calculations based
on the St. Louis Federal Reserve/U.S. Bureau of Economic Analysis.

185 *Two-thirds of the major business sectors*: Breakout Capital calculations based on data from Bank of America Merrill Lynch as of
December 31, 2017.

185 *During the pandemic, Americans*: Germán Gutiérrez and Thomas
Philippon, "Declining Competition and Investment in the U.S."
(National Bureau of Economic Research Working Paper 23583, July
2017), 7, https://www.nber.org/system/files/working_papers/w23583
/w23583.pdf.

185 *As small and young companies*: Breakout Capital calculation based on
data from the OASB.

186 *Using a standard index*: Grullon, Larkin, and Michaely, "Are US Industries Becoming More Concentrated?"

186 *extracting more monopolistic "rent"*: Jason Furman and Peter Orszag,
"Slower Productivity and Higher Inequality: Are They Related?"

187 *Politicians and economists on the left*: Eric Levitz, "The 'Greedflation'
Debate Is Deeply Confused," *New York*, July 8, 2023.

187 *One concern is the rise*: Lucian A. Bebchuk and Scott Hirst, "Big Three
Power & Why It Matters" (Discussion Paper No. 1087, Harvard University,
John M. Olin Center for Law, Economics and Business, December 2022).

187 *Even John Bogle, founder*: John C. Bogle, "Bogle Sounds a Warning on
Index Funds," *Wall Street Journal*, November 29, 2018.

188 *Many of the survivors*: Rachel Louise Ensign and Coulter Jones, "The
Problem for Small-Town Banks: People Want High-Tech Services,"
Wall Street Journal, March 2, 2019; Dan Alamariu, "If the Levee
Breaks: Political Fallout from the Banking Crisis," Alpine Macro Geo-
political Strategy Report, March 30, 2023.

189 *"Intangible" investments such as R&D*: James E. Bessen, "Accounting for Rising Corporate Profits: Intangibles or Regulatory Rents?"
(Boston University School of Law, Law and Economics Research

333

Paper No. 16-18, November 9, 2016), 51, https://papers.ssrn.com/sol3/papers.cfm?abstract_id=2778641.

189 *Cable profits and stock valuations*: Bessen, "Accounting for Rising Corporate Profits," 29–30.

189 *"Man's works have outgrown"*: Louis D. Brandeis, "The New England Transportation Monopoly," transcript of speech delivered to the New England Dry Goods Association, Boston, February 11, 1908, in Louis D. Brandeis, *Business—A Profession*, ed. and with a foreword by Ernest Poole (Boston: Small, Maynard & Co., 1914), 255–78, https://louisville.edu/law/library/special-collections/the-louis-d.-brandeis-collection/business-a-profession-chapter-16.

189 *"Paleolithic emotions"*: E. O. Wilson, interview, posted on YouTube by The School of We, https://www.youtube.com/watch?v=1DLW4TUb6Fg.

190 *By late 2023*: Adam Satariano, "In a First, Uber Agrees to Classify British Drivers as 'Workers,'" *New York Times*, March 16, 2021; "New EU Gig Worker Rules Will Sort Out Who Should Get the Benefits of Full-Time Employees," Associated Press, December 13, 2023.

190 *One tech analyst predicted*: Catherine Thorbecke, "How Uber Left Lyft in the Dust," CNN, March 29, 2023.

190 *Two companies make more than*: Eeckhout, *The Profit Paradox*, 27.

190 *dating sites*: Eeckhout, *The Profit Paradox*, 250.

190 *Former college backpackers*: Eeckhout, *The Profit Paradox*, 35–37.

191 *After the turn of the millennium*: John Haltiwanger, Ron S. Jarmin, and Javier Miranda, "Who Creates Jobs? Small vs. Large vs. Young" (U.S. Census Bureau Center for Economic Studies Paper No. CES-WP-10-17, August 28, 2010), https://papers.ssrn.com/sol3/papers.cfm?abstract_id=1666157.

191 *Many start-ups were simply disappearing*: Ryan A. Decker, John Haltiwanger, Ron S. Jarmin, and Javier Miranda, "Where Has All the Skewness Gone? The Decline in High-Growth (Young) Firms in the U.S." (National Bureau of Economic Research Working Paper 21776, December 2015), http://www.nber.org/papers/w21776.

191 *In the pharmaceutical industry*: Thomas Philippon, *The Great Reversal: How America Gave Up on Free Markets* (Cambridge: Harvard University Press, 2019), 82.

191 *The result by the late 2010s*: Grullon, Larkin, and Michaely, "Are U.S. Industries Becoming More Concentrated?"

191 *The battle over concentrated wealth*: Stoller, *Goliath*, 175.

192 *The first two postwar presidents*: Stoller, *Goliath*, 186.

192 *Half the veterans returning*: Stoller, *Goliath*, 183.

193 *Galbraith mocked a federal antitrust suit*: John Kenneth Galbraith, *American Capitalism: The Concept of Countervailing Power* (Eastford, CT: Martino Fine Books, 9th printing, Sentry Edition C, July 2012), 142.

193 *"We can rely on countervailing power"*: Galbraith, *American Capitalism*, 113.

193 *In 1975, heavily influenced*: Stoller, *Goliath*, 352.

194 *from tobacco and entertainment*: Leonard Silk, "The Peril Behind the Takeover Boom," *New York Times*, December 29, 1985.

194 *"The experiment of enforcing the antitrust laws"*: "Modern Antitrust Enforcement," Thurman Arnold Project, Yale School of Management, https://som.yale.edu/centers/thurman-arnold-project-at-yale/modern-antitrust-enforcement.

194 *After bringing a major Sherman case*: Alex Verkhivker, "Corporate Competition Is Healthier in the EU Than the US," *Chicago Booth Review*, January 28, 2019.

194 *In a separate branch*: Grullon, Larkin, and Michaely, "Are US Industries Becoming More Concentrated?"

194 *Before Biden started to revive*: "Modern Antitrust Enforcement," Thurman Arnold Project, Yale School of Management.

195 *While the United States*: Thomas Philippon, "The Economics and Politics of Market Concentration," *The Reporter*, no. 4, National Bureau of Economic Research, December 2019, https://www.nber.org/reporter/2019number4/economics-and-politics-market-concentration.

195 *This is one of the instances*: Germán Gutiérrez and Thomas Philippon, "How EU Markets Became More Competitive Than U.S. Markets: A Study of Institutional Drift" (National Bureau of Economic Research Working Paper 24700, June 2018), https://www.nber.org/system/files/working_papers/w24700/revisions/w24700.rev0.pdf.

195 *Their focus was on big tech*: Lina M. Khan, "Amazon's Antitrust Paradox," *Yale Law Journal* 126, no. 3 (January 2017): 710–805.

Chapter Twelve: How Markets Grew Too Big to Fail

198 *The U.S. economy was in recession*: "US Business Cycle Expansions and Contractions," National Bureau of Economic Research, March 14,

2023, https://www.nber.org/research/data/us-business-cycle-expan
sions-and-contractions.

198 *In the United States*: Blinder, *A Monetary and Fiscal History*, 153.

199 *Meanwhile, Wall Street had enjoyed*: Yun Li, "This Is Now the Longest
US Economic Expansion in History," CNBC, July 2, 2019.

199 *They wanted big banks*: Blinder, *A Monetary and Fiscal History*,
271–72, 276–77.

200 *In the central bank's internal*: Blinder, *A Monetary and Fiscal History*,
269.

201 *"The federal government is nationalizing"*: Jim Bianco, "The Fed's
Cure Risks Being Worse Than the Disease," *Bloomberg*, March 27,
2020.

201 *Three months later*: Henry Kaufman, "US Capitalism Has Been
Shattered," *Financial Times*, June 25, 2020.

201 *"The central bank had shown"*: Smialek, *Limitless*, 278.

201 *"they had become used to"*: Smialek, *Limitless*, 286.

202 *So it is that four decades*: Rochester Cahan, "Ballooning Borrowing
Costs and Bloated Inventories: How Bad?," Stock Selection Research
and Results, Empirical Research Partners, June 30, 2022; "Robots and
Artificial Intelligence: Margin Amplifiers," Empirical Research Partners,
December 2022.

202 *Before World War II*: Òscar Jordà, Moritz Schularick, and Alan
Taylor, "Leveraged Bubbles" (National Bureau of Economic Research
Working Paper 21486, August 2015), https://www.nber.org/papers/
w21486.

202 *Yet for the most part central*: Ruchir Sharma, *The Rise and Fall of
Nations: Forces of Change in the Post-Crisis World* (New York: W. W.
Norton, 2016), 259–61.

202 *Fed chairman Powell warned publicly*: Smialek, *Limitless*, 174.

204 *So more than half*: Breakout Capital calculations based on data from
Morgan Stanley Research, Bloomberg, and S&P LCD.

204 *The fear gripping the authorities*: Smialek, *Limitless*, 173.

204 *The result, argued political strategist*: Alamariu, "If the Levee Breaks:
Political Fallout from the Banking Crisis," 1.

204 *In fact, a growing expectation*: Bhargava, Gornicka, and Xie, "Leakages
from Macroprudential Regulations."

206 *As the government met each new crisis*: Jim Reid and Karthik Nag-
alingam, "2022: The End of the Ultra-Low Default World?," Deutsche
Bank Research, June 8, 2022.

206 *Tremors in stock and bond prices*: Cale Tilford et al., "Repo: How the Financial Markets' Plumbing Got Blocked," *Financial Times*, November 26, 2019.

207 *Podcaster and investor Joshua Brown*: Joshua M. Brown, "When Everything That Counts Can't Be Counted," *The Reformed Broker*, podcast audio, June 13, 2019, https://thereformedbroker. com/2019/08/09/when-everything-that-counts-cant-be-counted-2/.

207 *By late 2020, the market value of Uber*: Ibid.

207 *The roughly $6 trillion*: Sarah Ponczek, "Epic S&P 500 Rally Is Powered by Assets You Can't See or Touch," *Bloomberg*, October 21, 2020.

207 *"What if the cost"*: Brown, "When Everything That Counts Can't Be Counted."

208 *"Real life is factories"*: Erik Schatzker, "Grantham Warns of Biden Stimulus Further Inflating Epic Bubble," *Bloomberg*, January 22, 2021.

208 *By May, these small investors*: Breakout Capital calculations based on data from Morgan Stanley Research.

208 *Its stock rose sixfold*: Chris Isidore and Nathaniel Meyersohn, "JCPenney Files for Bankruptcy," CNN Business, May 15, 2020.

209 *"I mean, that can only happen"*: Sonali Basak, "Best of Bloomberg Invest 2023 Video," June 23, 2023, https://www.bloomberg.com/ news/videos/2023-06-23/best-of-bloomberg-invest-2023?s-ref=VpNSse6l.

209 *Yet the next summer*: Brian Cheung, "Warren Buffett: Zero Interest Rates Have Created a 'Sea Change' in Finance," Yahoo! Finance, May 2, 2021.

209 *The Fed controls interest rates*: Editorial Board, "Warren Buffett on Wall Street 'Gambling,'" *Wall Street Journal*, May 1, 2022.

209 *These money losers*: Dan Su, "Rise of Firms with Negative Net Earnings," April 6, 2022, rev. November 17, 2022, https://ssrn.com /abstract=4065772.

209 *Looking just at the persistently profitless*: Breakout Capital calculations based on data from FactSet and Bloomberg.

210 *Twenty-two start-up companies*: Sophia Kunthara, "These Are the Tech Companies That Went Public in a Blockbuster 2020," *Crunchbase News*, December 23, 2020.

210 *Capitalism had entered a dangerous phase*: Steven Pearlstein, "Socialism for Investors, Capitalism for Everyone Else," *Washington Post*, April 30, 2020.

210 *And most of the U.S. companies*: Michael L. Goldstein et al,
"Reshoring: A Paradigm Shift?" Empirical Research Partners,
Portfolio Strategy, February 9, 2024.

Chapter Thirteen: When Billionaires Do Best

211 *In the past, financial markets*: Savita Subramanian, "The Bull Case
for US Equities, China's Bumpy Recovery, and More," *Global Research
Unlocked* (podcast), Bank of America, May 25, 2023.

212 *"pitchforks"*: Eamon Javers, "Inside Obama's Bank CEOs Meeting,"
Politico, April 3, 2009; Ray Dalio, "Tackle Inequality or Face a Violent
Revolution," *Financial Times*, November 5, 2019.

214 *"often to be found parked on the street"*: Petrou, *Engine of Inequality*, 24.

214 *That is a striking sign*: Breakout Capital calculations based on fred
.stlouisfed.org; share of financial assets held by the top 1 percent;
share of corporate equities and mutual fund share held by the top
1 percent; share of corporate equities and mutual fund shares held
by the ninetieth to ninety-ninth wealth percentiles.

214 *When analysts break down*: "Distribution of Household Wealth in
the U.S. Since 1989," Distributional Financial Accounts, Federal
Reserve, https://www.federalreserve.gov/releases/z1/dataviz/dfa/dis
tribute/chart/; Moritz Kuhn, Moritz Schularick, and Ulrike I. Steins,
"Income and Wealth Inequality in America, 1949–2016," Federal
Reserve Bank of Minneapolis, June 2018, 33.

215 *Even Donald Trump*: Philip Bump, "On Trump's Once-Favorite
Metric—Stock Market Growth—He Trails Barack Obama," *Washington Post*, December 5, 2018.

215 *Suggestions that the stock market*: Federal Reserve Survey of
Consumer Finances, 2022

215 *Fisher may have sounded a bit*: Leonard, *The Lords of Easy
Money*, 182.

216 *Over the last two decades*: "McKinsey Global Private Markets Review
2022: Understanding ESG," November 22, 2022, https://www.lisc
strategicinvestments.org/post/mckinsey-global-private-markets
-review-2022-understanding-esg.

216 *"Because for the average family"*: Squawk on the Street, "Citadel
Founder & CEO Ken Griffin Speaks with CNBC's Sara Eisen," CNBC,
aired September, 14 2023, https://www.cnbc.com/2023/09/14/cnbc
-exclusive-cnbc-transcript-citadel-founder-ceo-ken-griffin-speaks
-with-cnbcs-sara-eisen-on-squawk-on-the-street-today.html.

216 *New York University urbanologist Mitchell Moss*: Joshua Chaffin, "Manhattan's Private Clubs Thrive in a New Gilded Age," *Financial Times*, September 7, 2023.

217 *"directly finance"*: Atif Mian, Ludwig Straub, and Amir Sufi, "The Saving Glut of the Rich," February 2021, 44, https://scholar.harvard .edu/files/straub/files/mss_richsavingglut.pdf.

217 *Setting out to "unveil"*: Pascal Paul and Joseph H. Pedtke, "Historical Patterns Around Financial Crises," Federal Reserve Bank of San Francisco Economic Letter, May 4, 2020, https://www.frbsf.org /research-and-insights/publications/economic-letter/2020/05/his torical-patterns-around-financial-crises/.

218 *Families headed by a person over sixty-five*: "Distribution of Household Wealth in the U.S. Since 1989," Distributional Financial Accounts, Federal Reserve.

218 *Three out of four adults under forty*: Petrou, *Engine of Inequality*, 81 and note 28 (Bank of America, "Millennial Report Winter 2020").

218 *The potential for generational conflict*: Petrou, *Engine of Inequality*, 21; Adrianne Pasquarelli, "Don't Count on the Kids for Your Retirement, Mass Mutual Says in New Ad Campaign," *Ad Age*, July 27, 2021.

218 *Today, half of American thirty-year-olds*: Ray Dalio, "Why and How Capitalism Needs to Be Reformed (Parts 1 & 2)," LinkedIn, April 5, 2019.

218 *Government's contribution to inequality*: David Willets, "Intergenerational Warfare: Who Stole the Millennials' Future?," *Financial Times*, July 2, 2019.

219 *Millennials were also nearly twice*: "Millennial Life: How Young Adulthood Today Compares with Prior Generations," Pew Research Center, February 14, 2019, https://www.pewresearch.org/social -trends/2019/02/14/millennial-life-how-young-adulthood-today -compares-with-prior-generations-2/.

219 *That summer, though the economic recovery*: Eric Milstein, Tyler Powell, and David Wessel, "What Does the Federal Reserve Mean When It Talks About Tapering?," Brookings Institution, July 15, 2021, updated January 27, 2022, https://www.brookings.edu/articles/what -does-the-federal-reserve-mean-when-it-talks-about-tapering/.

220 *The 2010s was the decade*: Ruchir Sharma, *The 10 Rules of Successful Nations* (New York: W. W. Norton, 2020), 55.

220 *Not since the first billionaire*: Annie Lowrey, "How the 0.00003 Percent Lives," *New York*, September 16, 2014.

221 *"It is fascinating"*: Catherine Clifford, "Bill Gates: 'For the First Time

in My Life, People Are Saying, Okay, Should You Have Billionaires?,"
CNBC, March 5, 2019, updated March 6, 2019.

222 *This second Gilded Age*: Ruchir Sharma, "The Billionaire Boom: How
the Super-Rich Soaked Up Covid," *Financial Times*, May 14, 2021.

222 *French luxury firms*: Ruchir Sharma, "Europe's New Success Stories
Are Built on High Luxury, Not High Tech," *Financial Times*,
June 4, 2023.

223 *The growing inequities*: Juliana Menasce Horowitz, Ruth Igielnik, and
Rakesh Kochhar, "Most Americans Say There Is Too Much Economic
Inequality in the U.S., but Fewer Than Half Call It a Top Priority,"
Pew Research Center, January 9, 2020, https://www.pewresearch.org
/social-trends/2020/01/09/trends-in-income-and-wealth-inequality/.

223 *Most Americans supported a wealth tax*: Howard Schneider and
Chris Kahn, "Majority of Americans Favor Wealth Tax on Very Rich:
Reuters/Ipsos Poll," Reuters, January 10, 2020.

223 *Even in late 2022*: Anand Giridharadas, "This Week, Billionaires
Made a Strong Case for Abolishing Themselves," *New York Times*,
November 19, 2022.

224 *In 2015, after his tenure was over*: Ben S. Bernanke, "Monetary Policy
and Inequality," Brookings Institution, June 1, 2015.

224 *By late 2023, its story*: See, for example, Dylan Matthews, "Do We
Really Live In an 'Age of Inequality'?" *Vox*, January, 11 2024, https://
www.vox.com/future-perfect/2024/1/11/23984135/inequality-auten
-splinter-piketty-saez-zucman-tax-data.

225 *More families saw their incomes fall*: Alan B. Krueger, "The Rise and
Consequences of Inequality in the United States," January 12, 2012,
5, https://obamawhitehouse.archives.gov/sites/default/files/krueger
_cap_speech_final_remarks.pdf.

225 *"income growth thus shifted"*: Levy, *Ages of American Capitalism*, 589.

225 *One in seven members of the top 1 percent*: Breakout Capital calculations
based on U.S. Bureau of Economic Analysis, National Data, National
Income and Product Accounts, Tables 6.2B. and 6.2D., "Compensation
of Employees by Industry": https://apps.bea.gov/iTable/.

225 *Incomes were also rising*: Levy, *Ages of American Capitalism*, 571.

226 *In a broad survey of the literature*: Henning Hesse, Boris Hofmann,
and James Weber, "The Macroeconomic Effects of Asset Purchases
Revisited" (Bank for International Settlements Working Paper
No. 680, December, 2017), https://www.bis.org/publ/work680.pdf.

226 *Other studies have confirmed*: Petrou, *Engine of Inequality*, 79.

226 *only slightly wider now than in 1980*: Jae Song et al., "Firming Up Inequality," *Quarterly Journal of Economics* 134, no. 1 (February 2019): 1–50, https://econpapers.repec.org/article/oupqjecon/v_3a134_3ay _3a2019_3ai_3a1_3ap_3a1-50..htm.

227 *During the pandemic*: Bivens and Kandra, "CEO Pay Has Skyrocketed 1,460% Since 1978."

227 *"all of the workers at successful companies"*: Furman and Orszag, "Slower Productivity and Higher Inequality: Are They Related?"

227 *The growing gap between firms*: Jae et al., "Firming Up Inequality."

227 *This is "one of the most robust" findings*: Eeckhout, *The Profit Paradox*, 131.

227 *"Just about everywhere you look"*: Furman and Orszag, "Slower Productivity and Higher Inequality: Are They Related?"

227 *Internal migration, long fundamental*: Grullon, Larkin, and Michaely, "Are US Industries Becoming More Concentrated?"

228 *There are many possible reasons*: Greg Kaplan and Sam Schulhofer-Wohl, "Understanding the Long-Run Decline in Interstate Migration," *International Economic Review* 58, no. 1 (February 2017): 57–94, https://www.jstor.org/stable/44280166.

228 *One of every five American workers*: Ryan Nunn, "Non-Compete Contracts: Potential Justifications and the Relevant Evidence," Brookings Institution, February 4, 2020, https://www.brookings.edu /articles/non-compete-contracts-potential-justifications-and-the-rel evant-evidence/; Evan Starr, "The Use, Abuse and Enforceability of Non-Compete and No-Poach Agreements: A Brief Review of the Theory, Evidence and Recent Reform Efforts," Economic Innovation Group, Robert H. Smith School of Business, University of Maryland, February 2019, https://eig.org/the-use-abuse-and-enforceability-of -non-compete-and-no-poach-agreements-a-brief-review-of-the-theo ry-evidence-and-recent-reform-efforts/.

228 *"Great Gatsby Curve"*: Timothy Noah, "The Mobility Myth," *New Republic*, February 7, 2012; Bhash Mazumder, "Intergenerational Economic Mobility in the United States," Federal Reserve Bank of Chicago Economic Mobility Project, April 2022; Robert B. Reich, "Income Inequality in the United States," testimony before the Joint Economic Committee, United States Congress, January 16, 2014, https://www.jec.senate.gov/public/_cache/files/121e5a80-61e2-4c 65-aa25-a06a1c0887d5/reich-testimony.pdf.

229 *Since 2008, by one estimate*: Alex J. Pollock, "Since 2008, Monetary Policy Has Cost American Savers about $4 Trillion," Wolf Street,

November 17, 2021, https://wolfstreet.com/2021/11/17/since-2008
-monetary-policy-has-cost-american-savers-about-4-trillion/.

229 *Below the top 1 percent*: "Economists are rethinking the numbers on
inequality." *The Economist*, November 29, 2019, https://www
.economist.com/briefing/2019/11/29/economists-are-rethinking-the
-numbers-on-inequality.

229 *A more limited government*: A more complex question on these
themes often arises here. Productivity growth, despite slowing sharply
since the 1970s, has outpaced median wage growth in that period—so
how would a government focus on boosting productivity address,
rather than magnify, income inequality? One answer is that whatever
wage gains have been achieved are a result of rising productivity, so
higher productivity should generate more gains, even if it does not
distribute those gains more fairly. Not an ideal outcome, but not bad.
Another is that slumping productivity and rising income inequality
appear to be closely related. Deglobalization will reduce the openings
for giant corporations, reducing the vast pools of capital they have
used to improve their own productivity, while starving rivals of
resources. Limited government again could play a role here, by increasing competition and raising productivity across a broader range
of firms, thereby reducing corporate inequality—the main driver of
income inequality.

Chapter Fourteen: A New Answer to the Productivity Paradox

231 *falling, as it has been for the last two decades*: Many recent histories
of capitalism cite a now famous chart on the "productivity-pay gap,"
which appears to show that "growth" in productivity has been steady
since World War II, while growth in wages stagnated in the 1970s.
What the chart actually shows is the productivity level, which did
continue to rise after the '70s—albeit at a much slower rate. Though
it's accurate, this chart has created some confusion, because it is the
slumping productivity growth rate (not the level) that matters most
for the economy.

231 *"you can see the computer age"*: Robert M. Solow, "We'd Better Watch
Out," *New York Times Book Review*, July 12, 1987.

231 *His evidence was from studies*: Erik Brynjolfsson, "The Productivity Paradox of Information Technology," *Communications of the
ACM* 36, no. 12 (December 1993): 66–77, https://dl.acm.org/doi
/10.1145/163298.163309.

232 *Some economists were even arguing*: Linn Slettum Bjerke-Busch
and Sebastian Thorp, "Overcoming the Productivity Paradox in the
Public Sector by Managing Deliberate Learning," *Public Management
Review*, June 2023, 1–27, https://www.tandfonline.com/doi/full/10.1
080/14719037.2023.2225510.

232 *Pessimists, led by*: Robert Gordon, "Is US Economic Growth Over?
Faltering Innovation Confronts the Six Headwinds" (National Bureau
of Economic Research Working Paper 18315, August 2012), https://
www.nber.org/papers/w18315.

232 *In this view, it is no surprise*: Ibid.

232 *By 2023, many commentators were saying*: Martin Neil Baily, Erik
Brynjolfsson, and Anton Korinek, "Machines of Mind: The Case for
an AI-Powered Productivity Boom," Brookings Institution, May 10,
2023, https://www.brookings.edu/articles/machines-of-mind-the
-case-for-an-ai-powered-productivity-boom/.

233 *As they fall deeper into debt*: Banerjee and Hofmann, "Corporate
Zombies: Anatomy and Life Cycle," 22–23.

233 *Compared to healthy firms*: Banerjee and Hofmann, "Corporate
Zombies: Anatomy and Life Cycle," 4, 5.

234 *Once they have transformed into zombies*: Albuquerque and Iyer, "The
Rise of the Walking Dead," 19.

234 *The heavier the congestion*: Banerjee and Hofmann, "Corporate
Zombies: Anatomy and Life Cycle," 31.

234 *The healthy firms that hang on*: Viral V. Acharya, Matteo Crosignani,
Tim Eisert, and Christian Eufinger, "Zombie Credit (Dis-) Inflation:
Evidence from Europe" (National Bureau of Economic Research
Working Paper 27158, May 2020), https://www.nber.org/system
/files/working_papers/w27158/w27158.pdf.

235 *But they suggested*: Jim Reid, Craig Nicol, Apurv Chaudhari, "2021:
Back to the Low Default, Low Productivity, Zombie World?" Deutsche
Bank Research, Credit Strategy Default Study, April 27, 2021.

235 *In the summer of 2019:* Chancellor, *The Price of Time*, 235.

235 *This sorting would only grow*: Viral V. Acharya, Simone Lenzu, and
Olivier Wang, "Zombie Lending and Policy Traps," September 2021,
https://papers.ssrn.com/sol3/papers.cfm?abstract_id=3936064.

235 *And going forward*: Banerjee and Hofmann, "Corporate Zombies."

236 *Should those estimates prove*: Ibid.

236 *Researchers at the OECD have warned*: Dan Andrews and Filippos
Petroulakis, "Breaking the Shackles: Zombie Firms, Weak Banks

and Depressed Economic Growth in Europe" (Organization for
Economic Cooperation and Development Working Paper No. 1433,
November 16, 2017), 7, https://www.oecd-ilibrary.org/economics
/breaking-the-shackles_0815ce0c-en.

237 *At a moment like that*: John Springer, "The Walmart Paradox," *Super-
market News*, June 10, 2010.

237 *Not only have sales been concentrating*: Philippon, "Causes, Consequences, and Policy Responses to Market Concentration."

237 *Productivity is falling across the board*: Furman and Orszag, "Slower
Productivity and Higher Inequality: Are They Related?"

238 *a new "unified explanation"*: Ernest Liu, Atif Mian, and Amir Sufi,
"Low Interest Rates, Market Power, and Productivity Growth"
(National Bureau of Economic Research Working Paper 25505,
August 2020), 3, 39–40, https://www.nber.org/papers/w25505.

238 *Starting around 1970*: Matias Covarrubias, Germán Gutiérrez, and
Thomas Philippon, "From Good to Bad Concentration? U.S. Industries Over the Past 30 Years" (National Bureau of Economic Research
Working Paper 25983, September 2019), https://www.nber.org
/system/files/working_papers/w25983/w25983.pdf.

239 *Stars of the digital economy*: Germán Gutiérrez and Thomas
Philippon, "Some Facts About Dominant Firms" (National Bureau of
Economic Research Working Paper 27985, October 2020), https://
www.nber.org/system/files/working_papers/w27985/w27985.pdf;
Philippon, "Causes, Consequences, and Policy Responses to Market
Concentration."

239 *This is also a serious drag*: Gary Hamel and Michele Zanini, "Excess
Management Is Costing the U.S. $3 Trillion Per Year," *Harvard
Business Review*, September 5, 2016, https://hbr.org/2016/09/ex
cess-management-is-costing-the-us-3-trillion-per-year.

241 *The Castro regime*: Sharma, *The Rise and Fall of Nations*, 86, 98,
125–26.

241 *Thus the anti-billionaire revolts*: Jonathan D. Ostry, Andrew G. Berg,
and Charalambos G. Tsangarides, "Inequality and Unsustainable
Growth: Two Sides of the Same Coin?," International Monetary Fund
Research Department, April 2014, 4.

241 *Nobel laureate Joseph Stiglitz*: Joseph Stiglitz, *The Price of Inequality*
(New York: W. W. Norton, 2012).

242 *Over the previous two decades*: "Focus on Inequality and Growth,"
OECD Directorate for Employment Labour and Social Affairs,

December 2014. See also: Orsetta Causa et al., "Growth and Inequality: A Close Relationship?," OECD Forum, October 1, 2014.

243 *In a 2018 study*: Stephen G. Cecchetti and Enisse Kharroubi, "Why Does Credit Growth Crowd Out Real Economic Growth?" (National Bureau of Economic Research Working Paper 25079, September 2018), https://www.nber.org/system/files/working_papers/w25079/w25079.pdf.

243 *In a 2020 paper*: Leonard, *The Lords of Easy Money*, 302.

244 *"There was a widespread"*: "The U.S. Productivity Slowdown: An Economy-Wide and Industry-Level Analysis," U.S. Bureau of Labor Statistics, April 2021, https://www.bls.gov/opub/mlr/2021/article/the-us-productivity-slowdown-the-economy-wide-and-industry-level-analysis.htm.

245 *In a 2021 study, the International Monetary Fund*: Lingling Wei, "China's Economic Recovery Belies a Lingering Productivity Challenge," *Wall Street Journal*, January 17, 2021.

245 *While the U.S. government does not meddle*: Ho-Fung Hung, "Zombie Economy," *New Left Review*, August 4, 2023, https://newleftreview.org/sidecar/posts/zombie-economy.

245 *By the 2010s, the productivity growth rate*: Roberta Capello, Camilla Lenzi, and Giovanni Perucca, "The Modern Solow Paradox: In Search for Explanation," *Structural Change and Economic Dynamics* 63 (December 2022): 166–80, https://www.sciencedirect.com/science/article/pii/S0954349X22001394.

245 *"transatlantic productivity gap"*: Ibid.

245 *For now, AI is more likely*: Joseph Briggs and Devesh Kodnani, "Upgrading Our Longer-Run Global Growth Forecasts to Reflect the Impact of Generative AI," Goldman Sachs, Global Economics Analyst, October 29, 2023.

246 *In recent years, global commentators*: Adam Tooze, "Welcome to the World of the Polycrisis," *Financial Times*, October 28, 2022; see also Edgar Morin and Anne Brigitte Kern, *Homeland Earth: A Manifesto for the New Millennium* (Cresskill, NJ: Hampton Press, 1999).

Chapter Fifteen: Where Capitalism Still Works

249 *"grow the pie"*: John Burn-Murdoch, "Are We Destined for a Zero-Sum Future?," *Financial Times*, September 21, 2023, citing Sahil Chinoy, Nathan Nunn, Sandra Sequeira, and Stefanie Stantcheva, "Zero-Sum Thinking and the Roots of U.S. Political Divides," September 7, 2023,

https://scholar.harvard.edu/files/stantcheva/files/zero_sum
_political_divides.pdf.

249 *"spirit of capitalism"*: Max Weber, *The Protestant Ethic and the Spirit of Capitalism* (New York: Scribner, 1930).

250 *The younger the respondent*: Burn-Murdoch, "Are We Destined for a Zero-Sum Future?"

250 *This trend was perhaps*: Ibid.

252 *These are just as wealthy and democratic*: Chris Moody, "Bernie Sanders' American Dream Is in Denmark," CNN, February 17, 2016.

252 *It delivers welfare benefits*: Nelson D. Schwartz, "Swiss Health Care Thrives Without Public Option," *New York Times*, September 30, 2009.

252 *Money is not the ultimate measure of success*: "World GDP per Capita Ranking 2022; Data and Charts," KNOEMA, https://knoema.com /sijweyg/world-gdp-per-capita-ranking-2022-data-and-charts.

252 *Wealth and income are distributed*: Breakout Capital calculations based on Gini index, per World Bank/Haver Analytics data.

252 *The big difference*: "Global Wealth Report 2023," UBS, 16, https:// www.ubs.com/global/en/family-office-uhnw/reports/global-wealth -report-2023.html.

252 *The Swiss model drew fifteen minutes*: Avik Roy, "Why Switzerland Has the World's Best Health Care System," *Forbes*, April 29, 2011.

252 *In 2015, Switzerland*: "Swiss Say Goodbye to Banking Secrecy," SwissInfoCH, SWI, January 1, 2017, https://www.swissinfo.ch/eng /tax-evasion_swiss-say-goodbye-to-banking-secrecy-/42799134; David Reid, "Swiss Banking Secrecy Nears End Following New Tax Rules," CNBC, January 2, 2017.

253 *And Switzerland is more open to trade*: Cristina Enache, "Top Personal Income Tax Rates in Europe," Tax Foundation, February 28, 2023, https://taxfoundation.org/data/all/eu/top-personal-income-tax-rates -europe-2023/.

253 *In the most recent ranking*: Observatory of Economic Complexity, https://oec.world/en.

253 *And most top Swiss firms*: Breakout Capital calculations based on FactSet, as of October 7, 2023.

253 *Traveling southwest from Zurich*: Ruchir Sharma, "The Happy, Healthy Capitalists of Switzerland," *New York Times*, November 2, 2019.

254 *Swiss critics called this proposal "money for nothing"*: Swaha Pattanaik, "Money-for-Nothing Idea Will Survive Swiss Rebuff," Reuters, June 6, 2016.

254 *Such is the reputation of its engineers*: Breakout Capital calculations based on IMF, Haver Analytics.

254 *Even in 2023, when stresses in global finance*: Karen Gilchrist, "The Small European Nation of Switzerland Beat Sky-High Inflation. Here's How," CNBC, February 27, 2023.

255 *The foreign-born population*: "Switzerland's History as an Immigration Destination," https://interactive.swissinfo.ch/2017_02_01 _evolutionForeigners/streamgraph_foreignersEvolution_EN.html; Julie Schindall, "Switzerland's Non-EU Immigrants: Their Integration and Swiss Attitudes, Migration Policy Institute, June 9, 2009, https://www.migrationpolicy.org/article/switzerlands-non-eu-immi grants-their-integration-and-swiss-attitudes.

255 *Since 2015*: OECD Better Life Index: see the chart at the top of the home page, click "by rank" in the lower right corner of the chart: www.oecdbetterlifeindex.org.

255 *Its government consistently ranks*: "World Competitiveness Rankings," IMD World Competitiveness Center, June 20, 2023, https://www.imd .org/centers/wcc/world-competitiveness-center/rankings/world-com petitiveness-ranking/.

256 *Government spending came down*: Alastair Levy and Nick Lovegrove, "Reforming the Public Sector in a Crisis: An Interview with Sweden's Former Prime Minister," *McKinsey Quarterly*, June 1, 2009, https:// www.mckinsey.com/industries/public-sector/our-insights/reforming -the-public-sector-in-a-crisis-an-interview-with-swedens-former -prime-minister.

256 *Sweden is now one of the few rich*: Susanne Alm, Kenneth Nelson, and Rense Nieuwenhuis, "The Diminishing Power of One? Welfare State Retrenchment and Rising Poverty of Single-Adult House-holds in Sweden 1988–2011," *European Sociological Review* 36, no. 2 (April 2020): 198–217, https://academic.oup.com/esr/art icle/36/2/198/5601460.

256 *By the eve of the global crisis in 2008*: Neil Irwin, "Five Economic Lessons from Sweden, the Rock Star of the Recovery," *Washington Post*, June 24, 2011.

256 *Gently scolding Americans*: Suzanne Daley, "Danes Rethink a Welfare State Ample to a Fault," *New York Times*, April 20, 2013; Matthew Yglesias, "Denmark's Prime Minister Says Bernie Sanders Is Wrong to Call His Country Socialist," *Vox*, October 31, 2015.

257 *a movement to repeal wealth taxes*: Sarah Perret, "Why Were Most

Wealth Taxes Abandoned and Is This Time Different?," *Fiscal Studies* 42, nos. 3–4 (October 25, 2021), https://onlinelibrary.wiley.com/doi /full/10.1111/1475-5890.12278.

257 *Ingvar Kamprad, founder of the IKEA furniture stores*: Daniel J. Mitchell, "Sweden Repeals Wealth Tax," *Cato Institute* (blog), March 31, 2007, https://www.cato.org/blog/sweden-repeals-wealth-tax.

257 *Growth revived, as the largest Scandinavian*: OECD's "Society at a Glance 2019 Report" looks at twenty-five social indicators, for thirty-six OECD member countries. Details available at https://www.oecd-ili brary.org/social-issues-migration-health/society-at-a-glance-2019 _soc_glance-2019-en.

258 *South Korea nurtured giant conglomerates*: Eleanor Albert, "South Korea's Chaebol Challenge," Council on Foreign Relations, May 4, 2018, https://www.cfr.org/backgrounder/south-koreas-chaebol-challenge.

258 *Taiwan cultivated smaller companies*: Ruchir Sharma, "World's Most Important Place: How Tiny Taiwan Came to Be the Epicenter of the Global Battle for Tech Supremacy," *Times of India*, December 15, 2020.

258 *Taiwan began, like many of its peers, by copying*: Cheng Tun-jen, "Transforming Taiwan's Economic Structure in the 20th Century," *China Quarterly*, December 15, 2020, 31–34, https://library.fes.de/li balt/journals/swetsfulltext/11241653.pdf.

259 *At a time when capitalism is bogging down*: Breakout Capital calcula- tions based on Haver Analytics, National Sources.

259 *The result is a record of extraordinarily*: "Statistical Appendix," World Economic Outlook—1997, 118, https://www.imf.org/external/pubs/weo may/part1.pdf.

259 *From 2020 to 2023, Taiwan's labor*: Breakout Capital calculations based on The Conference Board's Total Economy Database.

260 *The big powers racing to match*: Observatory of Economic Complexity, https://oec.world/en.

260 *Though foundries are a small corner*: Robert Casanova, "Despite Short-Term Cyclical Downturn, Global Semiconductor Market's Long-Term Outlook Is Strong," *Semiconductor Industry Association* (blog), February 8, 2023, https://www.semiconductors.org/despite -short-term-cyclical-downturn-global-semiconductor-markets-long -term-outlook-is-strong/.

260 *He bet big on multibillion-dollar*: "Taiwan's Dominance of the Chip Industry Makes It More Important," *The Economist*, March 6, 2023.

261 *Chang's fortune is just over*: Statista, "Leading Tech Companies

Worldwide 2023, by Market Capitalization," https://www.statista
.com/statistics/1350976/leading-tech-companies-worldwide-by-mar
ket-cap/; CompaniesMarketcap.com, "Largest Tech Companies by
Market Cap," 2023, https://companiesmarketcap.com/tech/largest
-tech-companies-by-market-cap/.

262 *Growth took off after*: Yasheng Huang, "How Did China Take Off?,"
Journal of Economic Perspectives 26, no. 4 (November 2012): 147–70,
https://dspace.mit.edu/bitstream/handle/1721.1/121058/jep.26.4.147
.pdf?sequence=1.

262 *By 2021, the once nonexistent*: Jennifer Conrad, "China Cracks Down
on Its Tech Giants. Sound Familiar?," *Wired*, July 29, 2021; "China's
Liu He Assures Business of Support, Amid Regulatory Crackdown,"
Reuters, September 6, 2021.

262 *There is a communist state*: Matthieu Francois, Thomas Hansmann,
Bo Huang, and Zoey Nguyen, "Boosting Vietnam's Manufacturing
Sector: From Low Cost to High Productivity," McKinsey & Company,
September 25, 2023, https://www.mckinsey.com/featured-insights
/asia-pacific/boosting-vietnams-manufacturing-sector-from-low-cost
-to-high-productivity.

263 *By the late 1980s*: U.S. Department of State, "Background Notes:
Vietnam, October 1998," Washington, DC, Bureau of East Asian
and Pacific Affairs, https://1997-2001.state.gov/background_notes
/vietnam_1098_bgn.html.

263 *Hanoi's answer was*: Anja Baum, "Vietnam's Development Success
Story and the Unfinished SDG Agenda" (International Monetary
Fund Working Paper, Asia Pacific Department, February 2020),
https://www.elibrary.imf.org/view/journals/001/2020/031/article
-A001-en.xml.

264 *Vietnam became a leading champion*: "Viet Nam Joins WTO with
Director-General's Tribute for True Grit," World Trade Organization,
January 11, 2007, https://www.wto.org/english/news_e/news07_e
/acc_vietnam_11jan07_e.htm.

264 *Global Trade Alert, which tracks*: "Number of New Interventions Per
Year," Global Trade Alert, https://www.globaltradealert.org
/country/228.

264 *Even as global trade slumped*: Ruchir Sharma, "Is Vietnam the Next
'Asian Miracle'?," *New York Times*, October 13, 2020.

264 *Since the late 1980s, its average income*: Ruchir Sharma, "The Next
'Asian Miracle': Vietnam Is Exporting Its Way to Prosperity, While

Leaving No One Behind at Home," *TOI Edit Page* (blog), October 15, 2020, https://timesofindia.indiatimes.com/blogs/toi-edit-page/the -next-asian-miracle-vietnam-is-exporting-its-way-to-prosperity-while -leaving-no-one-behind-at-home/?source=app&frmapp=yes.

265 *The blockbuster 2023 IPO*: "Pham Nhat Vuong $4.4B," *Forbes* Profile, November 3, 2023, https://www.forbes.com/profile/pham-nhat -vuong/?sh=75628c05382e.

265 *Vietnam, so far, is getting the balance*: Celina Pham, "Why Vietnam's Infrastructure Is Crucial for Economic Growth," Vietnam Briefing from Dezan Shira and Associates, September 9, 2022, https://www .vietnam-briefing.com/news/why-vietnams-infrastructure-crucial -for-economic-growth.html.

265 *"leaving no one behind"*: Era Dabla-Norris and Yuanyan Sophia Zhang, "Vietnam: Successfully Navigating the Pandemic," International Monetary Fund, March 10, 2021, https://www.imf.org/en /News/Articles/2021/03/09/na031021-vietnam-successfully-navi gating-the-pandemic#:~:text=Structural%20transformation%20 from%20agriculture%20to,account%20surpluses%20strength ened%20external%20resilience.

266 *The paradoxes of China's digital economy*: "Vietnam 22 Overview," Freedom House, https://freedomhouse.org/country/vietnam/freedom -net/2022.

267 *Vietnam's Communist Party has been in power*: Richard C. Paddock, "Term Limits Not for Vietnam's Hard-Line Communist Leader," *New York Times*, June 11, 2021.

268 *One no longer hears odes to Chinese bureaucrats*: Laura He, "Chinese Cities Are Struggling to Pay Their Bills as 'Hidden Debts' Soar," CNN, February 1, 2023.

268 *And in some cases American*: "Survey on Business Conditions of Japanese Companies in Asia and Oceania," Japan External Trade Organisation, December 15, 2022 [English-language version of press release, February 2023], https://www.jetro.go.jp/ext_images/en/re ports/survey/pdf/2022/EN_Asia_and_Oceania_2022.pdf.

268 *As the Biden administration rolled out*: "The South Is Fast Becoming America's Industrial Heartland," *The Economist*, June 12, 2023.

268 *All of the fifteen fastest-growing*: Migration Policy Institute Data Hub, "Top 25 Destinations of International Migrants," 2020, Migration Policy Institute, https://www.migrationpolicy.org/programs/data-hub /charts/top-25-destinations-international-migrants.

269 *By the 2010s, as the state reasserted control in China*: Jonathan Burgos, "Wealthy Chinese Lead Home Purchases in Singapore, Sending Prices Soaring," *Forbes*, November 9, 2022.

Chapter Sixteen: The Only Way Out Is Through

271 *Despite all its flaws*: Migration Policy Institute Data Hub, "Top 25 Destinations of International Migrants."

271 *That line goes back*: Edwin Kiester Jr. and Sally Valente Kiester, "Yankee Go Home—and Take Me with You!," *Smithsonian Magazine*, May 1999.

271 *One in ten Fortune 500 CEOs*: "10% of Fortune 500 Companies CEOs Are of Indian Ancestries, Says U.S. Envoy to India," *Business Today*, btTV, https://www.businesstoday.in/bt-tv/short-video/10-of-fortune -500-companies-ceos-are-of-indian-ancestries-says-us-envoy-to -india-387567-2023-06-29.

272 *"better off in five years"*: "Economic Optimism Collapses," 2023 Edelman Trust Barometer Report, Edelman.com, January 18, 2023, https://www.edelman.com/trust/2023/trust-barometer.

272 *Nearly four of five*: Janet Adamy, "Most Americans Doubt Their Children Will Be Better Off, WSJ-NORC Poll Finds," *Wall Street Journal*, March 24, 2023.

272 *An unlimited state is restricting*: Richard M. Salsman, "The Multiyear Decline in US Economic Freedom," American Institute for Economic Research, September 25, 2023, https://www.aier.org/article/the -multiyear-decline-in-us-economic-freedom/.

273 *When money is not free*: Basak, "Best of Bloomberg Invest 2023 Video," June 23, 2023.

274 *Even members of the political elite*: Viktoria Dendrinou, "Rubin Says US In a 'Terrible Place' on Deficit, Urges Tax Hikes," Bloomberg News, January 24, 2024, https://www.bloomberg.com/news /articles/2024-01-24/rubin-warns-of-enormous-risks-from-ameri ca-s-fiscal-trajectory.

276 *Liberal economist and columnist Noah Smith*: Noah Smith, "Progressives Need to Embrace Progress: Stasis Won't Lead to a Prosperous or Equitable Society," *Noahpinion* (blog), March 22, 2023, https://www .noahpinion.blog/p/progressives-need-to-embrace-progress.

276 *"are burning the flag"*: Jeremy Adelman, "The Two Faces of Neoliberalism," Project Syndicate, October 6, 2023, https://www.project -syndicate.org/onpoint/neoliberalism-friedrich-von-hayek

-milton-friedman-by-jeremy-adelman-2023-10?barrier
=accesspaylog.

276 *Oren Cass, a forty-year-old former adviser*: Oren Cass, foreword to
American Compass, *Rebuilding American Capitalism: A Handbook
for Conservative Policymakers*, https://americancompass.org/rebuild
ing-american-capitalism/foreword/.

276 *Christian political philosopher Patrick Deneen*: Patrick J. Deneen,
Regime Change: Toward a Postliberal Failure (New York: Penguin
Random House, 2023).

277 *It showed how less government*: Irwin, "Five Economic Lessons from
Sweden, the Rock Star of the Recovery."

278 *Starting with Portugal in the fifteenth century*: Ruchir Sharma, "The
Comeback Nation," *Foreign Affairs*, March 31, 2020.

278 *The share of countries*: Daniel Fried, "The U.S. Dollar as an International Currency and Its Economic Effects" (Congressional Budget
Office Working Paper 2023-04, April 17, 2023), https://www.cbo.gov
/publication/58764.

279 *Most made the leap from debtor to creditor*: Breakout Capital calculations based on National Sources, Haver Analytics.

279 *Brazilian president Luiz Inácio Lula da Silva*: "Brazil's Lula Calls for
End to Dollar Trade Dominance," *Financial Times*, April 13, 2023.

280 *Nine of the ten biggest central bank*: Ruchir Sharma, "What Strong
Gold Says About the Weak Dollar," *Financial Times*, April 23, 2023.

280 *Most of those efforts*: "Central Bank Digital Currency Tracker," https://
www.atlanticcouncil.org/cbdctracker/.

281 *Depending on the estimate, the dollar's reserve*: Fried, "The U.S. Dollar
as an International Currency," 18.

281 *"The crisis takes a much longer time"*: Rudi Dornbusch, transcript of
interview, *Frontline*, April 8, 1997, https://www.pbs.org/wgbh/pages
/frontline/shows/mexico/interviews/dornbusch.html.

282 *The health authorities have begun searching*: National Academies
of Sciences, Engineering, and Medicine, *Pain Management and the
Opioid Epidemic: Balancing Societal and Individual Benefits and
Risks of Prescription Opioid Use*, e-book (Washington, DC: National
Academies Press, 2017), https://doi.org/10.17226/24781.

282 *There is a long literature*: Livio Di Matteo, "Measuring Government
in the 21st Century," 11–17, Fraser Institute, December 2013, https://
www.fraserinstitute.org/sites/default/files/measuring-government
-in-the-21st-century.pdf.

283 *As the top rate came down*: Erica York, "Summary of the Latest Federal Income Tax Data, 2023 Update," Tax Foundation, January 26, 2023, https://taxfoundation.org/data/all/federal/summary-latest -federal-income-tax-data-2023-update; Andrew Lundeen, "The Top 1 Percent Pays More in Taxes Than the Bottom 90 Percent," Tax Foundation, January 7, 2014, https://taxfoundation.org/blog/top-1 -percent-pays-more-taxes-bottom-90-percent/.

284 *After 2008, global growth*: Breakout Capital calculations based on data from the World Bank.

284 *"modern supply-side economics"*: Janet L. Yellen, "U.S.-China Economic Relationship," Department of the Treasury, transcript of remarks at the Johns Hopkins School of Advanced International Studies, Baltimore, MD, April 2023, https://home.treasury.gov/news /press-releases/jy1425.

285 *"a belief in the perfected"*: Kevin Warsh, "Challenging the Groupthink of the Guild," *Business Economics* 51 (August 2016): 142–46, https:// doi.org/10.1057/s11369-016-0002-4.

287 *They found a set of factors*: Robin Greenwood, Samuel G. Hanson, Andrei Shleifer, and Jakob Ahm Sørensen, "Predictable Financial Crises," *Journal of Finance* 77, no. 2 (January 27, 2022): 863–921.

287 *Debt manias are visible*: "Global Waves of Debt: Causes and Consequences," press release, World Bank, December 19, 2019, https://www .worldbank.org/en/research/publication/waves-of-debt; Goldman Sachs Markets Institute, "Harnessing Global Capital to Drive the Next Phase of China's Growth, January 2015, https://www.goldmansachs.com/intelli gence/pages/us-china-bilateral-investment-dialogue/multimedia/papers /gir-chinas-growth.pdf.

287 *That finding aptly describes*: Sharma, *The 10 Rules of Successful Nations*, 160–164.

287 *A modern central bank*: Bernanke, *21st Century Monetary Policy*, 393–400.

INDEX

Bair, Sheila, 86
Bally's, 172
Bangladesh, 241
Bank for International Settlements
(BIS), 39, 71, 169, 171–73, 175,
225–26, 235
Bank of England, 26, 76, 224
Bank of Japan, 72
bankruptcy(-ies), 8, 15, 30, 40, 52,
53, 80, 84, 98, 120, 169, 173–75,
204–206, 208, 209, 274, 281
banks (banking industry), 26–28,
31, 36, 67, 73–76, 79–93, 86, 88,
90–91, 97–100, 134–38, 144, 160,
167–71, 173–74, 188–91, 199, 217,
233, 235, 252, 254, 256, 267, 275,
280, 286
See also central banks; shadow banks
Barstool Sports, 100
base rate, 52, 61, 65, 66, 69, 72, 77, 83,
86, 87, 90, 273, 275
Belgium, 170, 190
Berkshire Hathaway, 208
Berlin Wall, fall of the, 2, 250
Bernanke, Ben, 65, 69, 71–72, 75, 77, 87,
144, 199–200, 223, 224
Bernstein, William, 207
Bernstein Research, 161
Bessen, James, 189
Best Buy, 237
"Better Life" rankings, 255
Bezos, Jeff, 221–22
Bharatiya Janata Party (BJP), xii
Biden, Joe, and administration, xiii–xiv,
5, 16, 18, 19, 42–43, 43, 61, 92, 93,
105, 106, 110, 117, 118, 125–27, 194,
195, 210, 223, 246, 268, 285, 286
Bidenomics, 17–18, 43, 274, 275,
284–85
"Big Bang" reform (UK), 127
big government, 3, 5–7, 13, 15, 20, 40,
47, 49–51, 95, 102, 115, 192, 193,
227, 230, 241–46, 242, 273–77
billionaires, 4, 12, 15, 211–31, 240–42,
260, 261, 264–65, 274
birth rates, 13, 156, 157
Bismarck, Otto von, 114, 153
black Americans, 154
Black Monday, 63

BlackRock, 187
Blair, Tony, 8, 150
Blinder, Alan, 44, 45, 57, 58, 61, 145
Bloomberg, 91, 99, 117, 201
Boeing, 172
Bogle, John, 187
bonds and bond market, 2, 11, 12, 38,
55–56, 63–64, 68, 73–77, 79, 87,
90, 99, 100–101, 103, 106, 139, 141,
143, 149, 158, 174, 200–202, 204,
206, 209, 213, 215–16, 220, 225,
275, 287–88
See also government bonds; junk
bonds; U.S. Treasury bonds
Bordo, Michael, 104
Borg, Bjorn, 257
Boston College, 136
Bradford, Anu, 14, 128, 130–31
Brandeis, Louis, 189
Brazil, 87, 130, 279
Bretton Woods system, 47, 48
Brexit, 129
British Airways, 119
British Empire, 153
British Petroleum, 119
British pound, 47, 278
British Telecom, 119
Brooke, James, 168
Brookings Institution, 119, 181, 232
Brooks, David, 239
Brown, Joshua, 207
Brussels Effect, 130–31
Bryan, Vicki, 143
Buffett, Warren, 208, 209
bureaucracy, 8, 44, 49, 110, 111, 118,
121–27, 131, 154, 155, 195, 239–40,
263, 268, 277, 285
Bureau of Labor Statistics, 244
Burns, Arthur, 46, 80–81
Burt's Bees, 190
Bush, George H. W., and
administration, 53–56, 60, 65, 67,
111, 124
Bush, George W., and administration,
54, 56, 85, 110, 126, 162
Bush, Jeb, 162
business cycles, 26, 38, 45, 49, 60, 71,
157, 162, 174, 198, 203, 206, 274,
286, 289

ABOUT THE AUTHOR

RUCHIR SHARMA is chairman of Rockefeller International and founder and Chief Investment Officer of Breakout Capital, an investment firm focused on emerging markets. He moved to Rockefeller in 2022 after a twenty-five-year career at Morgan Stanley, where he was head of Emerging Markets and Chief Global Strategist. Based in New York, he is a contributing editor at the *Financial Times* and a former contributing opinion writer at the *New York Times*. His work has also appeared in the *Wall Street Journal*, *Foreign Affairs*, the *Atlantic*, the *Guardian*, and *Foreign Policy*. He is the author of four previous books, the international bestseller *Breakout Nations*, the *New York Times* bestseller *The Rise and Fall of Nations*, *Democracy on the Road*, and *The 10 Rules of Successful Nations*.